Although international finance and banking has been the subject of research and writing, the economic impact of banks on industrial structures and the relations between banking and industry in the twentieth century has remained a relatively unexplored area. This volume examines and interprets the economic effect of the financing of industry by banks and of the banks' credit intermediation in industrialized economies. Particular attention is given to the interplay of economics and politics, to the connections between bankers and industrialists, and to the significance of interlocking directorships. A special section is devoted to a hitherto wholly neglected problem in economic history: the vital influence of universal banking in small but highly industrialized countries in Central Europe and Scandinavia.

The role of banks in the interwar economy

The role of banks in the interwar economy

Edited by

HAROLD JAMES
Associate Professor of History, Princeton University

HÅKAN LINDGREN
Associate Professor of Economic History, University of Uppsala

and

ALICE TEICHOVA
Emeritus Professor of Economic History, University of East Anglia

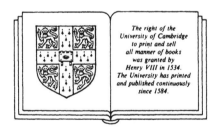

The right of the
University of Cambridge
to print and sell
all manner of books
was granted by
Henry VIII in 1534.
The University has printed
and published continuously
since 1584.

CAMBRIDGE UNIVERSITY PRESS

Cambridge
New York   Port Chester   Melbourne   Sydney

& EDITIONS DE LA MAISON DES SCIENCES
DE L'HOMME
Paris

CAMBRIDGE UNIVERSITY PRESS
Cambridge, New York, Melbourne, Madrid, Cape Town,
Singapore, São Paulo, Delhi, Tokyo, Mexico City

Cambridge University Press
The Edinburgh Building, Cambridge CB2 8RU, UK

Published in the United States of America by
Cambridge University Press, New York

www.cambridge.org
Information on this title: www.cambridge.org/9780521394376

First published 1991
First paperback edition 2002

A catalogue record of this book is available from the British Library.

Library of Congress Cataloguing in Publication data
The role of banks in the interwar economy / edited by Harold James,
Hakan Lindgren, and Alice Teichova.
          p. cm.
ISBN 0 52139437 6
I. Banks and banking – History – 20th century.   I. James, Harold.
II. Lindgren, Hakan.   III. Teichova, Alice.
HG1572.R65   1990
332.1´09´04–dc20   90-33164   CIP

ISBN 978-0-521-39437-6 Hardback
ISBN 978-0-521-52268-7 Paperback

Contents

List of contributors   *page* ix
Preface   xi

1   Introduction   1
HAROLD JAMES

2   Political disputes about the role of banks   13
GERALD D. FELDMAN

3   Universal banking in interwar Central Europe   19
FRITZ WEBER

4   Comparing the interwar banking history of five small   26
countries in North-west Europe
ULF OLSSON

5   American bankers and Britain's fall from gold   35
DIANE B. KUNZ

6   Banks and the problem of capital shortage in Germany,   49
1918–1923
GERALD D. FELDMAN

7   State, banks and industry in Sweden, with some reference   80
to the Scandinavian countries
MATS LARSSON

8   State, banks and industry in Belgium and The Netherlands,   104
1919–1939
GUY VANTHEMSCHE

9   Investment behaviour of industrial joint-stock companies   122
    and industrial shareholding by the Österreichische
    Credit-Anstalt: inducement or obstacle to renewal and change
    in industry in interwar Austria
    ALOIS MOSSER and ALICE TEICHOVA

10 Financing of Hungarian industry by the Commercial Bank   158
    of Pest: a case study
    ELIZABETH A. BOROSS

11 The rise and fall of German-inspired mixed banking in   179
    Italy, 1894–1936
    DOUGLAS J. FORSYTH

12 Banking and economic development in interwar Greece   206
    MARK MAZOWER

13 Why Canadian banks did not collapse in the 1930s   232
    IAN M. DRUMMOND

14 Japanese banks and national economic policy, 1920–1936   251
    W. MILES FLETCHER III

    Index   272

Contributors

ELIZABETH A. BOROSS, Department of History, Monash University, Clayton, Victoria, Australia.

IAN M. DRUMMOND, Trinity College, University of Toronto, Toronto, Ontario M5S 1HB, Canada.

GERALD D. FELDMAN, Department of History, University of California, Berkeley, California 94720, USA.

W. MILES FLETCHER III, Department of History, Hamilton Hall, University of North Carolina, Chapel Hill, N.C. 27514, USA.

DOUGLAS J. FORSYTH, Department of History, MIT, Cambridge, Massachusetts 02139, USA.

HAROLD JAMES, Department of History, Princeton University, 129 Dickinson Hall, Princeton, New Jersey 08544, USA.

DIANE B. KUNZ, Department of History, Yale University, P.O. Box 1504A Yale Station, New Haven, Connecticut 06520-7425, USA.

MATS LARSSON, Department of Economic History, University of Uppsala, Box 513, S-751 20 Uppsala, Sweden.

HÅKAN LINDGREN, Department of Economic History, University of Uppsala, Box 513, S-751 20 Uppsala, Sweden.

MARK MAZOWER, Department of History, Princeton University, 129 Dickinson Hall, Princeton, New Jersey 08544, USA.

ALOIS MOSSER, Institut für Wirtschafts- und Sozialgeschichte, Universität Wien, Dr Karl-Lueger-Ring 1, A-1010 Wien, Austria.

ULF OLSSON, Stockholm School of Economics, Box 6502, S-11383 Stockholm, Sweden.

ALICE TEICHOVA, London School of Economics and Political Science, Houghton Street, London WC2A 2AE, UK.

GUY VANTHEMSCHE, Sectie Geschiedenis, Vrije Universiteit Brussel, Pleinlaan 2, 1050 Brussel, Belgium.

FRITZ WEBER, Alserbachstrasse 18/10, A-1090 Wien, Austria.

Preface

The editors present this volume as a contribution to the Tenth International Economic History Congress which was held in Leuven, Belgium, in August 1990. The articles contained in it were devoted to Session C44 on 'The Role of Banks in the Interwar Economy'.

From the very start of our preparations of the Session, which began in 1987, our main objective has been to focus attention on a largely neglected field of research in economic and business history of the interwar period, that of mutual ties between banking, industry and the state in different countries in the context of the broader relationships between economics and politics. It has further been our aim to draw upon empirical work and, wherever source material allowed, to apply comparative and quantitative methods. We are happy that these objectives could be met satisfactorily, in general, because the authors agreed to produce papers emanating from their research and, in particular, that the contributions dealing with the Central European and Scandinavian countries offer certain findings of a research project in progress, conducted within the framework of an international research programme launched by Alice Teichova in 1986 on 'Bank–Industry Relations in Interwar Europe: Austria, Hungary and Sweden'. The Swedish part of the project is conducted by the *Bankprojekt* directed by Håkan Lindgren and Ragnhild Lundström.

The topics of the essays in the volume are divided into three problem areas: in the introductory chapters, authors discuss the developments of financial systems in the crisis-prone interwar world, examine the interactions of banking and politics, and compare and assess the complex aspects of universal or mixed banking in small but relatively industrially advanced countries of Central and North-west Europe. Further topics elucidate and interpret questions of monetary and banking policies in individual countries (USA, Canada and Japan), while the problem of capital scarcity is investigated with special emphasis on Germany. Finally, a considerable number of the contributions deal with the relations between banking, industry and the state in economies where universal or mixed banking predominated (Austria, Belgium, Greece, Hungary, Italy, Sweden and The Netherlands).

The editors wish to acknowledge that this volume is the product of many hands, and a large number of papers could not have been written without the generous support of institutions which funded the research work of the authors. We are happy to have this opportunity of expressing our sincere thanks to the British Academy, the Leverhulme Foundation and the Economic and Social Research Council of Britain as well as to the Bank of Sweden Tercentenary Foundation, the Jan Wallander Foundation and the Institute of Banking Research at the Stockholm School of Economics. Last but not least we should like to thank all authors, rapporteurs and commentators who took part in the preparation of the meeting at the Leuven Congress.

Harold James
Håkan Lindgren
Alice Teichova

1 Introduction

HAROLD JAMES

The financial history of the interwar years is turbulent. All the papers presented in this volume examine major crises in the developments of financial systems, and are concerned with the character of institutional responses to these crises, as well as with the pathology of financial behaviour.[1] Financial institutions frequently bore a great part of the strain of adjustment to profoundly altered conditions on the world market as well as in the world monetary system.

The First World War and the post-war inflationary and then deflationary traumas of the early 1920s described by Forsyth for Italy and Feldman for Germany set the points for policy responses, one decade later, to the world depression. Larsson tells the story of the major Swedish banking crisis of the early 1920s, and Vanthemsche develops a similar analysis of the severe shock given at the same time to Dutch banking. Boross looks at the investment strategies of one of the great Hungarian mixed banks, and Mosser and Teichova give an analysis of the first and most famous victim of the 1931 crisis, the Vienna Credit-Anstalt. Drummond looks at a country which experienced no major bank collapses, and explains why the Canadian system was so immune.

Kunz and Fletcher examine the debates about rejoining the international gold standard, and about how the international order might affect domestic conditions. They then detail the circumstances of 1931 in which Britain, in September, and Japan, in December, left gold. Mazower also deals with the Greek currency depreciation of April 1932. The weak attachment of Canada to gold plays a major part in Drummond's account. Vanthemsche considers the 1935 Belgian

1

devaluation, which followed in the wake of a severe financial panic and banking crisis. Mazower and Fletcher point out that their cases, Greece and Japan, which had undertaken very drastic currency depreciations, also had exceptionally impressive export perform-ances in the 1930s. Recovery in Sweden and Britain also followed devaluation, though it is much less certain that the mechanisms of recovery lay in export performance.

Two themes run through the papers: did adherence to the new monetary order of the international gold exchange standard in the 1920s increase vulnerability to financial disturbance? Secondly, were some kinds of financial structures – in particular those with a promi-nence of mixed or universal banks with long-term ties (credits but also equity participations) with industry – particularly vulnerable?

In making comparisons, one problem is instantly apparent. Clearly the countries considered here were at very different stages of develop-ment. Greece had the least advanced industry, and might be charac-terized as a dualistic economy, in which islands of modernity existed in the middle of a sea of backwardness. Japan also stood far back on the gradient of development, with a per capita productivity level esti-mated by Angus Maddison to be about a third of Britain's. Germany, Britain and Belgium were mature industrial economies, but suffered badly from the aftermath of war. The First World War did not affect the Netherlands or the Scandinavian countries directly, and the involve-ment of major industrial powers in combat offered non-belligerents a chance for accelerated development. By the end of the 1920s, Denmark and also Sweden had reached high levels of productivity.[2] Austria, Hungary and Italy were less advanced, and had sustained major wartime damage.

The financial systems of all these countries also stood at different points in their emergence; but if we use Raymond Goldsmith's financial intermediation ratios as a guide, we find a very different ranking order from that found for per capita income or labour pro-ductivity. In fact the correlation between the financial and the income or productivity indicators appears on the whole quite arbitrary.

It is perhaps unsurprising that in 1929 Greece came lowest in the financial rank order (financial assets were equivalent to 65 per cent of GNP), or that Germany's ratio (89 per cent) or Belgium's (85 per cent) represent figures much reduced in consequence of the after-math of great inflations, and below Italy (95 per cent), Canada (101 per cent) or Great Britain (131 per cent). But it is a surprise – though one that points optimistically into the future – that Japan appears in banking massively over-developed in relation to her income, with a ratio of 223 per cent, ahead even of the USA (129 per cent). The Scandinavian countries share these relatively high ratios: Sweden 138 per cent, Denmark 186 per cent and Norway 241 per cent. And, *before* the First World War, Germany like Japan had also been apparently over-banked also.[3] It is clear then that whatever else, the stages of financial development hardly coincide with the stages of economic development.

Moreover, there were dramatic and spectacular interruptions to the story of a progressive development of financial institutions and the economic order as a whole from one happy stage to the next. All these economies – from the most to the least developed – were affected by the great international crises – the post-war stabilization, and then the Great Depression and the currency destabilization that followed the sterling devaluation. One way of treating the issue of comparative analysis is to see how systems at different points in their emergence were altered under the impact of common international upheavals.

(1) What was the effect of adherence to an international system – that of the gold exchange standard – on domestic financial structure? Kunz points out that in the 1920s there existed an 'ideology of central banking', propagated by figures such as Montagu Norman, the long-serving Governor of the Bank of England, with a 'messianic fervour'. This doctrine required currencies convertible into gold at fixed rates, with independent central banks controlling domestic monetary developments in accordance with signals sent by movements of the international reserves (gold or convertible exchange – in practice dollars or pounds). The central banks would use their credit polity and their discount rate on bills supplied by the domestic banking system in order to regulate domestic conditions.

These institutions were supposed to recognize that in addition to domestic functions, they had an international role. As the advocates of central bank activity saw it, that role was not just to equilibrate international economic relations, but also to perform this by controlling the 'state of business activity', 'restraining where expansion seems secure and relaxing where business activity in the world at large is unduly declining'. In practice the task envisaged by Norman involved rather more restraint than expansion. He was shaped in his behaviour by the perception of the immediate post-war years that a shock was needed to weed out the unhealthy developments of the wartime inflationary period. As he formulated the view in 1921, 'a central bank should protect its own traders from the rapacity of other banks in his own country'.[4]

Adherence to this international system was invariably the price demanded in return for assistance and access to capital resources: either from the London or the New York markets, or from international agencies such as the League of Nations' Financial Committee, which was very much under the sway of the Norman doctrine. Being 'on gold' meant playing by the rules of an international game, and thus satisfying conditions for capital inflows set by the creditor countries – which in practice meant Britain and the USA, though by the end of the 1920s the French were also playing a major role. Adherence to gold would ensure that the excesses of the early 1920s, where (outside Britain and the USA) the belligerents of the world war or their successor states (in the case of the Habsburg and Ottoman monarchies) followed highly inflationary courses, could not recur. The gold standard provided a very visible marker for the ending of wartime inflationism and a return to responsibility.

Yet in the role expected of central banks there lay a problem. Their capacity to influence monetary developments varied enormously from country to country. In general, they could not use American-style open market operations to influence or control monetary aggregates, because the aftermath of inflationary government finance had brought very strict restrictions on Central Bank purchases of government securities. In Central Europe and Italy (which after the 1890s had developed a banking system that might be described as Central European in character), financial markets were dominated by large credit banks, which usually engaged in long-term financing of industry as well as in more conventional short-term businesses. They issued shares, gave current account credits and discounted bills; they often also held shares so that they often appeared to be industrial holding companies rather than banks more conventionally understood. Only in crises did central banks play a prominent role in discounting bills from the portfolios of commercial banks; in normal times the market operated relatively independently of central banks. In France the Banque de France very rarely held bills from the major banks; and in

Hungary the great banks prided themselves on never using the rediscount of the central bank. Forsyth traces the hostility to commercial banks on the part of the political establishment in Italy, and the relative weakness of the Bank of Italy, back to the pre-war Giolitti years.

Outside Britain where the contacts between the money market and the Bank of England were much more regular, central banks then needed to do something to assure the control that Norman, or the London and New York financial communities, or the League, believed to be an essential part of the confidence on which international capital flows might be based. But there was a paradox in that capital inflows – encouraged by the adherence to gold – were likely to give the commercial banks greater room for manoeuvre and to preserve an independence founded upon banks' access to domestic and increasingly international capital. They did not need to listen to the central banks. The result was that outside the Anglo-American world and Scandinavia, central banks were given an institutional interest in promoting crisis to guarantee their own control of markets. In such an event, the rediscount facilities of central banks might at last become central to the operation of the market.

Feldman describes the growing significance of the Reichsbank, the German central bank, as the post-war inflation developed, when he cites the Hamburg banker Max Warburg's description of the Reichsbank as 'our greatest helper': this was a novelty for Central European bankers. After the stabilizations of the German currency in 1923–4, the Reichsbank continued to play a major role – but only when foreign funds were unavailable.

Hungary and Austria had new central banks that were imposed as part of stabilization schemes under the auspices of the League of Nations; and most Latin American countries also only received central banks during the course of the interwar years. The same was true of Greece, where the largest commercial bank (the National Bank of Greece) simply issued notes. The new institution of 1927, the Bank of Greece, was created explicitly in response to Norman's international activity; but, according to Mazower, the abdication of central banking functions actually strengthened the old National Bank. It could now concentrate on its life as a powerful commercial institution, and did not depend on the rediscount of the central bank. The Greek problem then became the general one of Central Europe: strong commercial banks side by side with an inexperienced and weak central bank.

Drummond's counter-example offers an instructive test case of the consequences of not subscribing to the Norman regime of gold exchange standard and independent central banks. Canada, which until 1935 had no central bank, and where gold convertibility was mostly a fiction because the Dominion authorities would not release gold, in consequence was partially isolated both from external shocks and from domestic pressures for deflationary policies. Drummond presents a powerful case that 'if the Dominion authorities had really been attached to the gold standard, things might have been much more alarming'.

(2) It is easy to see why. Credit control and deflation looked like the easiest way of strengthening central bank influence. Yet financial structures and institutions are very vulnerable to deflation. The international interests of central banks in this way ran counter to the requirements of stability in the national system as a whole.

The deflationary experience of the interwar period can be summed up in this way: higher interest rate or restricted credit puts pressure on businesses to reduce inventories by lowering prices; falling prices reduce the value of securities against loans; banks at first demand additional securities to cover the loans, but when none are any longer forthcoming, they start to call in loans; borrowers are forced further to liquidate stocks; and prices fall still further in consequence. Banks call yet more loans, and the familiar vicious circle of 'debt deflation' described by Irving Fisher sets in.[5]

The deflationary process in the various national economies was a product of the international Norman system, a system which set its criteria for success in the degree of central bank control of domestic monetary markets as well as in central bank resistance to inflationary demands for government borrowing. Where central bank control was very limited, the economy might escape – at least to some extent – the deflationary pressure; such was the case in Greece in the early stages of the depression, when the Bank of Greece was expected to make credit scarce and tighten interest rates, but could not be effective because it had so little contact with the market. Obviously if other banks are able to lend more cheaply, and dare not depend on refinancing with the central bank, there is little that the central bank can do to restrict credit.

But there are other ways in which deflationary pressures were transmitted internationally. Falling world prices may have the same effect as deliberate attempts by national central banks to reduce loans. In this regard, Central European banking systems were especially vulnerable. Banks with large long-term loans to industry were threatened as price collapses threatened the value of their collateral. Banks with substantial share portfolios were vulnerable to declining security prices. They lost income as dividends were reduced or stopped; and in the longer run their solvency was affected by the declining value of their assets. This was a particularly powerful consideration in those countries with well-developed traditions of mixed banking: commercial and investment banking combined. Shares were sometimes also held in the expectation of favourable developments in the capital markets, and retained for longer than anticipated when those improvements did not set in. Here lay another cause of bank weakness in the later 1920s and early 1930s. The crises were particularly acute in the lands of the mixed banks.

Countries heavily dependent on primary products above all were vulnerable to a deflation transmitted through commodity markets. It was in particular the wheat price collapse that undermined both the Hungarian economy and the financial structure after 1929. This makes the Canadian example all the more remarkable. Here there was no universal banking tradition, so one potential source of trouble was removed. Most importantly, the government acted firmly to stop the transmission of a price decline affecting the debt pyramid and the whole financial structure. In early 1930 the provincial governments, and in late 1930 the central government acted to support the wheat price by guaranteeing the wheat purchasing pools of the prairie provinces. Drummond sees this as the crucial element in maintaining Canadian stability: 'A more serious collapse in wheat prices would have severely damaged Canada's banking system, and would probably have destroyed confidence in it.'

Several of the chapters focus on banking crises. Japan, where also there were many banks with long-standing industrial commitments, experienced a crisis in 1927: this collapse may have had the effect of convincing many leading bankers that it was better to obtain access to international capital markets that might be forthcoming under the gold exchange standard. The early crisis in Japan had, however, another effect: in retrospect it looks like a fine example of a preemptive purging. The financial restructuring that occurred in its wake was less painful and damaging in its effects on industrial lending than a similar operation carried out during the harshly deflationary conditions of the world economic crisis would have been. The Swedish and Netherlands crises of the early 1920s also similarly endowed those financial systems with increased immunity against the ills of the early 1930s.

1931 brought collapse in Austria, Hungary and Germany: destructively, in the middle of a world deflation as primary product prices suffered. In these conditions, the effects of deflation and the inherent weaknesses of mixed banking reinforced one another.

Italy had a latent banking crisis, as Forsyth demonstrates, as early as 1929: in other words, well before the events of 1931 in Central Europe could have had a contagious or knock-on effect. The crisis arose out of the declining prices and falling profitability of businesses: out of the pressure for deflation that followed Italy's choice of lira parity at the currency stabilization of 1927. The first banks to suffer were the small ones which did not possess the access to US capital markets enjoyed by their larger rivals.

By 1934, all the Belgian banks, with the exception of the giant Société Générale, were in such a weak position that they could no longer publish accounts; and the banking crisis required as a response the Belgian franc devaluation of 1935. Devaluation offered a path – one of the easiest and most promising – for the domestic management of monetary policy free of the need to transmit international deflationary pressures. In Central Europe, exchange control and voluntary agreements with creditors ('standstill agreements') or even moratoria on debt were another way of generating a new autonomy.

(3) Deflations and subsequent bank collapses led to large-scale restructurings of financial systems. Fletcher gives a powerful example when he describes the absorption of local – city and regional – banks in the course of an officially encouraged 'bank consolidation movement'. The 1927 Bank Law followed the severe financial crisis of that year, and the 'absence of opposition' (p. 260) to the new legislation was presumably a response to the destruction and havoc that had already been wrought. In Europe, the most dramatic restructuring took place in Italy. The large commercial banks were nationalized and their industrial participations separated out in the new state holding company Istituto di Riconstruzione Industriale (IRI). In Austria, the

Credit-Anstalt passed into state control, and two large Viennese banks – the Allgemeine Österreichische Boden-Credit-Anstalt and the Wiener Bankverein – were absorbed into it. For Germany, Feldman describes the 1933 Bank Inquiry and the 1934 Banking Law. In Sweden a law of 1933 attempted to halt an incipient mixed banking system by forbidding the ownership by banks of industrial shares (though the banks were given until 1938 to comply, and then they often evaded the control by setting up exempt non-banking subsidiaries). In Belgium, a decree of 1935 ended mixed banking and laid down auditing and supervisory requirements. In France in 1936 the Banque de France was put under state control, and schemes for the nationalization of private banks (actually put into effect only after the Second World War) prepared.

In all these cases, the position of banks became a highly political issue: not just one that could be examined from a pure standpoint of economic rationality. The reaction to crisis everywhere was greater state intervention in banking – ranging in scope from increased regulation (restrictions on activity; auditing requirements; limitation of credits in relation to size; limitation or prohibition of equity holdings) through state direct control (directed lending) and ownership as in Austria and Italy.

What consequences did restructuring – or attempts at restructuring, such as the hotly discussed Economic Bank described by Feldman – have on economic performance? The plan for an Economic Bank originated as a response to a widely perceived failure of German banks to play their historic role in assisting German industry and commerce. Larsson details a similar and contemporaneous proposal in his paper on Sweden, where during the early 1920s deflation the government sought not only to restructure banking but also to create a new publicly owned commercial bank as a result of the banks' neglect of their mission.

The issue of the relationship between finance and the rest of the economy has long posed difficulties for historians of financial systems, who are often surprisingly and distressingly reluctant to provide assessments of the macroeconomic implications of their work.

On the whole the contributors to this volume are not favourably impressed by the activity of interwar banks (the Canadian example is exceptional). Feldman's contribution demonstrates graphically how violent upheavals – in his case the post-war inflation and hyperinflation – can lead to the formulation of narrowly defensive strategies 'that betrayed [banks'] limited capacity to cope with the problems of industrial reconstruction'. This conservatism continued to characterize the approach of German bankers after the end of the inflationary period: indeed they frequently interpreted the stabilization as requiring a return to sobriety and modestly limited horizons. Teichova shows how the Credit-Anstalt was particularly heavily associated with the older and most traditional Austrian industries – mining and metallurgy, engineering, textiles, wood, and brewing. Mosser complains about the 'lack of growth strategies' in Austrian industry. Mazower shows for Greece how the world depression was not accompanied by the type of cleansing that classical economists believed should take place in depressions: there was no disappearance of small antiquated and inefficient firms. Japan and Italy saw much greater rationalizations in the wake of banking disasters; but in their adaptations public policy played an important part. There is, however, no evidence that the more prominent role of state institutions led to a more effective investment policy on the part of Japanese or Italian industry in the course of the 1930s.

Banks provide an institutional way of assembling and exchanging large quantities of information about the economy, and thus lay a basis on which decisions can be made. The superior and intimate knowledge of many branches derived by the German-style universal banks at the end of the nineteenth century provided a greater input to rational decision making than that derived from a stock market where the rewards for concealment were high. Some observers attribute faster growth in late nineteenth-century Germany to this superior supply of information.[6] Systems of interlocking directorates provided ways of reducing market uncertainty and risk, and represented a response to a high degree of competition on the financial market.

This leaves the important and interesting question of what went wrong in the interwar economy? An obvious answer is that the political disruptions and the consequent alteration of circumstances were at the same time so great and so frequent that information changed too quickly for its regular supply to offer major advantages on making long-term decisions. There was a general contraction of time horizons, a living of life for the moment, that deprived the universal banks of what had previously been a major asset – superior access to reliable flows of information.

It is easier to say what economic disturbances can originate from the financial system when we examine the bank failures which played a major role in the propagation of depression between the war. Banking crises provide an instance of specific institutional structures operating with an obvious and immediate effect on the whole economy. In crises information available changes with enormous rapidity. The special weaknesses of Central European mixed banking became glaringly apparent. While it may be possible to explain some of these failures by reference to the decline in commodity prices after the mid-1920s, bank crashes also had causes which lay within the operation of the international financial system: in particular in the institutional incentives to stage crises that the gold exchange standard provided. The pre-eminence accorded to central bankers under that system – even in countries where there was little tradition of central banking – represented an unprecedented development. Never before had central bankers had so idiosyncratically defined a role – and they were never to exercise it again. The effect of creating these new institutions at odds with older and established financial structures was deeply disruptive.

Central banks, however, emerged again: as also in some countries did the universal banks which had been the occasion of so much financial disturbance. Neither institution by itself is necessarily or inherently destabilizing; but in the interwar period the two sides had frequently been locked in a destructive conflict for control. In the post-war world these conflicts were limited: by public policy innovations, as well as perhaps more importantly by diversification and proliferation within the financial sector in part as a response to public policy. In addition, there was sufficient international co-operation or at least co-ordination to avoid a repetition of the global deflation of the early 1930s.

These papers open a perspective from a historical angle on the story of financial development. Their accomplishment is to show the interplay between finance and the rest of the economy, and they demonstrate – as Friedman and Schwartz have done for the US case[7] – how institutional structure and monetary policy decisions alter history.

12   Harold James

NOTES

1 On this theme, see, C. P. Kindleberger, *Manias, Panics and Crashes: A History of Financial Crises* (New York, 1978).
2 A. Maddison, *Phases of Capitalist Development* (Oxford, 1982), p. 212.
3 R. M. Goldsmith, *Financial Structure and Development* (New Haven, Conn., 1969), p. 209.
4 Bank of England archive OV 50/91, Principles of Central Banking. The first remarks quoted come from Kershaw's memorandum of 1935, 'Some observations on Co-operation'.
5 I. Fisher, 'The debt-deflation theory of great depressions', *Econometrica*, 1 (1933), 337–57.
6 W. P. Kennedy, *Industrial Structure, Capital Markets and the Origins of British Economic Decline* (Cambridge, 1987).
7 M. Friedman and A. J. Schwartz, *A Monetary History of the United States 1867–1960* (Princeton, N.J., 1963).

2   Political disputes about the role of banks

GERALD D. FELDMAN

The fundamental question I would like to raise in this comment is whether the political disputes about the role of banks in the interwar period are primarily disputes about positions taken and claims made by banks in contention with the state, central banks, industrial and other members of the business community or whether they are not in the main disputes originating in the disappointment of non-banker institutions and agencies with the results of the tasks which they had assigned to the bankers or permitted bankers to take on during the interwar period. When Diane Kunz argues, quite correctly, that one of the consequences of the depression and Anglo-American decisions to go off gold was that 'economic questions had become a matter for governments, not bankers', she implicitly argues that previously economic questions had been a matter for bankers. In so far as they were dethroned, they must have once been enthroned, all of which raises the question of how and why they became the subject of political disputes in the first place.

One of the realities demonstrated by the papers under discussion here, however, is that the kind of political disputes over the role of banks which one finds in Great Britain, Germany, Austria, Belgium and Italy were not universal. The Canadian case analysed by Ian Drummond shows that banking systems which were not enmeshed in the conditions, ideologies and practices that caused or deepened the Great Depression could escape political debates about their role as well. In Canada, there was no central bank until 1935 and no real attachment to the gold standard. There did exist a complicated system of mutual support between the government and the banks in which

13

the banks could count on the government as a lender of last resort while the government could rely on the banks for short-term credits. The banks were not heavily engaged in industrial lending, and government guarantees prevented the banks from succumbing to the dangers of that area of lending in which they were most involved and most vulnerable, the so-called wheat pools. Thus, however nasty the depression in Canada, its tribulations did not include political conflicts over banks.

This was more or less the case in Greece as well, where the low level of industrialization and the limited industrial investment on the part of Greek commercial banks should have been a political issue but was not because neither the government nor industry were prepared to make it one. In contrast to Canada, Greece had a well-established and well-developed banking system and the capital needed to promote modernization, but neither the banks nor the regimes that ruled Greece in the interwar period were prepared either to encourage the banks to engage in long-term industrial investment or to provide an alternative to such financing. While Greece followed the English lead in going on to gold and created a central bank in 1928 and then went off gold in 1932, the English 'model', as Mazower shows, had very limited consequences in promoting either further industrialization or rationalization. Both the central bank and the largest commercial bank, the National Bank, co-operated in the liberal lending policy encouraged by the Venizelos government but were immune to the kind of crisis which hit Romanian banks because of their involvement in industrial finance and to the distress experienced in Yugoslavia because of the policy of contraction pursued there. The government preference for giving industry a protectionist regime rather than promoting technological progress reinforced the tendency towards inertia, and it was a policy with which the banks were in harmony with the government's low expectations of their performance in industrial financing.

In Japan, as Fletcher shows, there were few political disputes about the role of banks, not because there was the kind of relative uninvolvement of banks in industry and parallel attitudes on the part of banks and governmental leaders that one finds in Canada and Greece, but rather because government, banking and industry worked in relatively close collaboration in attempting to define policy and because, I would suggest, the primacy of national policy, reinforced by the interpenetration of elites, muted or obviated the kinds of overt conflicts over the relative positions of banks, industry and government that one finds in the Central European and in the Anglo-American situations. The debate over the timing of the reintroduction of the gold standard, for example, seems to have taken place within the banking community, government and industry as a mutual problem of common concern and national interest. Positions appear not to have been fixed but rather to have changed and been modified in pragmatic response to developments. The final decision to return to gold, however ill-timed in the wake of the 1929 New York Stock Market crash, was taken by the government 'only after broad-based consensus had been formed'. Similarly, there seems to have been remarkable consensus concerning the 1927 Bank Law, which promoted a policy of mergers of regional banks and which appears to have been conducted in a manner that was at once sensitive to regional and small business requirements and responsive to the necessity of creating strong financial institutions capable of servicing the large capital needs of industry. In contrast to Germany and Italy, where interwar societal corporatism and state corporatism[1] often functioned in an atmosphere of competition, tension and hostility among the various interests, the Japanese version of corporatist decision making, if it can be called that, seems uniquely harmonious. Obviously, there was jockeying for advantage and banks sought to reduce government controls and interference, but these do not appear to have been political issues except in the context of the much broader political conflicts pertaining to Japanese imperialism and the role of the army in the 1930s. Indeed, the abandonment of the gold standard seems to have taken place as harmoniously as its reintroduction a few years earlier. Banker objections to government fiscal irresponsibility and to the extreme merger policy pursued in the late 1930s were less conflicts over the role of banks than over the implications of a triumphant militarism and imperialism for the nation's economy and finances.

If one wishes to find real political conflicts over the role of banks, then one has to look elsewhere, and the most extreme example of political strife over the role of banks in the interwar period is supplied by Italy. Forsyth's description of the German-inspired mixed banking system in that country suggests that the Italians had taken over everything about that system except what made it work. The German system, at least before the First World War, rested on a very symbiotic relationship between the Reichsbank and the large universal banks and a hands-off policy on the part of the government. The Reichsbank functioned as a lender of last resort and a regulator of the credit market through its discount policy, and the banks engaged in innovative risk taking to promote industrial development. At the same time, they controlled the size of their portfolios through the timely floating of shares on a reasonably strong securities market and furthered stability in the economy by encouraging concentration and cartelization. In Italy, security market weakness made the banks especially vulnerable to crisis, while tensions between the great Milan banks and the Bank of Italy over the latter's attempts to regulate interest rates and credit and save failing banks exacerbated the vulnerabilities.

Forsyth also suggests that tensions between the Bank of Italy and the Milan banks were heightened by the fact that the leading director of the Bank of Italy, Bonaldo Stringher, and the officials of the bank came from the civil service rather than the world of finance and 'were more sensitive to the goals and concerns of the Italian state's political and administrative leadership than they were to those of the financial community'. This kind of explanation may indeed be helpful for Italy, but it does not hold for Germany, where the head of the Reichsbank from 1908 to 1923 was a career civil servant, Rudolf Havenstein, who proved a good servant of the state, the banks and industry. The fact that he died the world's greatest hyperinflationist as a result of allowing an excessive 'tanking up' by all three at the Reichsbank should not obscure the fact that the relatively smooth interrelationships and interpenetration of the state, banking and industry were made possible by a political economy in Germany that operated very differently from the one which prevailed in Italy.

In Germany, capitalism was highly organized on the basis of an ecology in which live and let live was the rule in so far as the various organized sectors of the economy could come to mutually acceptable compromises and in which that state tacitly subcontracted the management of the economy to the private sectors. What Forsyth shows is that the Prussian liberal economic model did not work in Italy because of basic economic liabilities, on the one hand, and because of banker ill-discipline and a hopeless intertwining of insolvent banking and industrial interests on the other. There was no ecology at all, and it was precisely the fact that the role of the banks was a major political issue well before the Fascists came to power that created the foun-

dation for the drastic solution taken in Italy through the nationalization of the banks and the creation of a huge publicly owned industrial
sector in the form of the IRI.

All this is not to suggest that the role of banks in Germany was not a
political issue, but what I believe my own contribution to this volume
suggests is that what I have here called the 'ecology' of the German system, while dramatically disturbed by the war and its aftermath, nevertheless continued to function and to move along lines true to its
previous evolution. Industrial self-financing had diminished the role
of the banks even before the war, and the major industrial sectors were
not tied up with the banks in the way they were in Italy. As in Italy, there
was dissatisfaction with the role being played by the banks in the post-
war economic reconstruction, but in Germany it was certain portions
of industry and a very small group of government officials who pressed
for an Economic Bank, a German IRI, while the central bank and the
leaders of the government joined the banks in opposing such a
scheme. At the same time, however, the German banks were not
powerful enough to stand in the way of the evolution of the banking
system at those moments when it was bursting the bonds of their own
conceptions. Like their Italian counterparts, the great Berlin banks
lost in their struggle to keep the savings banks from engaging in industrial investment, but the German battle was more painless because
here industry and the government came down on the side of the
savings bank. In short, where the German system of mixed banking
had, under Italian conditions, created a banking system that was a
major bottleneck in the economy and a source of severe political conflict, that same system in Germany had evolved into something much
less formidable and problematic by the time the banking crisis of 1931
came.

It was, of course, problematic enough, but I would argue that the
deficiencies of the banking system must be seen in the context of the
post-1924 financial and political settlement, and this was not the
creation of the German bankers. It was that settlement which had
enthroned Montagu Norman along with what Diane Kunz describes
as the 'Morgan ideology' – the return to the gold standard at pre-war
parities in England, Germany and certain other key countries, the
faith in central bank co-operation to make the system work, and the
policy regimes of balanced budgets which so exacerbated the problems when the Great Depression hit. As Kunz shows, there came a

point where political survival took precedence over Anglo-American banker orthodoxy and where the English bankers themselves bowed to reality. When J. P. Morgan went travelling about Europe in 1922, he was viewed as the potential saviour of the continent. In 1931–3, he could save the gold standard neither in Europe nor in the United States and one looked, sometimes with miserable results, to politicians, not bankers, for salvation.

In the last analysis, the political disputes about the role of banks in the interwar period were less about banks than about whether finance or economics were to have primacy. Inflation, war debts and reparations had placed finance in the forefront and encouraged rather erroneous conceptions about the true sources of prosperity in the pre-war period. Bankers were natural and important perpetrators of these misconceptions, but they were also their victims. When, as in Italy, they truly stood in the way of what Fred Hirsch and Peter Oppenheimer have called 'the subordination of finance to economic management',[2] which was one of the chief outcomes of the depression, they were true political losers. Where, as in Germany, Sweden, Japan, Great Britain and the United States, they abdicated in the face of political realities, they had only to bear the yoke of relatively mild regulation and recognition of the fact that banks were too important to the economy to be allowed to go unregulated or insufficiently regulated. Most importantly, they were also forced to recognize that economic and sociopolitical, that is, national interests demanded that banks and bankers not be allowed to play the kind of role they had been allowed to play in the period between the end of the First World War and the World Economic Crisis. This was the central political dispute about the role of banks. Whether or not it was finally settled in the 1930s, or subsequently, remains to be seen.

NOTES

1 For the application of this distinction first developed by Philippe Schmitter to the German case, see U. Nocken, 'Corporatism and pluralism in modern German history', in D. Stegmann, B.-J. Wendt and P.-C. Witt (eds.), *Industrielle Gesellschaft und politisches System. Beiträge zur politischen Sozialgeschichte. Festschrift für Fritz Fischer zum siebzigsten Geburtstag* (Bonn, 1978), pp. 37–56.
2 F. Hirsch and P. Oppenheimer, 'The trial of managed money: currency, credit and prices 1920–1970', in C. M. Cipolla (ed.), *The Fontana Economic History of Europe. The Twentieth Century. Part Two* (Glasgow, 1976), pp. 603–97, quote on p. 621.

3 Universal banking in interwar Central Europe

FRITZ WEBER

For the Central European banking system the interwar years meant a period of crisis which reached its dramatic peak in 1931 with the collapse of the Austrian Credit-Anstalt in Vienna and the Danatbank in Berlin. One has to bear this in mind when analysing bank–industry relations during the 1920s. The extent to which the Central European banks were hit by the world depression of 1929 was due to historical as well as contemporary reasons. It was a consequence of the fitful performance of regional industry after the First World War, characterized by cataclysmic developments like disintegration of the Danubian area and hyperinflation in various countries. Moreover, the banking crisis was aggravated by the symbiotic relationship between banks and industry inherited from the pre-1914 era.

Already in the nineteenth century, when – according to Alois Mosser and Alice Teichova – the Crédit Mobilier banks started to carry out the 'functions of a capital market', they had been extremely exposed to the storms of the business cycle, especially in periods of persistent stagnation such as after 1873. But even on the eve of the First World War the state of the Viennese banks was worse than was believed by contemporaries as well as by later historians like the mentor of Austrian banking history, Eduard März, who tended to underestimate the sneaking problems bottled up during the pre-war boom.[1] In 1913 one could, however, observe signs of frozen industrial credits and an over-accumulation of the banks' share portfolios.[2] The unwelcome results of this development were repressed only by the lucky chance of the war boom, which forestalled the onset of an economic depression.

Nevertheless, the nostalgic review of the interwar Viennese bankers identified the pre-1914 decade with a sound world without business cycles – to such an extent as to believe in a rapid return of a similar prosperity at any moment until 1930.[3] Some of the German bankers did so, too, whereas their Czech colleagues had a much more realistic insight into the economic environment.

The Czechoslovakian and German case will, however, be excluded from the following considerations, because the two countries represent a picture too different from Austria and Hungary. That Czechoslovakia avoided hyperinflation altered somewhat the pattern of bank–industry relations and brought forth a different attitude towards short-term credits offered by Western lenders. Foreign credits never played an important role as a means of financing industrial projects by the Prague banks. In inflation-shattered Germany industry succeeded – as K. E. Born has shown[4] – in loosening the ties with banks in the inflationary period. Moreover, the German giant industrial companies later had direct access to capital markets at home and abroad as well as to the credit facilities of foreign banks.

The parallels between Austria and Hungary, however, are striking: in both countries the dependence of industry on bank credit had already been closer than in Germany before the war.[5] In the stages of hyperinflation and deflation the links between banks and industry were considerably strengthened. Both economies were plagued by similar defects due to inflation: a substantial weakening of the capital basis of the banks,[6] an almost complete disappearance of the industrial working capital, and high interest rates following the end of inflation.

But why was the Austrian banking system hit harder than the Hungarian one? One explanation could be sought in different growth rates, since Hungary experienced a somewhat better economic performance than Austria. A second answer would be that Austrian banks suffered supposedly higher losses through both inflation and altered geopolitical circumstances. But thirdly, we have to look at the business strategies pursued after 1918.

Speaking about the inflationary period, Elizabeth Boross seems to lay the emphasis on a quasi 'rational' behaviour on the part of the bankers, determined by the long-term interest of the institutes they represented: that is, banks tended to look at clients as future profitable customers. But it is clear that – under inflationary circumstances – banks are forced to invent short-term tactics to avoid becoming net losers of the depreciation of money value.[7] The desire to defend a bank's traditional 'sphere of interest' in the industrial sector can, for instance, easily conflict with short-term profitability of banking business.

In Austria (and, incidentally, in Germany, too) the big commercial banks for an astonishingly long period charged – even if we take into account the various 'commissions' and other surcharges invented to cover credit costs – interest rates far below the inflation rate.[8] Only in the very last stage of hyperinflation did they introduce inflation-indexed interest rates and grant credits only in foreign currency. Thus, even though the risk of negative interest rates[9] was borne – to the greatest extent – by their creditors, the banks must have suffered from losses, at least to that extent to which they granted advances from their own capital funds.

The counter strategy developed by the Viennese banks was, increasingly, forcing firms to repay credits by new share issues (or persuading them to change the legal form into joint stock companies). This policy of 'Veraktionierung', which was part of the common 'flight into assets', resulted in a huge holding of industrial equities at the end of the inflationary period.[10] And the Viennese banks – although trying to do so during the stock exchange boom in 1923 – never succeeded in getting rid of their over-expanded equity hoard until the economic depression of the thirties, when they had to write off a large part of the shares almost to nil. The 'marasmus of the stock exchange'[11] frustrated every attempt to sell those 'old' security packages as well as to convert industrial advances into new share capital.

The stock exchanges in Prague and Budapest seem to have functioned better. At least Agnes Pogány reports that the Hungarian banks were able to sell off a great many of their huge equity portfolios after 1924.[12] Moreover, the Hungarians successfully introduced a new type of long-term industrial credit, mortgage loans, at the end of the 1920s. In Austria there was some discussion about corporate bonds; in reality, however, only a few big companies like the Alpine Montangesellschaft or the Krupp works in Berndorf and the Electrical Power Companies were in a position to approach foreign capital markets.

It should be clear now, that the question, to what extent industrial investment projects were determined by banking policy in a period in which access to external capital sources was decisive, affects also the status of the lender. In Austria, there was no alternative to financing by short-term credits. The minutes of the Viennese banks confirm the findings of Mosser and Teichova. They show – not counting exceptions – a continuous rise, but only a short period of really rapid credit expansion, starting in 1927 and ending in 1929. These few years sufficed to create unsolvable difficulties, since the borrowers proved to be unable to pay interest and amortization, and an ever-rising portion of the advances started freezing, at the latest with the onset of the world depression.

Pretty often investment projects proved to be callow and unconsidered, because bank managers did not waste much time examining them. The checking of debtors – as a more widely spread policy – started very late and was employed only if a company obviously had been declining into a very bad state.[13] The examination usually was only a bookkeeping one, not aiming at scrutinizing the commercial and technological aspects of investment decisions.

Nevertheless, the banks performed, as Boross states for Hungary, a 'progressive credit policy in promoting technological advances' in interwar Austria too, especially in automobile production and in the development of hydro-electric power plants. But this was rather smelling the rat, and presentiment rather than rational strategy: automobile production as a whole expected to become a profitable field for the future. The majority of those projects (as well as linkage investments in oil extraction in Galicia) proved to be detrimental, as will be shown elsewhere.[14]

The depression of the stock exchange forced the banks to finance client firms, as Boross formulates, to an extent 'at times going against sound banking principles'. The indebtedness of Austria's greatest automobile producer, the Steyr works, vis-à-vis her patron bank surmounted even the latter's share capital in 1929. Besides those excess advances a long list of instances of negligence could be computed, such as enhancing automatically credits to the extent of unpaid interest rates, and credits granted for the sole purpose of putting a client into the position to pay dividends (since the bank managers hoped to sell those shares later); it also meant the creation of such tricky instruments as 'Besserungsscheine' (bills of betterment) and 'bedingte Nachlässe' (qualified discounts), which were designed to enable the banks not to reassess and write off doubtful debts at an early date.

Thus the high interest rates and commissions the Viennese banks were charging should not only be interpreted as an outcome of inflation and deflation,[15] but also as an attempt to pass on the low returns and losses of the bad clients and the high costs of the bank apparatus to the shoulders of the good ones. This procedure cannot be regarded as far-sighted because even the best debtors were unable to bear such high burdens for any length of time, and the banks received the repercussions with a certain time lag, being forced to increase advances involuntarily.[16]

As in Hungary (and Germany) the Austrian banks tried to ease the weight of interest rates by procuring cheap Western credits to industrial companies. However, since only big firms could benefit from this privilege, a split credit market was created, with small and medium-sized firms as underdogs paying interest rates often twice as high as for dollar or sterling advances. And since the foreign short-term money was used for long-term investment, the latent danger of the different time structure of liabilities and lendings soon turned into actual dangers: yet it was not the withdrawal of foreign credits (as is often believed) that pulled banks into the abyss after 1929, but rather the cessation of the inflow of new funds from abroad, combined with the freezing of advances and the fall in value of securities. The recalling of foreign money was only the ominous last drop which made the barrel overflow.

Emergency mergers between banks could postpone only for a short while the difficulties of institutions, which had been heavily hit by inflation, and were – for better and for worse – chained to an industry addicted to bank credit: the bigger the industrial empire of a bank grew by absorbing another one, the worse were the potential dangers originating from the 'Konzern'. After a series of mergers the Credit-Anstalt combined two-thirds of the total of Austrian bank debtors in 1930, the total balance sheet equalling the budget of the national government.

When the bank got into troubles in 1931, its problems could therefore only be solved by the public hand: the state and the National Bank had to step in to prevent the closing of the counters. The main argument for state intervention (and, at the same time, the reason why even the Social Democrats were in favour of the rescue action) was to thwart the repercussions of the bank collapse on industry.

Indeed, the Credit-Anstalt was kept alive by heavy sacrifices of the state. And only after the government had assumed the financial burden of the bank vis-à-vis the National Bank and the foreign creditors[17] could the path of reconstructing the industrial combine be entered. The method usually chosen was the extensive writing off of advances, the cancelling of shares (lying in the portfolio of the Credit-Anstalt) and the conversion of a part of the credits into new share capital.

This policy can be regarded as a conscious part of a fundamentally supply side oriented strategy. It meant indirect state subsidies for the industry and aimed at facilitating the starting position of the Austrian economy for a future international upswing. Financing industrial investment, however, was never resumed by the banks during the 1930s. The bankers had, as one of their representatives stated, learnt the lessons of the twenties and restricted themselves within the confines of short-term lending.[18]

The failure of the Austrian Credit-Anstalt was only the worst (and most costly) outcome of the crisis of the Central European universal banking system. The biggest German banks had to be supported by the state,[19] and in both Czechoslovakia and Hungary banks were forced to considerably reduce their share capital to cover losses. In Austria only the subsidiary of the French-owned Banque des Pays de l'Europe Centrale got over the years of crisis without serious trouble. Even the well-conducted Wiener Bankverein had to be amalgamated with the Credit-Anstalt in 1934, after having received considerable public aid in 1933.

In an unfriendly interpretation one could call the years of the banking crisis the farewell to a period of illusions. Thinking positively, the historian should consider the early thirties the failure of an historical experiment – of the attempt to create an almost *anti-cyclical banking policy*, by which banks tried to counteract the adversities of the business cycle as well as of structural economic changes within the topsy-turvy Danubian territory. Obviously the task exceeded the contingencies of the banks.

NOTES

1 Cf. E. März, *Österreichische Industrie- und Bankpolitik in der Zeit Franz Josephs I.* (Vienna, 1968).

2 In 1913, a greater part of the share capital of the Viennese banks was tied by the security portfolio than was the case in the German banking community.

3 The same was true for the idea of Vienna remaining the financial centre of Central

Europe, which resulted in the costly attempt to carry on financing firms and banks in the successor states of the Monarchy.

4 Cf. K. E. Born, 'Die Deutsche Bank in der Inflation nach dem Ersten Weltkrieg', *Beitrage zu Wirtschafts- und Währungsfragen und zur Bankengeschichte,* 17 (1979), 27–8.

5 In that sense the Finance Capital 'reached its purest form' in the pre-1914 Habsburg Monarchy. See A. Teichova, *Rivals and Partners: Banking and Industry in Europe in the First Decades of the Twentieth Century,* Uppsala Papers in Economic History, no. 1 (1988), p. 3.

6 In Hungary the leading bank, the Hungarian General Creditbank, had preserved 37.4 per cent of her pre-war capital, the Commercial Bank of Pest about 25 per cent. In Austria the figures varied between 19 and 34.5 per cent. In Germany the average of the preserved capital was about 21 per cent.

7 Cf. H. Kernbauer and F. Weber, 'Die Wiener Grossbanken in der Zeit der Kriegs- und Nachkriegs inflation (1914–1922)', in G. D. Feldman, C.-L. Holtfrerich, G. A. Ritter and P.-C. Witt (eds.), *Die Erfahrung der Inflation im internationalen Zusammenlung und Vergleich* (Berlin and New York, 1984), pp. 153–75.

8 A possible explanation could be found in illusions of the bankers, concerning a future revaluation.

9 Until autumn 1921 interest rates for advances did not exceed 20–25 per cent, whereas the inflation rate amounted to 100 per cent.

10 Cf. Kernbauer and Weber, 'Die Wiener Grossbanken'.

11 Rudolf Sieghart, *Die letzten Jahrzehnte einer Grossmacht* (Berlin, 1932), p. 115. Sieghart was the President of the Boden-Creditanstalt, one of the leading Viennese banks during the 1920s.

12 Cf. A. Pogány, *From Cradle to Grave? Banking and Industry in Budapest in the 1910s and 1920s,* Uppsala Papers in Economic History, no. 6 (1988), pp. 13, 14.

13 The controlling department of the Credit-Anstalt, for instance, the 'Industrie-Inspektorat', was installed and extended in the years 1925 and 1926.

14 The author is preparing a detailed study of the Credit-Anstalt 1918–38 forthcoming soon.

15 The exact reasons for the high charges in Hungary have yet to be investigated.

16 The high charges were considered necessary, since the net profits of the banks were far below the pre-1914 level. Nevertheless, the banks paid relatively high dividends, showing profits which had been artificially created by dissolving 'hidden' and 'latent' reserves allegedly lying in the equity portfolios.

17 Cf. D. Stiefel, *Finanzdiplomatie und Weltwirtschaftskrise* (Frankfurt on Main, 1989), pp. 187–230.

18 Cf. J. Joham, 'Banken und Industrie im Dienste der Volkswirtschaft', *Österreichische Zeitschrift für Bankwesen* (November 1937).

19 Cf. K. E. Born, *Die deutsche Bankenkrise. Finanzen und Politik* (Munich, 1967).

4 Comparing the interwar banking history of five small countries in North-west Europe

ULF OLSSON

Banks, growth and industrialization

It should surprise no one that banks and banking systems have been popular subjects for economic historians. The relations between debtors and lenders and the power that goes with money have been important aspects of societies from time immemorial. The gradual process of commercialization in Western Europe and the capital-demanding industrialization naturally brought banks and the financial sector of the economy into focus. Several functions had to be fulfilled: trade needed credits as did investment in fixed capital. The need for secure – and preferably profitable – deposit possibilities grew as a result of the monetary penetration of the economy. In the development of European history as a field of study attention to financial aspects was crucial. Some of the earliest publications of business historians consisted of monographs dealing with banking. Often these studies include an analysis of what role the banks played in financing the industrial revolution. When the monographs deal with big, influential commercial banks or with central banks, they provide valuable information also on a more general level. The historical and monographical approach to banks could thus form a basis for general conclusions up to a certain level of aggregation, more seldom, though, above the national level. Traditional business historians have only reluctantly developed quantitative or formal models of bank behaviour.

For economists too, money and banking have been natural foci of investigation. On the macro level the financial sector enjoyed a special

26

interest after the Second World War, when many economists engaged in studying the so-called underdeveloped countries. Starting from rather unsophisticated and 'economistic' models they tried to measure the role of capital in the growth process, normally presuming there was a scarcity of capital. The Harrod–Domar model was the point of departure and in the impressive line of researchers we find names such as W. W. Rostow, A. Lewis and R. Nurkse. In retrospect, it might be argued that these approaches were rather unproductive; no general correlations between savings, capital accumulation and economic growth were established. The exercises were carried out on a level of aggregation where little of the empirical realities could be explained and little advice could be given to concerned governments. In his ambitious attempts to explain the long-term economic behaviour of modern industrial nations, using rather rough macro data for the financial sector, Simon Kuznetz likewise enjoyed limited success. The need for a broader view, including institutional factors also, became obvious.

Capital has played a less significant role in the analysis of economic growth since the 1970s as economists have become more humble in their attempts to explain the economic development of national economies.

From an economic historian's point of view, Rondo Cameron and his group used more attractive models when in the 1960s they ventured to explain the role of the banking system in industrialization in a number of foreign countries. The starting-point was the same: it was assumed that a well-functioning banking system would facilitate an industrialization process and a badly working system would hamper such a process. Early on the results seemed to verify the hypothesis, but as the research has progressed doubts have increased. Summing up in *Banking in the Early Stages of Industrialization* Cameron concludes that it is hard to establish significant general connections between the system of commercial banks and economic growth. He finds, however, normally higher figures for – or a spurt in the relative size of – the banking sector, i.e. the ratio of bank assets to national income, during the industrial 'take-off' of a specific country.[1] The causal meaning of such a finding is hard to establish, since the banking systems have been very different in individual national economies.

One of the crucial difficulties in comparing the role of banks in different economies is the very delineation of banks. It is normally possible to isolate commercial banks from the rest of the banking system, but the division of labour between them and savings banks, mortgage banks, state central banks, etc., differs immensely. Looking at relations with industry it is also worth remembering that industry sometimes satisfies its need for different financial services itself, completely without help from banks. The famous observation by Alexander Gerschenkron – that banks seem to perform a more central function in the industrialization process of nations like Germany, being more 'backward' than England, but not as backward as the late-comers in Eastern or Northern Europe – has had a restricted validity when tested more systematically. Gerschenkron's concept of back-wardness, as well as Rudolf Hilferding's concept 'Finanzkapital', has helped to structure our thinking about the role of banks, without, how-ever, being particularly useful in more quantitative or comparative attempts at general model-building.

These rather disappointing experiences in looking for regularities through comparative banking studies have not stopped economic his-torians from going on to explore the fascinating history of commercial banks and banking systems. As institutions banks stand in the focus of both the real economy and economic policy and their behaviour influ-ences both the nation as a whole and the individual as a depositor or a borrower. The papers that I have been asked to comment upon belong to a series of institutional and qualitative – rather than formalized or quantitative – studies, aspiring to cross-national conclusions. Once more economic historians heroically try to combine agent-oriented history with a more structural approach and to bridge the gap between narrative history and theory-building social science.

Model time meets historic time?

The two papers by Larsson and Vanthemsche deal with, respectively, Sweden, including an outlook on Denmark and Norway, and Belgium and the Netherlands. Both papers analyse the relations between the state, banks and industry during the two decades between the world wars. The five countries are small and situated in the north-western part of Europe. From a global point of view there certainly are other similarities too between them, but if we look at the banking system, and more specifically, the relations between the banks, industry and the state, there are also important differences. These can partly be explained by the diverging paths that were chosen by governments or financial authorities or by various influences from neighbouring countries. Looked at more closely, however, the banking systems of the early 1920s reflect the stage of general economic development and the degree of industrialization that the different countries had reached by the time of the First World War. The five pictures we are confronted with resemble five frozen frames from different parts of five motion-pictures. It could be argued that a better point of departure for a comparative study would have been to use a 'model' time concept, i.e. to start from frames from the same part of the film, for example scenes from the industrial breakthrough which did not take place at the same time in the five countries.

Three cases can illustrate the problem. In Norway the system of commercial banking was late and the numbers of banks and bank offices were still growing around 1920. The banks played an unimportant role for industrial development mainly because the country was still dominated by agriculture, fishing and trading but also because early attempts to establish banks of the Crédit Mobilier – or universal – type had failed. While Sweden at the end of the nineteenth century developed strong, regionally based commercial banks, Norway was still dominated by small, local savings banks. State discount commissions also played an important role at a late stage. The Bank of Norway never gave the private banks the privilege of issuing notes. As a result they could never build a position strong enough to resist the banking crises around 1880. It was foreign capital, not least from Swedish commercial banks, that financed the crucial wave of Norwegian industrialization around the turn of the century. Another ambitious attempt to establish a domestic investment bank, 'Central-banken for Norge', was hit by the crises of the early 1920s and the bank had to liquidate.

By that time the Swedes could already look back to a long period of successful universal or mixed banking. The private commercial banks enjoyed the right of issuing notes during the nineteenth century, but they had in addition expanded their depositing services, as had the new joint-stock banks. In a big trade-off with the Bank of Sweden, they ceded the privilege to issue notes, but managed to keep the advantage of direct contact with the customers, among which the growing industry soon was the most interesting. The commercial banks acted both as investors and entrepreneurs in the 'continental' fashion. When the Swedish process of industrialization accelerated, with a breakthrough during the 1890s, the banks were not hampered by restrictive legislation from supplying venture capital, but they also had a long experience of the risks involved. Consequently, compared to the Norwegian banks, the Swedish banks were economically stronger and functionally better suited to play their part in the reconstruction of the Swedish economy following the crisis after the First World War. Both the Swedish economy and Swedish commercial banks fared better during the post-war crisis than was the case in many other countries. In the Netherlands and in Denmark, as well as in Sweden, the system of commercial banking was by that time more developed than in Norway, reflecting the more versatile industrial character of these countries.

The Belgian example, finally, is of course the extreme case in this connection. Regions within the country were among the first to be industrialized on the European continent and developed the type of basic industry that needed heavy and sustained capital investment. Not surprisingly Belgium also pioneered the area of investment or mixed banking. The banks expanded in number, volume and influence right up to the 1920s. By that time, Société Générale and Banque de Bruxelles were the dominant institutions both as lenders and owners of manufacturing firms. During the post-war reconstruction of the economy, the banks became still more heavily involved with the industrial sector. The degree of domination of industry by the banks that we find in Belgium had no parallels in Sweden, which represented something of a middle way between the Belgian and Norwegian examples. The drawbacks of this policy for the Belgian banks themselves became visible first during the depression of the 1930s. According to critics, this involvement hampered the national economy for decades.

It is obvious that there were basic differences in the characters and roles played by the commercial banks in the small countries in Northwestern Europe at the beginning of the 1920s. The reasons for this situation are only to a very limited extent political decisions taken by parliaments and governments. Analysing the Scandinavian banking laws before the 1920s, Sven Fritz has emphasized the passive character of the legislation: 'Banking legislation was enacted after the fact, so to speak, and to a very great extent its purpose was to counteract conditions that were considered damaging or as being abuses of the system. In only a few exceptional cases was it intended to open new areas for banking activity.'[2] Laws and banking regulations probably had still less direct influence on the development of banking during the interwar period. In his paper Larsson presents little evidence for the role he sometimes ascribes to the earlier banking legislation in explaining what happened to the Scandinavian banks and economies after the First World War. Good explanations of the different outcomes in this respect mainly have to be built on the 'real' preceding history: the behaviour of the entrepreneurs, be they private or state-controlled, the stage and character of the ongoing process of industrialization, as well as the direct effects of the war and the post-war depression. This is not to say that the legislative aspect should not be studied.

The two papers we are discussing thus deal with five different banking systems partly because the systems represent different stages in a similar development pattern. They are the results of the gradual industrialization during the period before the First World War. The fates of these banking systems are then traced through the interwar period, which has a profoundly different character. The national as well as the international financial systems were disintegrating and the national economies were subject to external strains. All five economies were simultaneously hit by the same international shock-waves. Governments were forced to deal with similar and partly related problems, including the protection of their financial systems.

The fact that the papers we are discussing here deal with the interwar period makes a historical comparative approach especially attractive. The studies of banking and industrialization often compare developments and events that normally take place at different points in time. For an economist this is acceptable, since he is used to substituting model time for 'historical' time. An economic historian is normally more sceptical of these methods, since such an 'ahistorical' approach severely restricts the explanatory power of the analysis. Comparisons of 'historically' simultaneous sets of events should have a much better chance of revealing fundamental mechanisms in the systems involved.

Legislation and state control of banks

The post-First World War crisis hit the industrial and financial systems of all European economies. Depending on the severity of the problems and on the character of the relations between industry and banks, the latter experienced more or less damage. In Belgium the commercial banks were strong enough to move in and finance the reconstruction of industry. The 1920s thus saw the climax of the system of mixed banking. In contrast to the situation in Belgium, the Dutch banks had only recently started to finance industry on a large scale. Being inexperienced in the field, they were dangerously exposed to the industrial crises of the early 1920s and many had to be supported to avoid failures. The same type of public 'emergency treatment' was practised also in Sweden. As a result of the problems in industry, many banks were in the danger zone and the depositors' money could be saved thanks only to mergers and outside support. Financially sounder commercial banks as well as the government thus took part in the reconstruction of the banking system during the first half of the decade. A similar, but much more dramatic development occurred in Norway and Denmark. In both these countries depositors lost money as a result of bank failures, even though the governments intervened to stabilize the banking system. In Denmark the government was reluctant to do so, but finally had to support one of the biggest commercial banks facing liquidation. After serious losses many Norwegian banks were put under direct state administration to be subsequently liquidated. This abnormal situation reached its peak as late as 1927, when almost half of the commercial banks belonged to the group under state administration. This system was, however, completely wound up during the following years.

There are striking parallels in the stories of the five countries during the 1920s. Even if the problems varied in degree they mainly had their roots in the engagement in domestic industry. The state had to support the banks in order to protect depositors, but state involvement was seen as temporary and not as a step towards structural changes in the financial systems. Discussions about bank legislation and control got started, but the political will to enforce new rules was obviously not strong enough. In this field as well as others the economic policy of the 1920s aimed at returning to 'normal', pre-war conditions.

With the new international depression, first evident in 1929, the attitude towards the commercial banks changed. In all five countries new laws were enacted and new rules for regulation and supervision were enforced; this does not necessarily mean that the banks were in fact affected. In Belgium such a development seemed rather natural, since the problems for the commercial banks became formidable in 1934–5. The system of mixed banking was regarded as responsible for the severity of the crises. In addition to the financial short-term support of banks on the verge of bankruptcy, new laws were therefore enforced, confirming the rupture in the old symbiosis of banks and industry. Without real conflicts between the business community and the government a system for supervising commercial banks was gradually forced into a system of reporting to the central bank. The creation of publicly owned banks in order to achieve more support for industrial growth in the Netherlands is a very interesting development; the banks were in focus also for the Dutch discussion and blamed for the bad economic situation in the country. Here they were accused of being too little involved in industry; in Belgium they were accused of being passive because they were overly involved.

The radical critique against the banks was aired also in Sweden, even if the financial problems were much less threatening now than during the 1920s. The Kreuger crash, however, put the second biggest commercial bank in peril and it had to be rescued with the help of the government. Groups to the left of the social democratic majority asked why the bank should be saved after having taken part in the dirty business of an international swindler like Kreuger. They argued that a socialization of the banks or the creation of public alternatives would make more sense. However, the reformist policy won the day, and a 'Belgian' system was introduced also in Sweden. The banking law of 1933 did not allow banks to own industrial shares except as securities against claims in default, complementary rules were introduced to guarantee the solidity of the banks and the security of the depositors, and the position and authority of the Inspection Board was strengthened. No public alternatives to the private commercial banks were created.

In Denmark similar laws and regulations were introduced in 1930, while bank failures and depositor losses in Norway led to the introduction of basically the same policy some years earlier.

It is obvious that state involvement and legislation in the banking field generally increased as a result of the depression of the 1930s. Behind this development there seem to be political rather than economic reasons. The banks were accused of being too passive in their relations with industry, either because they were too much or too little involved. The commercial banks were, as usual, seen as nuclei of

the capitalist system, a system that according to many observers now
was finally breaking down. The anathema of the free market system
could be heard also from non-socialists like Keynes. His theories
furthermore gave a new role for the state in economic policy, as well as
putting the credit market in focus. The anti-capitalistic wave that put
an end to international free trade and the gold standard also necessarily influenced the financial system and the degree of freedom for the
commercial banks. This was true also within the five nations we are discussing here. They remained democratic, neither turning to fascism
nor to communism in these years of hardship. The five nations were
politically influenced from leading European centres, but they also
had many political and cultural links directly with one another. It
would probably be worth investigating to what degree they influenced
one another in the field of banking policy.

In his book *A Financial History of Western Europe* Charles P. Kindleberger distinguishes between three types of comparative history: 'the
impressionist or romantic that searches for parallels; the quantitative
of the sort undertaken by Bairoch, Chenery, Goldsmith, Kuznets, or
Maddison; and the sociological or model building that provides
criteria for looking from one country to another for general explanations'.[3] The two papers discussed here certainly have ambitions to
go beyond the first type and are obviously not aiming at the second.
They are rather aspiring to the third, and further work in this direction
should concentrate on improving the model to make it still more useful for comparisons. The framework for analysing relations between
banks and industry has so far received more attention than have the
links between banks and governments. Public opinion and the political processes behind changes in rules and legislation are probably one
of the areas worthy of more attention.

NOTES

1 R. Cameron, *Banking in the Early Stages of Industrialization. A Study in Comparative Economic History* (Oxford, 1967), pp. 300ff.
2 S. Fritz, 'Frågan om bankernas aktieförvärvsrätt under 1900-talets första decen-
nium', in *Från vida fält. Festskrift till Rolf Adamson 25.10.1987* (Stockholm, 1987),
pp. 1ff.
3 C. P. Kindleberger, *A Financial History of Western Europe* (London, 1984), p. 2.

5 American bankers and Britain's fall from gold

DIANE B. KUNZ

> ... when I remember that the men responsible in America for working with us ... are Mr. Mellon, the Secretary of the Treasury, the Governor of the Federal Reserve Bank and Messrs. Morgan I should like to say as my convinced opinion that in these men we are dealing with men [of] whom there are none higher for financial ability and moral rectitude.[1]
>
> Prime Minister Stanley Baldwin, May 1925

The 1920s and early 1930s marked a high-water mark in the influence and power of private bankers. In particular, the association between American bankers and the British government during the summer of 1931 became one of the most famous examples of the power of private finance. Indeed, the London *Daily Herald*'s accusation on 25 August 1931 that an American 'bankers' ramp' had caused the fall of the Labour government soon became established fact. But what actions did American bankers really take during that *annus terribilis*? The purpose of this chapter is to examine their role during Britain's battle to remain on the gold standard in 1931.[2]

i

The role of American bankers in international finance had continually expanded during the two decades preceding the British financial crisis of 1931. In part this evolution occurred because of the tremendous shift in world economic patterns caused by the First World War. The United States had been transformed from a debtor to a creditor nation while Britain, formerly the world's largest financial centre, had emerged from the war with massive debts to both the American public and private sectors. The European need for continual cash infusions for post-war reconstruction and restabilization greatly enlarged the role of the country with the deepest pockets.

Into this changed environment stepped men well suited to adapt to this 'brave new world'. Benjamin Strong, first Governor of the Federal Reserve Bank of New York (FRBNY), occupied a key position in the post-war new order. The Federal Reserve System, having begun operations only in 1914, remained in its formative stages. Because of Washington's indifference and his own inclination, but without real statutory authority, Strong transformed the FRBNY into an American central bank for international transactions. From 1918 until his death in 1928 Strong worked to restore the European financial system. In this endeavour he co-operated with his British counterpart, Montagu Norman, who for twenty-four years, beginning in 1920, autocratically ruled the Bank of England.[3] With messianic fervour Norman preached his ideology of central banking. At a time when the world-wide maintenance of the gold standard had changed from a relatively painless task to a difficult endeavour, the Governor of the Bank of England urged that central bankers should be independent of government control. Insulated from public pressure by their autonomy, central bankers could manage the technical and fiscal aspects of each nation's finances, while governments would attend to political and financial considerations.[4] No one yet perceived that this was a false dichotomy. Governments approved because Norman's theory meshed with their ideological and political preconceptions and allowed elected leaders to blame unpopular political choices on the central bankers. Central bankers welcomed this bifurcation because it aggrandized their positions and also protected monetary policy from the actions of 'weak' politicians who might be willing to barter fiscal prudence for votes.

The gold standard being central to Norman's *Weltanschauung,* clearly Britain, which had slipped from its golden anchor during the First World War, itself needed to return the pound to a gold basis.[5] On 28 April 1925, with the help of Strong and the House of Morgan, Norman met this goal: the pound had returned to a gold bullion standard at the pre-war parity of £1 = 4.86.[6]

During the 1920s the House of Morgan clearly reigned supreme as the leading American bank. It consisted of three interrelated houses: J. P. Morgan & Co., New York, Morgan Grenfell (London) and Morgan Harjes, later Morgan et Cie (Paris).[7] While the foreign branches lacked the market dominance of the New York head-quarters, they each had their special cachet.[8] Edward Grenfell, later Lord St. Just, head of the London branch, also served as Conservative Member of Parliament for the City of London and a Director of the Bank of England while the Paris house maintained close ties with all the French governments of the 1920s.[9]

J. P. Morgan occupied the central position in the bank his father, J. Pierpont Morgan, had led to wealth and notoriety. While he lacked his father's ambition and presence, 'Jack' dominated the House of Morgan.[10] Not the least of Jack's talents was his ability to gather around him men of exceptional talent, particularly Thomas W. Lamont, Russell C. Leffingwell and Dwight Morrow. All four individuals shared an ideology of public service. Certainly they intended that their transactions be profitable, but they also hoped to contribute to society, specifically by advancing the return to world-wide financial stability.

For the first year after Britain's return to the gold standard, matters proceeded smoothly but by early 1927 the Bank of England began to feel the strain of higher American interest rates. In July 1927, at a bankers' summit held in Long Island, New York, Strong pledged to lower the FRBNY's discount rate in order to diminish the attraction of the New York market. While London and other European financial centres benefited from this action, lower American rates fuelled the Wall Street boom.

Still the pull of the Wall Street money market proved increasingly irresistible to lenders seeking the maximum return on their money. During 1928, as central banks dealt with this problem, Strong died, and was succeeded by his deputy, George L. Harrison. A lawyer by training, Harrison had spent his entire career in the Federal Reserve System, joining the Washington board in 1914 as Deputy General Counsel (later General Counsel) and moving to New York, as Deputy Governor, in 1920. In the beginning doubts were expressed about his ability to step into Strong's role. But Leffingwell reassured Grenfell that 'George Harrison has been under the disadvantage of being young and new and a promoted subordinate and he has inherited all the antagonisms that poor Ben left behind him. But I have confidence in the soundness of his views and his ability to work out the situation ultimately.'[11]

At first the Wall Street crash of October 1929 seemed a blessing; no less worthy an observer than John Maynard Keynes welcomed the removal of the 'incubus' of the Wall Street market from European shoulders.[12] But during the next year it became increasingly apparent that world-wide economic conditions were rapidly deteriorating. The second renegotiation of reparations, known as the Young Plan, did not receive the same warm welcome as had the Dawes Plan five years later. An increasingly deep recession gripped the United States and international commodity and primary producer prices continued to tumble downwards. While observers had predicted an economic upturn during early 1931, the banking collapse of Central Europe ended any talk of recovery.

The chain of events began with the failure of the Credit-Anstalt, Austria's largest bank, on 15 May. In response Norman authorized a credit to the Austrian National Bank and convened an English creditors' meeting which included a reluctant Charles Whigham, a senior partner of Morgan Grenfell. Across the Atlantic, Harrison discussed the situation with Secretary of State Henry Stimson. This act had significance because under President Herbert Hoover, Washington had followed a rigorous 'hands off' policy towards European financial issues.

At the beginning of June Lamont took the initiative and discussed the world economy with Hoover directly. Sharing the conviction of most informed observers that the war debts/reparations burden was contributing to the financial crisis, on 5 June Lamont called Hoover to urge the President to advocate a moratorium on intergovernmental payments. Lamont's plea came at an opportune moment and the backing of this seemingly radical idea by the influential House of Morgan gave the plan respectability. Yet the President initially replied that 'politically it was quite impossible'.[13] For two weeks Hoover continued his resistance because, among other things, any action would require the American government to make an explicit connection between war debts and reparations, something that Washington had resisted for over a decade. But under pressure from various quarters the President finally decided to plunge in and on 20 June announced the Hoover Moratorium. It provided for a one-year suspension of all war debts and reparations payments. This intervention represented a significant reorientation for an administration which had resisted involving itself officially in European financial problems.

Unfortunately, the two-week delay dissipated the moratorium's effectiveness. Instead of preventing a German collapse, it came just as the Governor Hans Luther of the Reichsbank appealed to fellow central bankers for a support loan. On 16 June Norman and Harrison, together with Gates McGarrah, President of the Bank for International Settlements, and Clement Moret, Governor of the Bank of France, agreed that each of their institutions would lend the Reichsbank $25 million.

This massive credit did not stop the haemorrhage of German funds. The initial refusal of the French government to agree to the Hoover Moratorium exacerbated the burgeoning financial crisis. US Senator Dwight Morrow, formerly a Morgan partner, had urged Hoover to consult the French privately before announcing his plan. Hoover did not follow his advice and when French leaders learned that they were expected to agree to the postponement of all reparations, not just the softer conditional annuities, they reacted angrily. In the end the French government agreed to the moratorium but only after procrastinating until 7 July. This second delay, coming at a crucial point in the German crisis, squandered any remaining benefits which the moratorium might have brought. In a panic, Luther proposed a flying tour of European capitals to raise money for Germany. But it was too late. 13 July proved the crucial day. The *Darmstädter und Nationalbank* (or Danat), one of the large German banks, failed. Concurrently, the British 'Committee on Finance and Industry', popularly known as the 'Macmillan Committee', released its report.[14] Not only did the report damn the gold standard with faint praise, but it revealed that British banks had outstanding liabilities in Germany of £267 million or over twice the amount of the reserves of the Bank of England. In response the Bank of England began to lose reserves as holders of sterling exchanged their pounds for dollars and francs. Even Norman was disheartened. That apostle of central bank independence told his fellow bankers on 13 July that the world's financial problems were now too big for the central banks and must be handled by governments.[15] However, governments were not yet fully ready to assume this role. Therefore, Norman's allies in the battle to save the gold standard were his American counterpart and the Morgan Bank.

ii

All three Morgan branches had been paying close attention to the German crisis. When the New York partners learned about Luther's trip and his goal of a new German credit of $500 million, they cabled Grenfell on 10 July in astonishment. Instead of new loans, Morgan's (NY) advocated austerity, i.e. raising the discount rate and further credit restrictions. The partners felt that the failure to take these steps created a bad impression among American banks as did the fact that German nationals had withdrawn their funds from Germany while simultaneously asking foreigners to continue their lines of credit. The cable ended on a stern note: 'the rest of the world is thoroughly tired of the incapacity which the Germans have shown to deal with their own problems and that the Germans themselves might as well understand here and now that they are not going to be babied any longer and if they get future credits it will be only because they deserve them'.[16]

The significance of this cable lies in its encapsulation of the Morgan ideology. The partners could not be accused of taking a parochial attitude towards financial issues. The Morgan bank had been heavily involved in the major currency restructurings of the 1920s, most importantly the Dawes and Young loans and the French stabilization. Yet they subscribed to the traditional banking orthodoxy which emphasized the importance of both the gold standard and a balanced budget. Further, they espoused belt-tightening and deflation as the remedy for a currency under siege. But their philosophy is most notable for its ordinariness. Bankers, eager to protect their investments, are rarely innovative thinkers and the Morgan partners were no exception. American governmental leaders espoused a similar set of beliefs as did most British politicians and their French and German counterparts. Mindful of the German inflation of the 1920s, men worried that any laxity in fiscal orthodoxy would set off what British economist H. D. Henderson termed 'a real degrinolade'.[17] Rather than imposing its views on governments, the House of Morgan was echoing the viewpoint of their contemporaries.[18]

While the German crisis intensified, the Morgan bankers became more concerned at the sudden weakening of the British position. After 14 July sales of sterling steadily increased. On 22 July the Bank of England raised the bank rate 1 per cent to $3^1/2$ per cent and then raised it a further 1 per cent on 30 July. However, as representatives of seven major nations met in London to discuss the German financial crisis, Norman grew more and more panicky. Indeed Prime Minister and Labour Party leader Ramsay MacDonald described the Governor as 'frightened to death and scared'.[19] As it happened, J. P. Morgan had already left the United States for his annual British summer holiday. Immediately upon docking in Southampton, he journeyed to London for a conference with Norman. The Governor expressed himself concerned at the continued willingness of the British government to tolerate unbalanced budgets. Norman then asked Morgan about the possibility of a British government borrowing in the United States. Morgan replied that it seemed to him that 'before they could wisely borrow in the U.S.A. the government would have to show at least some plan of restoration of financial stability and should at least have expressed the intention to reduce the expenditures to come within their means'. Norman replied that this 'was quite right' and that Chancellor of the Exchequer Philip Snowden had authorized him to discuss this matter with Morgan and to report to him on the result.[20] Clearly Morgan's views were shared both by Norman and by the British Minister charged with responsibility for the Treasury.

In the event, on 1 August the FRBNY and Bank of France each lent the Bank of England £25 million ($125 million). The prevailing orthodoxy held that a large support credit would stop a run on a currency since its availability would convince holders that the currency would not be devalued. However, three factors prevented this massive credit from working its magic. First, on 1 August the British government released the report of the May Committee which predicted a British government deficit of £120 million. At a time when an unbalanced budget seemed the height of financial irresponsibility, this report apparently indicated an imminent disaster. Secondly, in what appears to have been a deliberate attempt to increase the pressure on the government, the Bank of England allowed the pound's value to drop on the Paris bourse.[21] Finally, the London Conference and follow-up experts' meeting in Basle resulted in the so-called 'Standstill' or *Stillhaltung* Agreement which provided for a freeze on German debts. The continued illiquidity of British bankers' German loans, initially blocked in the wake of the Danat bank's failure and subsequent closing of all German banks, now further increased the strain on sterling.

By 20 August a British government crisis was clearly in the offing.

Norman, having suffered one of his periodic nervous breakdowns, had left Britain for Canada. In his absence Deputy Governor Ernest Harvey and E. R. Peacock, head of Baring Brothers and Norman's intimate friend, informed the government that the maintenance of the pound on the gold standard required another and larger borrowing. But significant budget cuts were a prerequisite to any foreign loan. Again, this accorded completely with the sentiments of Conservative and Liberal leaders as well as the Prime Minister and his Chancellor.[22]

The showdown came on 23 August. MacDonald had requested that Harvey ask Morgan's (NY) if it would make a loan to the British government should significant budget cuts be made. The Morgan partners, assembled at the Long Island house of F. D. Bartow, told Harvey by telephone (confirmed by cable) that while a public loan would be out of the question until after Parliament met, a private credit might be possible. If the British government desired such a credit, the partners would canvass the New York banking community. They did enquire: 'Are we right in assuming that the program under consideration will have the sincere approval and support of the Bank of England and the City generally and thus go a long way towards restoring internal confidence in Great Britain?'[23] The purpose of their question was not to put pressure on the British government. Rather, the Morgan partners realized that the Bank of England, not they, should decide if the economic programme made sense. Morgan's (NY) did not want responsibility for judging the wisdom of the British government's decision; that was for the Bank of England. And if the City did not approve of the measures, British holders would no doubt continue to dump sterling, thus nullifying the usefulness of the loan.

MacDonald conveyed this message to his Cabinet late on 23 August.[24] After heated debate the Cabinet split on the issue of further cuts of £12 million in unemployment benefits. MacDonald went to the King to tender his resignation but by the next day had been persuaded to stay in office at the head of a National Government. With Conservatives and Liberals agreeing to serve, it seemed as if the battle to save the gold standard was a success.[25]

iii

The new government in place, Morgan, Grenfell formally requested Morgan's (NY) to consider a short-term loan to the British government. Unfortunately, the outlook was already less than cheerful. MacDonald's action had split his party. Violent recriminations had already begun, fuelled in part by the *Herald* article of 25 August which alleged that on 23 August George Harrison had demanded cuts in the dole as the *quid pro quo* for arranging British government credits.[26] On 24 August a leading article in *The Times* revealed that the central bank credits were almost exhausted.[27] At a time when prevailing theory held that smoothly working markets required minimal information, this disclosure caused alarm in financial circles, depleting the climate of optimism Morgan bankers hoped the National Government would engender. Yet by 25 August Morgan's (NY), following its long-held view that the bigger the credit the better, suggested an American loan of at least $150 million if not $200 million, to be accompanied by a simultaneous borrowing in Paris. This operation would be the largest support credit ever assembled. What made it even more remarkable was that the Morgan Bank put together an offering at a time when American banks were under great strain, both because of their German exposure and from the worsening domestic American financial crisis. As J. P. Morgan told British Treasury officials: 'there is not a single institution in our whole banking community which actually desires the British Treasury Notes on any terms'.[28] But the Morgan Bank used its considerable influence to create an American syndicate of 110 banks and fund a loan of $200 million. The partners took this action, which involved what Lamont tactfully labelled 'difficulties', in part because as prime sellers of British government notes, they were eager that their borrower's credit rating remain acceptable.[29] But more importantly, the Morgan partners believed that staying on the gold standard was the high road, which all countries would do well to follow.[30] Having helped Britain to return the pound to gold in 1925, how could they not aid this noble quest, particularly when the Bank of England, with which they had worked for the previous decade-and-a-half, requested their help?

The British government loan agreement was signed on 28 August and borrowings began immediately. Simultaneously British Treasury officials arrived in Paris to negotiate a similar credit which was signed on 10 September. Unfortunately by that time the British situation had clearly deteriorated. The reconvening of Parliament on 8 September revealed deep fissures in the House of Commons as Labour Party MPs subjected MacDonald to vicious attacks. Having hoped for a united country, the Morgan partners expressed dismay at what Grenfell termed this evidence of hatred.[31] Further, the new Cabinet was bitterly divided over the question of protection. But just as they had done all summer, the American bankers were forced to watch events from the sidelines, taking no part in these crucial matters. The Bank of England even ignored their input on financial matters. From 31 August New York partners had been worried by the discrepancies between the spot and forward rates for sterling and the different sterling rates in various markets. They remained troubled also by the Bank's failure to raise its bank rate – the classical remedy in a crisis of this sort. But their comments were ignored even when the drawings under the American tranche reached the 40 per cent level on 7 September.[32]

The mutiny of sailors at Invergordon on Tuesday, 14 September set in train a seemingly inexorable series of events. Losses from the Bank of England's reserves amounted to £5 million on Wednesday, and £10 million on Thursday. On Friday, 18 September Harvey and Peacock informed a bewildered MacDonald that the battle for Britain's gold standard had been lost. It was not until late that night that Harvey told the grim tidings to Harrison and the Morgan partners. The Americans expressed astonishment and dismay; Harrison, for one, enquiring repeatedly on Saturday if there remained any way to save the gold standard.[33] During Sunday Morgan's (NY) cabled the London House suggesting that if the Bank of England raised the bank rate and enacted controls over trading in sterling, the gold standard could yet be rescued.[34] The Bank of England ignored these appeals and on Monday, 21 September Parliament approved the requisite legislation. Britain had left the gold standard.

Traditional wisdom has it that the Bank of England had absolutely no choice in this matter – outside forces pushed the pound off the gold standard. Yet an examination of the evidence reveals that Harvey and Peacock, without consulting their American allies, took the decision that it made no sense for Britain to keep fighting what appeared to be an increasingly futile battle.[35] Three reasons support this conclusion. First: the Bank of England never followed Bagehot's advice to lend dear but to lend freely. It refused to raise the bank rate until after 21 September and never let gold go in the quantities that contemporaries expected.[36] Second: during August and September Treasury and Bank of England officials as well as various Conservative Party politicians began expressing doubts about the gold standard. Early autumn also saw the beginning of an increasing xenophobic condemnation of the United States and France for supposedly violating the rules of the gold standard game. This change of attitude permitted the directors of the Bank not only to think the unthinkable but permitted them to conclude that a decision to depart from gold would be welcomed by their countrymen.

Finally, during the 1956 British financial crisis, Sir Humphrey Mynors 'recalled the precedent of 1931 when the gold standard was maintained until the reserve had fallen to an amount approximately equal to the total of short-term credits which had been taken and used in order to maintain the standard. Some objective test of this kind is a line of defence against the accusation of having abandoned the fight too soon.'[37] As Mynors was a confidante of Harvey, the veracity of his comment may be assumed.[38]

What stands out is the clear lack of any input by American bankers. Harrison was neither consulted nor even informed about the decision until it was irrevocable. The Morgan partners found themselves in the same unenviable position. They were kept in the dark, not only by Harvey and Peacock but by Edward Grenfell who in his position as Director of the Bank of England knew well the Bank's intentions. Grenfell had put his loyalty to the Bank above his loyalty to his partners. As a Morgan's internal memorandum delicately put it: 'J. P. Morgan had a very great grievance against Grenfell.'[39]

However, within three weeks Morgan partners found themselves occupied with an equally difficult task: convincing European banks that the massive withdrawals of gold from the FRBNY did not signal an American departure from the gold standard. When, in April 1933, the American government took this action, the Morgan partners would again find themselves ignored. Norman proved prophetic: economic questions had become a matter for governments, not bankers. Not for another forty years would bankers have significant financial power. When they did, during the petro-dollar recycling of the 1970s, bankers would face problems similar to those which had bedevilled their predecessors.

NOTES

1 Morgan Grenfell Papers, London, British Gold Standard Gold Credit-1925, Grenfell and Lamont to Morgan, no. 25/4615, 5 May 1925.

2 For a more detailed history of the events of 1931, see D. B. Kunz, *The Battle for Britain's Gold Standard in 1931* (London, 1987). The legend of the 'bankers' ramp' has also been addressed by Philip Williamson in 'A bankers' ramp? Financiers and the British political crisis of August 1931', *English Historical Review*, 99 (October 1984). Other articles include D. Williams, 'London and the 1931 financial crisis', *Economic History Review*, 15 (April 1963), and D. E. Moggeridge, 'The 1931 financial crisis – a new view', *The Banker*, 120 (1970). However, neither Williams nor Moggeridge had access to significant documents which became available in the 1980s.

3 The Bank of England at this time was a privately owned institution which, among other things, acted as the bank for the British government.

4 Bank of England, London, G 15/7, Note of a conversation between Norman and Snowden, 4 September 1929.

5 Although sterling officially remained on the gold standard during the war, trading in the pound had been curbed since 1914. On 1 April 1919 the export of gold was prohibited under regulations promulgated pursuant to the Defence of the Realm Act. These restrictions were re-enacted in the Gold and Silver (Export Control) Act 1920 which would expire in December 1925.

6 The FRBNY provided a loan of $200 million and Morgan's (NY) assembled a credit of $100 million. No drawdowns under either credit were necessary. For the best account of the British government's return to gold, see D. E. Moggeridge, *British Monetary Policy 1924–1931: The Norman Conquest of $4.86* (London, 1982).

7 The authoritative book on the first half-century of J. P. Morgan & Co. is V. P. Carosso, *The Morgans: Private International Bankers 1854–1913* (Cambridge, 1987). Kathleen Burk has written an authorized history of Morgan Grenfell: *Morgan Grenfell 1838–1888: The Biography of a Merchant Bank* (London, 1989).

8 During the 1920s the House of Morgan possessed the largest interest in foreign banks of any American lending institution. In 1931 the Commerce Department estimated the American investment in foreign banking institutions at $125 million. Of this Morgan's accounted for $5.5 million, namely from the par value of the paid-up portion of Morgan Grenfell & Co. shares plus a pro rata equity in the surplus of the London Company plus their large interest in Morgan et Cie. See C. Lewis, *America's Stake in International Investments* (Washington, D.C., 1938).

9 A comparison of Morgan Grenfell with Baring Brothers will yield a picture of the relative size of the institutions. In 1929 Morgan Grenfell had a capital of £2,582,958, gross earnings of £670,039 and a net profit of £533,370. In contrast Barings had share capital of £1,025,000, gross profits of £646,724 and net profits of £405,963. Indeed the 1920s saw Morgan Grenfell's profitability increase steadily. Net profit, at £195,561 in 1920, increased throughout the decade until in 1930 it stood at £533,370. In 1931 the firm sustained its first loss in almost two decades but then returned to profitability in 1932. See Burk, *Morgan Grenfell*, pp. 268–9; P. Ziegler, *The Sixth Great Power: Barings, 1762–1929* (London, 1988).

10 For example, Anne Morrow Lindbergh recalls that her father, Dwight Morrow, and all his partners remained in awe of Mr Morgan. Author's interview with Anne Morrow Lindbergh, 3 March 1989.

11 Russell C. Leffingwell Papers, Yale University, New Haven, Conn., I/3/69, Leffingwell to Grenfell, 29 May 1929.

12 J. M. Keynes, *The Collected Writings of J. M. Keynes, Vol. XX – Activities 1929–1931* (Cambridge, 1981), p. 1.

13 Lamont Papers, Harvard University, Boston, Mass., 99–18, Lamont Memorandum, undated.
14 Report of the Committee on Finance and Industry, Cmd 3987.
15 Federal Reserve Bank of New York, New York, Harrison Papers, 3115.2, Harrison Memorandum, 14 July 1931, concerning telephone conversation with Norman, 13 July 1931.
16 B/E, G 1/43, J. P. Morgan, NY to Morgan Grenfell & Co., no. 31/2313, 10 July 1931.
17 Public Record Office, Kew, MacDonald Papers, 30/69/260, Henderson, 'Notes on the Economy Issue', 27 August 1931.
18 For a masterful chronicle of the evolution of British economic thought during this period, see P. Clarke, *The Keynesian Revolution in the making 1924–1936* (Oxford, 1988). For another view of the same issue, see R. W. D. Boyce, *British Capitalism at the Crossroads 1919–1932* (Cambridge, 1987).
19 Stimson Papers, Yale University, New Haven, Conn., Stimson Diaries, reel 3, vol. 17, 22 July 1931.
20 Morgan Grenfell & Co., London, German Crisis 1931, MG to JPMNY, no. 31/4894, 29 July 1931.
21 Kunz, *The Battle for Britain's Gold Standard*, pp. 91–3.
22 MacDonald and Bank of England officials had been briefing Conservative and Liberal party leaders about the crisis since 12 August.
23 MG, BG Credit-1931, JPMNY to MG, no. 31/2383, 23 August 1931.
24 Harvey conveyed the comments of Morgan's (NY) to MacDonald. This message laid the basis for the 'bankers' ramp' myth. Among other things, politicians assumed the message was from Harrison, who occupied an official American government position. However, the real explanation for the popularity of the legend lies in the fact that American bankers provided politicians with a convenient scapegoat.
25 Baldwin, former and future Prime Minister and Leader of the Conservative Party, for one wanted Labour to remain in power because 'Labour had to look after their own chickens as they come home to roost'. Neville Chamberlain Papers, Birmingham, 7/11/24-1, Baldwin to Chamberlain, 15 August 1931.
26 *Daily Herald*, 25 August 1931.
27 *The Times*, 24 August 1931.
28 MG, BG Credit 1931, JPMNY to MG, no. 21/2401, 27 August 1931.
29 A sterling devaluation, however, would not affect British government debt issued in the United States because it was denominated in dollars. For Lamont quote, see MG, BG Credit 1931, Lamont to Grenfell, 10 September 1931.
30 See, e.g., MG, BG Credit 1931, Leffingwell to Sanchez, 2 October 1931, where Leffingwell, the most philosophical of the Morgan partners, expounds at great length on his ideas about the gold standard.
31 MG, BG Credit 1931, Grenfell to Morgan, 17 September 1931.
32 MG, BG Credit 1931, JPMNY to MG, no. 31/2417, 31 August 1931, no. 31/2418, 1 September 1931, no. 31/2437, 7 September 1931, MG to JPMNY, no. 31/4987, 8 September 1931.
33 George L. Harrison Papers, Columbia University, Binder 59, Harrison Memorandum dated 19 September 1931 concerning telephone conversations with Harvey at 6.30 a.m. and 8.35 a.m.
34 MG, Gold Standard-Bundle 133, JPMNY to MG, no. 31/2461, 20 September 1931.
35 However, it would appear that they spoke with Norman. Although most accounts

such as those by Sayers (cited above), Sir H. Clay (*Lord Norman*, London, 1957) and Boyle (*Montagu Norman*, London, 1967) state that Norman knew nothing of the departure of the pound from the gold standard until his return to Britain on 23 September, from recently available evidence it appears quite likely that Norman was involved in this crucial decision. Contrary to his usual practice when undergoing a *crise de nerfs*, Norman had gone not to South Africa where he would have been incommunicado but to Canada. While there he stayed in touch with Harrison, cabling him on 22 and 23 August to give an evaluation of the Labour government's last-ditch budget-cutting proposals. Among other things, the texts of these cables show that the Governor of the Bank of England was in command of his faculties and fully abreast of the situation at Threadneedle and Downing Streets. Thereafter Norman stayed in touch both with the Bank of England and with Harrison. Indeed the two central bankers spent the crucial days of 14 and 15 September together in Quebec. Obviously their rendezvous included a discussion of the crisis facing the Bank of England. Accordingly, Norman was aware both of the plight of sterling and the American reaction to the latest financial crisis. Under these circumstances, it is impossible to believe that Norman, on the one hand, and Harvey and Peacock, on the other, were not in communication between 13 and 16 September, the day on which the governor boarded the *Duchess of Bedford*, bound for Liverpool. (The last surviving cable between Norman and the Bank of England is dated 10 September.)

Furthermore, given Norman's belief that 'La Banque, c'est moi', it beggars the imagination to conclude that he was not part of the seemingly abrupt decision to jettison the gold standard. The fact that in years subsequent to the crisis Norman grew closer to Peacock and Harvey, substantiates the conclusion that Norman felt that his lieutenants had played their parts faithfully in his absence. Finally, Norman having been in a precarious political position during the summer of 1931, his apparent absence during the climactic decision to jettison the gold standard would have been desirable as it could serve, *inter alia*, to protect him should any recriminations follow the débâcle of the policy which he had for so long championed. For a complete explanation of Norman's actions during August and September 1931, see Kunz, *The Battle for Britain's Gold Standard*, pp. 121–34.

36 See, e.g., B/E, G 14/316, Niemeyer Memorandum, 21 September 1931.

37 B/E, G 1/99, Mynors to Bolton and Parsons, 11 December 1956.

38 See R. S. Sayers, *The Bank of England 1891–1944* (Cambridge, 1976), vol. II, pp. 437 and 444.

39 MG, BG Credit 1931, Memorandum concerning 1931 Crisis, undated, p. 19.

6 Banks and the problem of capital shortage in Germany, 1918–1923

GERALD D. FELDMAN

Finding a satisfactory point of departure for the analysis of the role of Germany's banks and banking system in the Weimar Republic presents some very special difficulties despite the progress that has been made in the history of German banking in recent years. On the one hand, the 'capital' required by the historian, namely the unpublished records of banks, bankers and their associations, is available in much more limited quantity than the business records at the disposal of students of German industrial history, either because of physical destruction and barriers – temporary, one hopes – to access, or because what is available is not generally known and has not been much used. On the other hand, there are great uncertainties facing the historian who wishes to provide a comfortable interpretation of the place of interwar German banking in the short-term and long-term history of German banking. The two sets of problems are, of course, intimately related since more sources and more research would help to clarify our explanatory options.[1]

What context is one to emphasize, for example, in dealing with the responsibility of German banking organization, practices and policies in the unleashing of the banking crisis of 1931? One may, of course, stress the 'sins' of the banks, transgressions to many of which their leaders themselves confessed in the famous investigation of 1933 into the causes of the banking crisis: excessive competition within the banking sector as a whole, overexpansion and concentration by the great Berlin banks at the expense of the provincial and private banks and to the detriment of small and medium-sized business borrowers, inadequate resistance to the demands of public and private borrowers and, above all, the dangerous practice of granting short-term credits for long-term investments often against the better judgement of the lenders. Given the scope of the bank crash, a trip to the confessional was unavoidable, but the bankers who survived to testify about the débâcle had no intention of overdoing their penance either in word or in deed. The explanatory context they employed to account for their failures, by and large, was one that attributed the banking collapse to causes beyond their control: the depletion of Germany's capital by war and inflation; reparations; unavoidable but excessive dependence on foreign, primarily American, capital; harmful government policies of overtaxation, excessive expenditure for social and other purposes, and promotion of high wages, all of which led to harmful competition between the public and private sectors for capital, and exaggerated demands by private industry forced to undertake an 'overrationalization' of its plants because of high labour and social costs. It was obviously more politic to echo the charges of industry against the 'Weimar system' than to overdo the notorious abuse of the credit system by certain industries and firms, and it would have been absolutely suicidal to more than hint that the Reichsbank had undermined the efforts to procure long-term credit from abroad in important instances or that the Reichsbank had not done all it could have as a lender of last resort in the crisis. Hjalmar Schacht, after all, was the *Dirigent* of the proceedings in 1933, gently chiding State Secretary of Economics Gottfried Feder for digressions on matters of *Weltanschauung* instead of sticking to business, affording National Socialists the opportunity to air their discontents and present reform ideas but not the opportunity to have them seriously considered, and ensuring that the banks would be spared the socialization or extreme controls which National Socialists, but not only National Socialists, thought they deserved. Germany's banks and bankers did not suffer the fate of their Italian counterparts. The investigation ended in a paean to conciliation by Schacht and a strengthening of the position of the Reichsbank. It also eventuated in the Banking Law of 5 December 1934 which, given the ideology and character of the Nazi regime, was by no means extreme. Germany was hardly alone in legislating increased state control and surveillance of the banking and credit system at this time.[2]

If economic historians have not fully accepted the self-exculpation of the bankers in all its facets, above all not with respect to the bankers' political judgements of the Weimar regimes, they have nevertheless been remarkably 'sympathetic' to the basic explanatory context provided by the bankers. Thus, the East German historian Manfred Nussbaum, while criticizing the great banks for paths not taken to increase their long-term assets and for faulty credit policies, emphasizes structural changes in the international and national credit markets and the credit shortage in explaining the banking collapse.[3] Gerd Hardach, while conceding that 'the banks had become somewhat careless in their drive for financial reconstruction',[4] provides a similar explanation and hastens to point out that a more cautious policy in the context of the gold standard and Reichsbank restrictions might have made things worse. This view is shared by Carl-Ludwig Holtfrerich, who views the sharp diminution of the capital stock and reserves of the banks relative to deposits as part of a secular trend. The real issue was the shortened term-structure of credit operations after the inflation, and the only way in which the banks could have protected themselves against the bank-run was by reducing the credits they granted between 1924 and 1929 until they could 'refill' their balance sheets. The price of such a policy, however, probably would have been higher unemployment than the 10 per cent average between 1924 and 1929.[5] Knut Borchardt goes even further in suggesting that the trap was inescapable, not only absolving the German banking structure of responsibility for the collapse by pointing out that the entirely different systems in France and the United States proved no protection against disaster, but also arguing that the really astonishing thing was that the system survived the severe crisis of 1929–31 and insisting that 'the banking crisis was a part of a state crisis, not an autonomous development which might easily have been avoided by some more adroit behaviour on the part of the bankers'.[6] Lastly, Harold James, in the more detailed account provided in *The German Slump*, places the blame for the toppling of 'a fundamentally unsound structure'[7] characterized by insufficient capital, low liquidity ratios and conservative investment policies squarely on the shoulders of the German government, which tolerated a massive flight of capital and mismanaged its debt. The political crisis at once triggered the banking crisis and exaggerated the political crisis by inflaming populist anti-capitalist paranoia which tended even in its more latent phases to focus on financial institutions.

One of the many virtues of James' *German Slump*, however, is that he makes some attempt to place the behaviour of the German banking community during the Weimar Republic in the context of its long-term role in providing and/or mobilizing capital for German industry and trade. From this perspective, if I read James correctly, the leadership of the great banks suffered from a special threefold slump of their own, some aspects of which have already been elaborated upon by other historians. First, the relative role of the banks in the financing and guidance of German industrial development had been declining even before 1914 thanks to increased industrial self-financing. It would seem that the dominating influence of finance capital was coming to an end even as its leading theoreticians were describing it before 1918. In addition to increased industrial self-financing, the need to form consortia for the amassing of capital and the tendency of great bankers to accumulate supervisory board (*Aufsichtsrat*) seats in numbers that far exceeded their capacity to follow the affairs of the individual firms and concerns with which they were involved also served to check their influence. My own research on Hugo Stinnes and his enterprises suggests that where the bankers with whom he dealt played close attention to technical and managerial issues of the Stinnes-owned or -influenced enterprises in which they invested during the first decade of the twentieth century, they tended to be much less active in the five years before the war and seemed most intent on using their supervisory board positions to get Stinnes' commercial business.[8] Secondly, James accepts the general argument made by other students of the period that the war and inflation greatly increased these tendencies. Government contracting and subsidization of new plant as well as the generally high liquidity made self-financing more possible than ever and virtually eliminated even the need to turn to the banks for operating capital in the form of commercial bills. There can be little question that the banks reached the nadir of their influence on industry between 1914 and 1923. Thirdly, the great banks emerged from the war and inflation with their capital greatly depleted and yet an important measure of their power restored. The recovery of power was parlous because of the depletion of their capital and dependence on short-term foreign money. The post-war great banks owed much of their putative strength to the absorption of provincial banks during the inflation and to major fusions, a concentration process that was to continue until the depression, and to their role as conduits for American capital flows. At the same time, alterations in the banking laws and inflationary conditions had given rise to new sources of competition from the savings banks, government-owned banks of various types, and banks established by various industries and economic sectors. Where James' analysis moves beyond that of other analysts, however, is in his argument, based on contemporary investigations and findings in 1930 and 1933, that the bankers of the period were a far cry from their pre-war predecessors in the quality of their entrepreneurship and that they directed what limited resources they had at their disposal towards old industries like textiles and food and government-guaranteed investments. They put their money where they thought it was 'safe' and had so little confidence in their own judgement that they continued to put their money into such enterprises even when they were visibly unsafe.[9]

This charge raises important questions relating to the yet-to-be-undertaken full-scale investigation of the quality and character of Germany's interwar economic reconstruction and the investment policies pursued by Germany's economic and financial leadership. In the context of the present paper, the issue is whether there was any alternative to the defective mobilization of Germany's scarce capital in the manner described by James. Needless to say, one can speculate about theoretical alternatives for ever and a day, but the issue necessarily becomes less speculative if the problem has genuine historicity, that is, if it was so perceived by contemporaries and if alternatives had been contemplated. This, however, is precisely what did happen in 1920–1, and it is to the debate over proposals for alternative modes of mobilizing capital for industrial investment, the responses by the German banking community and their relationship to subsequent developments that this paper will now devote the bulk of its attention.

The proposals for a restructuring of Germany's credit market had their origins in the responses of a relatively small group of high government officials, publicists and industrialists to the problems and prospects of German reconstruction as they were perceived at the beginning of 1920. The first great post-war inflationary surge that began in the summer of 1919 and ended in the early spring of 1920 did much to expose the difficulties facing Germany's reconstruction effort. It demonstrated that firms and concerns with control of or access to raw materials and foreign exchange were clearly at an advantage under existing post-war conditions, while manufacturers of finished products and small and medium-sized enterprises found themselves short of credit, subject to harsh payment conditions and threatened in their independence. Despite the high liquidity of the economy, operating capital was a serious problem for many enterprises. Furthermore, the sources of the liquidity were problematic. Much of it came from the Reichsbank's continuation of its wartime practice of funding the government debt by discounting treasury bills. Another, certainly more welcome source, was foreign speculative engagement in marks and mark-denominated assets, which probably accounted for between 30 and 40 per cent of the accounts of the major German banks in 1920. If foreigners were willing to speculate on the future of the German economy, however, many Germans were not. The lost war, looming reparations burdens, the desire to evade the draconian taxes of the Erzberger tax reform passed in late 1919, anxieties over socialization and general distrust of political and economic conditions within Germany had resulted in the hoarding of money by farmers and others with cash reserves and a substantial flight of capital abroad. While knowledgeable Germans understood that the long-term reconstruction of Germany's industry would require foreign capital in any case, they were concerned that foreigners might take advantage of the inflation to buy up and control German enterprises although many realized that foreigners would be reluctant to make long-term investments in the German economy until social and political conditions appeared more stable and the economic prospects more inviting. It was in truth easier to create barriers to 'foreignization' through the use of preferred shares and other devices than it was to convince the outside world that investment in Germany was something more than a speculation.[10]

The great German banks and bankers seemed to view the situation with considerable complacency. Thanks to the inflationary conditions, they were 'swimming in money' and overloaded with work, and the evidence suggests that the expansion of their staffs, burgeoning paperwork, need to service the rising speculative tendencies in the economy and preoccupation with their own reconstruction through the buying up of provincial banks left them with little inclination to think in the long term. Undoubtedly, the fact that the great concerns were quite liberated from dependence on the banks acted as a further disincentive to excessive rumination about the future and to a concentration on making a maximum profit on such services as they could perform for industry, that is, daily commercial services, the floating of new stock issues and the granting of short-term credits to those industries and firms which were not self-financing for rather high charges.

Some industrial leaders, however, thought that this complacency was very dangerous. They feared that some major untoward development or combination of circumstances would lead foreigners to cease their speculation in favour of the mark. The massive deposits held in Germany would then be liquidated along with the money and assets held abroad. Germany would thus be deprived of this crucial source of foreign exchange. At the same time, the mark would sink into worthlessness, especially if the foreign flight from the mark were accompanied by the resale of treasury bills to the Reichsbank by the banks in order to satisfy the cash demands of their customers. As the paper products manufacturer Hans Kraemer expressed the ultimate nightmare in October 1920:

> The banks are 'swimming in money'. What will happen, however, at the moment when one really goes about collecting taxes in Germany . . . ? This time will perhaps also come some day, even if I do see some smiles of doubt on many faces. Above all, how will things be when . . . the boundless increase of the currency is finally dammed and when the outside world one day for foreign or domestic reasons takes its deposits, which have reached 30 billions in my view and which constitute a very substantial part of the deposits of the German banks, out of Germany . . . [11]

In his view, the existing situation was nothing but a 'gigantic soap bubble'. In so far as the vaults of the banks were not filled with foreign speculative capital, they were filled with Treasury bills, that is, the floating debt of the Reich which 'will float until the whole business bursts'.[12] Hans Kraemer was one of those who was convinced that German industry could not afford to surrender to the monetary illusion if it was to have a successful economic reconstruction and that ways and means had to be found to master the credit crisis that would inevitably strike the economy once the excess liquidity had been removed by taxation and stabilization. Industry, therefore, had to give some thought to other sources of money. This view was promoted above all by the then State Secretary in the Economics Ministry Julius Hirsch and by another influential industrialist and member of the Presidium of the Reich Association of German Industry, Hans Jordan of the synthetic textile industry. It was also vigorously supported by the influential editor of the *Vossische Zeitung* and of the economic journal *Plutus*, Georg Bernhard, who was a left Democrat and a member of the Reich Economics Council. There was thus nothing surprising about the fact that the March 1920 issue of *Plutus* provided Hirsch and Jordan with an opportunity to present their schemes for the co-operative organization of industrial credit in Germany.[13]

Within the confines of the Reich Cabinet, Hirsch had warned as early as September 1919 that if those in possession of capital continued to withhold it because of the political and economic uncertainty and to flee taxes, then 'a taking over of capital formation by the state will have to be considered in the form that the state itself undertakes the building of new plants for important industries, finances them and then runs them in the form of mixed economic enterprises'.[14] The tone of his memorandum on 'Capital Formation and Capital Creation'[15] argued that the supply of capital from private sources was not keeping pace either with the need for operating capital or, more importantly for Hirsch, with the need for long-term capital to renew and rationalize Germany's industrial plant. He was particularly concerned about the dangers of 'foreignization' (*Über-fremdung*), that is, that Germans would sell their firms to foreigners or be bought out because of their financial problems. Yet, Germans were sending their capital abroad, hoarding it at home or investing it in 'cubist paintings of uncertain colour' and other such non-productive investments. The problem, in Hirsch's view, was how to put this capital to use in the service of the national economy before foreigners would gain enough faith in Germany's long-term productive capacity to buy up German industry on the cheap. One of his particular concerns was mobilizing the large amounts of German money abroad for capital investment at home, and he was convinced that it might be possible to bring together Germany's industries and banks in a co-operative effort to turn those holdings as well as a portion of industry's export profits into a source of credit for industry based on the issuance of bonds backed, on the one hand, by a Trusteeship Bank (*Treuhandbank*) organized with industrial and banking participation and, on the other hand, by the Reich itself.

While Hirsch placed major emphasis on self-organization by the business community to secure credit, he considered state investment essential to further guarantee the credit and also emphasized the need for a measure of control and direction of investment. As he pointed out, there were precedents for this. During the war, the nitrates industry had created an equalization fund to use part of its profits to help the less developed plants in the industry, and a portion of the coal industry profits were being used to support the construction of miner housing. Finally, the proposed bank could be employed at once to attract foreign capital and prevent foreign control. In so far as it was in whole or partial control of certain enterprises to be socialized, such assets could not be expropriated to pay for reparations as they would not lie in the hands of the Reich. At the same time, it could make provision against foreign control a condition for support in securing foreign credit by private firms.

While the leaders of German industry were anxious to reduce the government role in the economy as much as possible, they were 'very sympathetic'[16] to the idea of an industrial bank, and this combination of motives triggered Hans Jordan's memorandum of February 1920 calling for a 'credit co-operative of German industry'.[17] Jordan agreed with Hirsch's diagnosis of the problem, but he placed much more emphasis on Germany's long-term ability to secure foreign, especially American capital, if she balanced her budget and offered enough security. The speculative American engagement in Germany was taken as evidence of confidence in 'our basically industrious population, our valuable highly developed industrial plant, the personality of our entrepreneurs and our technical intelligence'.[18] To secure American aid, however, German industry had to take the path of self-help. Neither the government, already burdened with reparations and subject to political pressures, nor the banks could do the job. What was needed, according to Jordan, was an organization of German industry to produce credit through co-operation and solidarity within the industrial community, while the banks and the Reichsbank would lend their technical assistance to this effort. Such a 'general credit cooperative' would place its combined resources and credit behind the new institution as a guarantee both for the credit provided to its members and for the credits received from foreign sources. Jordan went so far as to suggest that the new bank be in a position to issue what was tantamount to its own money for foreign trade. Jordan proposed that the organization be permitted to issue a commercial paper of its own which could not be used in domestic commerce. This short-term paper was to bear 2 per cent interest and attain its face value in the course of the year, at which time it would have to be turned in for payment in the currency of a foreign state based on gold. Basically, the cooperative was to control all imports of raw materials and to mediate all foreign credits for such purposes. Furthermore, it was to do more than secure short-term credits and issue short-term paper. It was also to issue long-term bonds bearing 6 to 8 per cent interest based once again on the security provided by the combined resources and credit of its membership. Jordan felt that such debentures

> would probably be taken by American banks, because the costs could be recovered by selling them again to the public. Such long-term loans in dollars based on a broad guarantee of the co-operative membership would be suitable to replace the missing operating capital needed for foreign trade, to relieve the passivity of the balance of payments and, together with the short-term bills and foreign exchange from abroad, to ensure orderly private economic intercourse with the outside world.[19]

While Jordan's plan was much influenced by current difficulties in purchasing raw materials from abroad and securing operating capital, and was thus criticized by Hirsch for failing to consider long-term reconstruction problems, it was quickly shot down as an attempt by industry to set up a state within the state that would virtually issue its own currency and determine economic policy. Neither the Reichsbank nor the banks, whose traditional roles were seriously threatened by the plan, showed the slightest enthusiasm for it any more than they did for Hirsch's scheme. The plan was most popular in industrial circles, where one of its leaders pointed out that foreigners would not give Germans credit simply because of their 'beautiful eyes', and that they would demand securities. Therefore, 'we can do nothing more wrong than to sit down and wait until the outside world becomes so friendly as to help us recover with a large-scale credit action'.[20] He strongly urged that industry help itself and do something about its own situation so as to attract foreign financial assistance.

Nevertheless, virtually nothing was done until the late summer of 1920, when the 'discussion' of the problem was suddenly revived in the form of virulent attacks by the Reichsbank, the banks, various chambers of commerce and the Finance Ministry in response to reports that the plan for what was now being called a Reich Economic Bank (*Reichswirtschaftsbank*) was going to be implemented through the use of foreign exchange taken by the government from export profits. Where the impulse for earlier versions of the plan had come from the difficulties of securing operating capital to purchase raw materials during the inflationary surge at the turn of 1919–20, now the inspiration was being provided by the increased unemployment during the relative stabilization that began in the spring of 1920 and was to last for a year. Hirsch was now arguing that the fundamental reason for creating a Reich Economic Bank was social, namely, the giving of credits as a means of fighting unemployment, and he seems to have planned to have labour represented on the board of the new bank. His boss, Economics Minister Ernst Scholz, after some hesitation also began to show interest in the idea of helping cash-starved factories to provide more employment and even contemplated tapping of the resources of the savings banks and the clearing centre (*Girozentrale*) of the municipal banks, which he himself had helped to establish in 1907–8.[21]

Whatever the case, the mere report of such intentions was sufficient to provoke a massive and, in its attacks on Hirsch's motives, even scurrilous reaction that was led by the Hamburg Chamber of Commerce, which represented a powerful combination of commercial and banking interests. They warned that the plan would lead to a revival of the controlled economy in new guise, that the 'centralization and monopolization of foreign exchange' would lead to the further burdening of commercial activity and the hated tendency of excluding the commercial sector from economic life, that it would produce unnecessary and undesirable competition for the banks, and that it would lead to a redistribution of capital from the deserving to the undeserving because there was no real mechanism by which the new agency could determine who was worthy of credit and who was not.[22]

This missive was followed by an open and behind-the-scenes struggle against the economic bank scheme. Most impressive from a public relations point of view was a declaration by the leading Berlin banks of 28 September 1920 which appeared in the advertisement section of major newspapers declaring that the banks were 'in a position to meet every justified credit requirement of industry and commerce, that they have always done so readily in the past and will also do so in the future'. The banks pointed out that numerous chambers of commerce, the Reichsbank president and leading experts supported this position and warned against 'an enterprise that will not bring the hoped for advantages but will lead to a waste of Reich resources'. The 'newly planned clothing of the project in the form of unemployment support' in no way altered this negative judgement in the eyes of the leading banks.[23]

The attitude of the banks was strongly seconded by the Reichsbank and the Finance Ministry, both of which feared the inflationary effects of the programme and which criticized it as a mechanism for the supplying of credit to the undeserving. The counter-cyclical implications of the plan appeared as yet another of that surfeit of violations of sound economics which had produced Germany's economic malaise. This was echoed by Jakob Goldschmidt of the National Bank, who warned the government that 'The placing of fresh means at the disposal of industry and commerce can only produce a temporary improvement, which will then lead to an even more severe collapse. The German economy is already in the middle of a crisis. He [Goldschmidt – GDF] wishes, in the interest of the German economy, that an elemental crisis will occur as soon as possible . . . '[24]

Such remarks, however, could only confirm the arguments of proponents of the plan that something had to be done to break the monopoly of the banks over credit, which placed many businesses at the mercy of the banks, and gave the banks a 'horrendous power position in economic life'. These critics charged that 'Lately, the great banks have decided to undertake a cleansing of German economic life by limiting the granting of credits in order to force the death of those plants less capable of survival, and this to be sure in the hope of bringing about a rehabilitation of those plants that remain . . . '[25] The Deutsche Bank, for example, had denied its branches the right to grant credits in excess of 100,000 marks without permission, and its Berlin office almost without exception refused the granting of larger credits. If this continued, proponents of the economic bank argued, then there would be increasing shut-downs and massive unemployment, so that the Reich would end up having to pay huge sums in unemployment relief. The economic bank, therefore, lay very much in the interests of industry, and the plan's proponents could not understand the opposition of the chambers of commerce or industrial groups in certain regions, such as Saxony, where unemployment was such a problem.

One reason for the opposition was fear of reviving government controls, and another might have been the commitment to traditionalist capitalist principles as expounded by Goldschmidt. To an industrialist of the stamp of Hans Kraemer, who was willing to trade a certain amount of government economic involvement in return for the positive results it could bring, and who did not feel bound by the rigid rules of classical doctrine, the position of Goldschmidt was nothing more or less than a 'capitalist catastrophe policy', and he felt that 'everything had to be done to avoid the catastrophe'. Goldschmidt, however, was relentless and insisted that

> The German economy is in the middle of a catastrophe that has to run its course with the elimination of small enterprises. A support of enterprises that are not capable of survival must not occur . . . He has long given up prophesying how the future will be . . . It is impossible to bring about a general remedy for the collapse which stands before us. If a guarantee of the Reich is necessary for the various credits that are given, then a further monetary inflation is unavoidable. The credit question can only be solved in each case on an individual basis. One cannot operate according to a bureaucratic scheme.[26]

Even critics of the proposals and those with reservations, however, were not prepared in most cases to go quite as far as Goldschmidt and share his enthusiasm for an enlivening and refreshing economic *Götterdämmerung*. Reichsbank director Friedrich admitted that there might be a need for assistance of some kind, while others pointed out that the banks had denied certain industries and plants credit in a manner that seemed unjustified and that had even necessitated Reich intervention. Such persons admitted that a distinction had to be made between the purely private economic perspective and the broader perspective of what was best for the economy. A means had to be found, they argued, to funnel and channel credit for the latter purpose. As everyone recognized, however, the use of the central clearing agency of the savings banks, which largely handled savings bank funds, would require a Reich guarantee because of the legal requirements that savings bank funds be placed only in absolutely secure (*mündelsicher*) investments. This was not the most welcome of solutions, and there continued to be division over whether there was a problem, that is, a true credit shortage, and what should be done if there were.

Given the fact that the Reichsbank, the banks, the leading chambers of commerce and the Chancellor of the Reich, Josef Wirth, along with leading ministries, were totally opposed to the plan for an economic bank, it was something of a miracle that the project received any further discussion. The continued debate over the issue was largely due to Hans Kraemer, one of the most active industrialists on the Reich Economic Council (Reichswirtschaftsrat – RWR), who joined forces with Jordan and Georg Bernhard as well as with Hirsch in keeping the issue alive by establishing a sub-committee of the Reich Economic Council to take testimony and explore the credit problems of industry further.

The sub-committee to 'Investigate Measures Against the Financial Distress of the Productive Estates' began its meetings on 19 October 1920 and held a total of eleven meetings between that date and 14 July 1922. The first ten of these were held between 20 October and February 1921, that is, at the height of the relative stabilization when the problems of credit shortages and unemployment which were to plague the post-inflationary Weimar economy appeared to be matters of some urgency.[27] These sessions were largely devoted to hearings in which experts from the world of banking and industry were interrogated as to whether there was in fact a capital shortage and what means could or should be taken to relieve the credit problems of industry. The last two meetings, in November 1921 and July 1922, took place during entirely different phases of the inflation, and are mainly interesting for the light they shed on the changes that had taken place. These lengthy meetings, like most meetings of the RWR and its committees, produced no practical results whatever, but they provide a revealing picture of both credit and banking conditions and the economic thinking of many of Germany's most important and influential economic leaders.[28]

No one contested the fact that the banks were 'swimming in money' or claimed that there was a credit shortage because of insufficient liquidity. What emerged from the testimony and discussion, however, was that since 1 January 1920 the conditions being offered by the banks for credit had become considerably more severe than before, amounting to an increase of 15 to 20 per cent and that there was a serious disproportion between the interest that the banks were giving on deposits and what they were charging for credit. While offering only 1.5 per cent interest on deposits – and in some cases actually charging customers for holding their money – they were asking between 9 and 12 per cent interest for credit and often even more. The formal interest charge was usually 7 per cent, the rest being accounted for by a variety of commissions (*Provisionen*). Customers with a credit line, for example, were charged each quarter for that portion of the credit they did not use in order to compensate the bank for keeping the money available. Other imaginative provisions had also been introduced. As a representative of the Berlin clothing industry, which was apparently particularly hard hit by these credit conditions, complained, the banks had a cartel with a monopoly of credit through which they were able to enjoy a 'monopolistic' position in economic life:

> The banks today form a cartel. We have to deal with a condition cartel in banking. I am a convinced supporter of cartels, but this support means in my case also that the limits of cartels must be drawn, and these are determined by the general economy because otherwise cartels cannot perform the functions which are expected of them. This monopoly by the banks lacks any control by competition or the public. This makes it possible for the banks to exploit – I mean this in the best sense without any other implications – the need for credit and leads to a situation in which production is hampered to such an extent that its justification needs to be considered . . . If one thinks of credit as a means of production, and if that means of production stands today at 10% and is 2% too expensive, then there is a burden placed on production which, at a time when price reduction is more necessary than ever, can and should be borne only if its inner justification and necessity can really be indisputably demonstrated.[29]

Thus, while credit was available in the formal sense, businessmen of this kind found it more satisfactory to reduce their production than to expand it because the credit they needed simply was too expensive. Finally, there were loud complaints that in many instances the banks were offering particular customers credit only on condition that they paid interest as high as 20 per cent with the obvious object of cutting them off altogether.

The bankers had a relatively simple response to these charges, namely, that all costs had risen since the war, and that it was hardly to be expected that the cost of money would not do so as well, especially given the increased staffs and other costs of the banking business and the irritating government reliance on the banks for the depositing of paper assets and their reporting in connection with the new tax programmes. They also found it somewhat odd that the textile cartel was complaining about the banking cartel. Under such circumstances, it was impossible to give higher interest on deposits or demand less for credit, the bankers argued. They claimed that credit in Germany was cheaper than in other industrial countries, which was true if one took only the Reichsbank discount rate into account, and that one should not forget the factor of risk. One banker reminded the committee that there had been relatively few bankruptcies in Germany during the spring when the mark suddenly rose in value, and this was because the banks had stepped in and helped, as apparently was the case in the textile and shoe industries. 'Just think what kind of risks have resulted from these credits given by the banks', he told the committee.[30]

Rudolf Hilferding, another expert witness, viewed the bank charges somewhat differently. While agreeing that increased costs and risks played a role, the banks also could take advantage of certain circumstances that operated very much in their favour. They were able to offer such low interest on deposits because people were unwilling to put their money into government bonds and other long-term fixed interest-bearing assets. The banks could thus offer a repository for money upon which one could draw at any time and which had nowhere else to go. Similarly, the commissions and interest being charged by the banks were possible, not only because there was a condition cartel in banking, but also because the Reichsbank had not been providing industrial operating credit in the form of commercial bills so that businesses were being compelled to turn to the private banks when they were short of operating capital. In Hilferding's view, the distinction between commissions and interest was purely verbal and arbitrary. The banks decided what they could charge, 10 per cent for example, and then divided up the amount in categories they thought most palatable psychologically.[31]

In response to these points, the bankers insisted that the risk they were running and their costs justified high commissions and interest as well as the differential between interest paid on deposits and charged for credit. Only Max Warburg expressed a mild dissent, admitting that the latter gap was perhaps too great and suggesting that the banks had been overly inventive in concocting new kinds of commissions. He preferred that interest be called by its name, but pointed out that 'if you see the costs and burdens which the banks have today and how through a strike of bank employees they shoot up by millions, then one cannot think ill of the banks and bankers if they create a certain reserve through the invention of commissions'.[32]

Warburg also tended to dismiss the anxieties of the proponents of the economic bank about the danger of a shortage of long-term investment capital, their arguments that the entire credit structure was extremely vulnerable, and their fears of a severe credit crisis. He insisted that the banks actually wanted to give industry credit since their investment in Treasury bills and other forms of government paper could only be viewed as 'second class'. He knew of no deserving firm that had been denied money and suggested that the banks had found a solution to the great sums needed as a result of the inflation by forming credit consortia to help out firms where necessary. As he colourfully explained:

> When today a great industrial enterprise, which earlier needed 3 million now needs 30 million and the individual bank is unwilling to give this credit . . . then a credit consortium is formed, and this type of credit consortium is actually a post-war phenomenon and will undoubtedly be maintained at least for the near future. With the help of this credit consortium and with the help of our greatest helper, the Reichsbank, which ceaselessly prints notes, we will always be in a position to give every credit that is demanded. (Laughter.) The credit shortage will only start at that moment when the Reich and the currency becomes solid and we no longer, as before, have inflation. There can be no talk of a credit shortage until now.[33]

Needless to say, this was no answer to the argument that a credit shortage was in the offing, but Warburg seems to have maintained a measured optimism that Germany could pull through her credit difficulties if she was smart and lucky. He warned against a complicated scheme like that proposed by Jordan, pointing out that foreigners did not take kindly to the German penchant for complexity and would not go along if 'we demand complicated brainwork'. They wanted clear security and not so insecurable a security as the 'solidarity' of some collectivity of industries and firms. Warburg shared the view of others that no one would be impressed by the guarantee contained in a credit co-operative because there would be no way of monetizing it if the credit could not be repaid. Foreigners would give credit, Warburg argued, for the purchase of raw materials that would be turned into finished goods in Germany and resold abroad (*Veredlungskredit*), and he pointed out that they were flooded with credit offers of this nature on excellent terms from the United States, England and Holland which they were turning down because of domestic and world market conditions. These offers were being given because the mark 'enjoys an unbelievable confidence in the outside world which we ourselves do not share'. Germany was living on 'the credit of earlier decades' and the belief that she would recover. At the same time, the excess production abroad was so great, that the outside world had to offer credit, and it was because of Germany's inability to take advantage of all of it that 'England, etc. are choking on their raw materials, and that is why there is the terrible crisis which we will, I hope, be partially spared in our misfortune, even if we unquestionably will partially experience it...'[34]

In contrast to Warburg, Jakob Goldschmidt positively relished the idea of Germany's undergoing a major crisis along Anglo-American lines and warned against trying to prevent this crisis with 'brute force and bureaucratic organization' and thereby prolonging it. In his view, interest rates could and should go higher.[35] Goldschmidt denied that there was a capital shortage or a credit shortage and pointed out that twelve times as much capital had gone into industry through the founding of corporations and the increase of capital stock in 1920 than in 1913. 7.5 billion in capital stock increases and 909 million in incorporations in 1920 stood over against, respectively, 440 million and 212 million in 1913. Additionally, 1.5 billion in industrial bonds had been sold. From such increases, nominal to be sure, Goldschmidt concluded that the capital market could hardly be said not to be functioning, and he, like his colleague Arthur Salomonsohn, argued that the banks were not and should not be in the business of providing credit for long-term plant expansion and renewal. This had to come through the traditional means of incorporation and capital stock issues, and while many private firms were reluctant to surrender their independence or family character by becoming corporations, there were important tax inducements for doing so and it was, in any case, unfair to ask either the banks or the taxpayers to bear risks that could be properly distributed by such readily available and traditional means. The bankers insisted that the banks only had a responsibility to provide operating capital, and then only to firms which were good credit risks, and even then not for the production of goods for which there was no market and that would only make things worse. Throughout the hearings, they were strongly supported in this posture by the availability of a lengthy Reichsbank memorandum of 8 November 1920. While this memorandum did irritate the bankers by suggesting that interest rates for borrowers were too high and interest rates on deposits were too low, it compensated for this 'deficiency' by sharply and unconditionally opposing the artificial easing of credit through an economic bank or the other plans that had been suggested.[36]

Georg Bernhard and his allies were well aware that it was not customary for banks, at least officially, to grant credit for long-term capital improvement or to grant operating credit on anything other than traditional banking principles, and he was also aware that the larger and richer industries themselves were often playing the banker for their daughter companies and customers by granting credits. He questioned, however, whether the existing state of affairs was either equitable or economically sound. It was, after all, not entirely an accident of fate that certain firms were in a position to raise their capital, grant credits and receive credits from bank consortia or simply do without banking help. Firms which had not been in a position to make war profits and which had obeyed the spirit and letter of the tax laws were less advantaged than war profiteers and tax evaders. Bernhard rejected the simple equation between what the bankers declared sound practice and the general welfare of the economy. He argued for an economic bank because 'such a bank would be in a position to supply the difference between the credit that is privately possible economically and that which is necessary from a [national – GDF] point of view'.[37]

Under existing circumstances, this was an argument which addressed itself to the problems of medium- and small-sized industry, and especially to the industries which manufactured finished products. As the General Director of the Allgemeine Elektrizitäts-Gesellschaft, Felix Deutsch, pointed out:

It is true that the great firms can get any capital they need. The issue is largely one that concerns the smaller and medium-sized firms and manufacturers. They need many times more capital than they needed in peacetime. Raw materials and semi-finished products have become much more expensive. The banks demand very high interest rates. The result is that the manufacturers demand very large credits from their suppliers. The great firms have lately once again become the bankers of the small and medium-sized companies and private persons. Now the banks come along and say: this is only because you charge much lower interest rates than we banks. If you charge the same rates as we, then the people involved will see that they have to come to terms with the banks and we will give them as much credit as our practices permit. But that won't work in industry. Suppliers have never charged their customers interest in the manner of the banks . . . The question therefore is: are the banks in the position and willing to give the small and medium-sized firms the much higher credits which are necessary to do business today . . . [38]

The answer was less than reassuring if one considered the treatment of small and medium-sized firms without access to credit from their suppliers. Such industries were often compelled to make immediate payment to their suppliers while giving credit to their customers. They were an important source of employment, and were barred from shutting down their plants by Weimar social legislation. They were often highly dependent on provincial banks, but such banks were coming more and more under domination by the great banks. Under such circumstances, they naturally began to cast an eye on the resources of the savings banks, but here too they found the great banks standing in their way and objecting to any expansion of the functions of the savings banks.

It was indeed true that the great banks and their provincial branches did not simply oppose an economic bank organized by industry and/or the state but were also adamant in their opposition to increased competition from within the traditional banking sector. They unswervingly opposed every suggestion that the reserves of the savings banks be tapped for capital investment in industry. Under the Prussian Regulation of 1838, savings banks were permitted to invest only in first-class paper, usually various types of government bonds and mortgages. These investment limitations along with the desire to promote savings served as the justification for their tax-free status. In reality, the savings banks were already undergoing a major transformation before the war, especially after being allowed by legislation of 1908 to engage in checking and clearing (*giro*) services. The pace of such change increased during the war, when the savings banks were used by the Reichsbank to place war loans and when these savings banks, either individually or in consortia, took over all municipal loans and thus began to administer securities. The post-war tax legislation of the autumn of 1919, which required that all securities be deposited in banks for tax purposes, could not be implemented without the use of the savings banks. The government was thus forced to concede to the savings banks the right to hold and administer all types of securities and by decrees of 9 October 1920 and 15 April 1921 to enter into the business of buying and selling on the securities market. In many frontier and occupied areas, as well as in important business centres, the savings banks were allowed to deal in commercial securities for their customers, and they were also called upon to administer the multiplying financial activities of municipalities arising from the purchase and distribution of food and clothing.[39] Given the deterioration in the real value of mortgages and government securities, it was natural for the savings banks to show an increased interest in dealing in industrial securities and for industry to see this as a new source of capital. As Hans Kraemer pointed out:

> If the tax legislation will be carried out in the sense desired by the Socialist portion of the German people, it will lead to a levelling of capital to the greatest extent and then the money will no longer flow through the great channels of the banks but will flow through a countless number of small channels into the repositories of the savings banks ... I would consider it economically short-sighted if we would not today give timely thought that these billions – which today come from the *Mittelstand*, the chief depositors of the savings banks – which are flowing into this great gathering point of the Reich Clearing Centre, be directed back into the great pot from which German industry can be nourished.[40]

Not only the *Mittelstand* but also the workers were known to be using the savings banks to build up some savings wherever possible, and here too good political and social as well as economic arguments could be made for tapping these resources. As another committee member noted:

> the entire social development which gives the broad masses enormously increased rights also without a doubt places upon them the responsibility to help the credit needs of the economy and to make the means which they have made available useful for this. It will be impossible to have the savings of the large mass of our people continuously go into the savings banks and then go the not-very-productive route of municipal loans, as is now largely the case. Also, the concept of first-class security has become so fluid, that in many cases it can no longer seriously play a role. It must in my view be possible to fill the saving impulse of the broad masses with confidence in the productive tasks of our industry.[41]

All such arguments were rejected by representatives of the great banks, underlying all of whose contentions about the laws governing savings banks investments was a profound irritation over the expansionist tendencies of the savings banks evidenced in their creation of city, district and communal banks which were guaranteed by the savings banks but which were free to invest as they wished. The Siegen Savings Bank, for example, attained considerable notoriety for its plan to open a municipal bank. It justified its intention in a memorandum of January 1921 by bluntly stating that it was in competition with the great banks. The Siegen Savings Bank argued that the growing concentration of Germany's banking system, the decreasing autonomy of the old provincial banks, their lack of interest in lending to craftsmen, merchants and workers, as well as their reluctance to lend to municipalities, required countermeasures if the great banks were not to dictate terms on the local level. The Siegen bank claimed that savings banks and municipal banks would strengthen one another, the former placing its resources at the service of the latter, while the municipal banks, with their resources guaranteed by both the savings banks and the municipalities, would be placed in a position to service the needs of the community and its citizens. It was a measure of the aggressiveness of the Siegen Savings Bank, the municipality and their supporters that they sabotaged efforts of the Deutsche Bank to take over the provincial Siegen Bank for Industry and Commerce. Indeed, the Deutsche Bank's opponents thought that it would be better if the Siegen Savings Bank were to do the taking over and thereby get the office space it needed and avoid having to erect a new building. It was useless for the allies of the Deutsche Bank to protest against this 'confusing of the boundary between savings bank and bank' and 'mixing of public and private activities'.[42] By April 1921, government decrees permitted savings banks to deal in all forms of security transactions except those involving foreign exchange.

The leading bankers were less pronounced in their opposition to proposals that the workers be encouraged to invest in industry by being offered small shares (*Kleinaktien*) at favourable terms with the object both of getting capital and giving them a sense that they were participants with a stake in productive enterprise. Warburg and Goldschmidt feared that it would encourage speculation without being particularly effective, an argument that was criticized as pointless 'moralizing' since a veritable speculative fever was gripping large portions of the population in their efforts to escape the consequences of the inflation.[43]

Throughout the sub-committee discussions, probably the greatest degree of consensus revolved about the billions of marks privately hoarded by Germans in an effort to escape taxation and which they did not want to keep in the banks because of the abrogation of their rights of privacy. The expert witnesses were convinced that 'millions and billions' would flow in, especially from the farmers. The Reichsbank itself took up the cause of abrogating or at least relaxing some of the legislation designed to prevent tax evasion, especially through the restoration of the privacy of bank accounts, pointing out that 'the state, even against its own wish and desire, is binding the capital market through its legislation and is now faced with the consequence of its own actions if industry now comes and asks it for the credit help which it had previously been able to procure itself'. The legislation had to be changed so that 'capital can move freely again without being followed every step of the way for tax purposes'.[44]

Here the bankers and the Reichsbank were at one, and they were especially enthusiastic about the one major proposal of the Reichsbank for relieving such operating capital needs as existed, namely, the reintroduction of commercial bills. Because of the wartime government payments in cash, high liquidity and the demand by industrial trade associations for immediate payment in cash in the post-war inflation, commercial bills had virtually disappeared from use. The Reichsbank viewed the reintroduction of 'solid commercial bills' as an excellent means of relieving operating credit difficulties in a safe manner. In the Reichsbank's view, commercial bills had a host of advantages. They permitted a three-month delay in cash payment; a portfolio of such bills, if solid, could be used to procure further credit. They also reduced cash requirements in the economy and thereby would make it possible for the Reich to reduce liquidity through taxation and long-term loans from the domestic economy without bringing the economy to a standstill because of a credit shortage. The Reich would then be in a position to purchase back its Treasury bills, while the Reichsbank and other banks would once again have reliable portfolios of commercial bills instead of dubious Treasury bills. That this vision of the pre-war order of things, where credit for operating capital was given with solid bills based on real production and sales, proved so palatable to everyone was not very surprising. Only Kraemer expressed concern that the reintroduction of commercial bills might produce a fantastic credit demand by industry, but this arose from his worry that the banks might not be able to meet the demand, an anxiety which the banks declared unfounded.[45]

Thus, the one point on which the sub-committee on industrial credit could reach a measure of harmony was with respect to doing something old rather than to creating something new. By the time it finished hearing testimony in February 1921, all the various projects proposed since early 1920 had been successfully buried by their opponents inside and outside the government. The chambers of commerce and bankers fired salvo after salvo against the plans, especially at the bankers' convention in Berlin on 25–27 October 1920.[46] Reference was made to the Brussels Financial Conference of the previous month, where the European financial leaders and experts attacked all forms of unproductive spending and deficit spending and called for a return to traditional fiscal and financial practices. While the Jordan Plan could be rejected on the grounds that it would be impossible to organize industry for the purposes intended and that a credit co-operative would not have the experience, knowledge or personnel to review credit applications effectively, the economic bank scheme and all notions of the Reich serving as a guarantor of industrial credit could be attacked on the grounds of violating economic orthodoxy and as potentially inflationary. As the Frankfurt banker L. Hahn argued in the *Frankfurter Zeitung*:

> We have until now, and that is bad enough, a financial inflation, i.e. an artificial excessive creation of purchasing power to satisfy the financial demand. One must guard against adding to this financial inflation an industrial and commercial inflation, which perhaps already exists latently in many places. Whether the interest rates in giving credit to industry and commerce are to be raised or lowered – in Brussels as is known the overwhelming inclination was the view that the interest rates are in general too low – over this one can argue, but there can be no doubt that the firm boundary of every credit expansion is the possibility of its being repaid . . . Our financial inflation had its beginning at the moment when the Reichsbank, hardly noticed by the broad public, began to discount Reich Treasury bills instead of commercial bills, whereby the fate of the currency became tied to the fate of the state finances. The creation of an economic bank with the goal of giving credits when repayment is insecure would be a step of no less major significance. It would place a new burden on the currency at a time when the old is threatening its collapse . . . [47]

Defeating the economic bank and related schemes proved much easier than avoiding the destruction of the currency through the combined public and private credit inflation which was in full swing two years after Hahn wrote these lines thanks to precisely those conditions predicted by the proponents of the economic bank and to the reintroduction of commercial bills so warmly recommended by the Reichsbank and bankers. German domestic conditions and international developments on the reparations front had combined to produce a loss of confidence in Germany's future and her currency by mid-1922, and the answer to the cutting off of foreign speculative engagement in the German currency was a Reichsbank decision, made in response to the desperate urgings of industry and the banks as well as to the inclinations of its leadership, to relieve the credit crisis through the massive rediscounting of commercial bills. Although the Reichsbank tried to limit its credits to 'credit-worthy' concerns and firms, these were precisely the customers most in a position to take greatest advantage of the low Reichsbank interest rates and repayment in depreciated currency and to obfuscate the distinction between good commercial bills backed by real orders and credit to increase company liquidity (*Finanzwechsel*) for which there was no real security at all. The less 'credit-worthy' were thrown on the tender mercies of the banks, who apparently were charging as much as 67 per cent interest in the autumn of 1922 and who, as most 'credit-worthy' institutions, were in a position to discount their commercial bills at the Reichsbank for 6 per cent. By late 1923, there was genuinely explosive hostility towards the *Zinswucher* of the banks, who were charging between 6 and 18 per cent daily interest for paper marks after the stabilization and 18 per cent yearly interest for Rentenmark credits. One employer organization called for the creation of a Reich Supervisory Agency for banks at the end of December 1923, while another thought it remarkable that no one had thought of socializing an economic sector so essential to the economic welfare of the nation. Such complaints and comments continued through 1924 and abated but never disappeared afterwards. As has been shown, these charges had been levied early in the inflationary period and thus constituted a continuing source of hostility to the banks throughout the Weimar Republic.[48]

More serious, however, were the complaints about the uncreative role of the banks which, as has been shown, had their origins in the 1920–1 period and are thus not simply the product of the historian's hindsight. The expanded role of the great banks during the war and inflation was largely a function of their involvement in state finances and foreign exchange transactions, activities which undoubtedly promoted their increased take-over of provincial banks, as did the subsequent depletion of their monetary assets because of the inflation. The great German banks do indeed seem to have been bogged down in purely defensive strategies, and it can be argued that even their expansion took on the character of a compensation for depleted resources rather than an increase of their 'radius of action'. Even more telling was that, despite all their complaints about the proliferation of banks and industrial self-financing, their conservative posture towards the establishment of gold accounts in 1923 and resistance to valorized credits and even towards the currency reform of November 1923 on the grounds that stabilization had to come from without and that all such measures from within were doomed to failure could only have the effect of increasing the number of banks providing valorized credits.[49] Many of these institutions survived the inflation. While one may agree, with Knut Borchardt, that Germany's two inflationary experiences have provided her with a modernization advantage today by forcing a more flexible, multi-purpose banking system, this did little to serve the Weimar Republic.[50] In the Weimar Republic, with its limited capital resources, the expanded role of the savings and municipal banks and proliferation of public and private credit institutions were a source of tension and conflict over the direction and character of investment and especially the use of the foreign capital that flowed into Germany. The banks were not merely pulled down by the general political crisis that led to Weimar's collapse: they were caught up in the latent political crisis before the crisis.

If it is possible to raise very serious doubts about the possibility and desirability of public direction and steering of investment in advanced capitalist societies, such doubts are especially appropriate in the case of the Weimar Republic, where 'organized capitalism' and corporatism appear to have promoted stagnation and ossification more than innovation and growth.[51] Furthermore, one can reasonably argue that the Weimar governments were too weak to do any more 'steering' than they were doing already, and that the international and national capital markets were in such condition that those seeking to direct the economy were being forced to make bricks without straw in any case. This is not to say that the performance of the banks both before and after the stabilization did not justify the criticisms made of them and that the efforts to create an alternative mode of dealing with the credit shortage in 1920–1 lack significance. Given the political constellation, however, there was less a lost opportunity than a revealing moment of truth in which the banks employed a purely defensive strategy that betrayed their limited capacity to cope with the problems of industrial reconstruction. The answers provided by their critics, however, were not very inspiring either because, as the hearings progressed, they tended to lose sight of the general problems of industrial investment and reconstruction in their concentration upon immediate difficulties of providing for medium- and small-sized business at reasonable interest rates. Both sides set the pattern for the post-stabilization period.

It was simply disingenuous of some bankers at the 1920–1 hearings to claim that they were not in the business of providing long-term capital. As one of them pointed out in contradiction to this contention, the granting of short-term credits as a preliminary to the issuance of debentures and new shares had been common practice before the war:

A separation of capital credit and revolving credit cannot be strictly made . . . If this had been done in the past then Thyssen and Stinnes would today still be small potatoes instead of great industrialists. Everyone in the business world knows that the credits which these firms and the great corporations took were first short-term and the transformation into debentures only occurred after it was clear which of these credits were to be turned into debentures.[52]

When the banks with the enthusiastic concurrence of their customers took short-term foreign credits to finance long-term investments after the stabilization, they were simply conforming to previous practice. This was clearly recognized by State Secretary Hans Schäffer in a memorandum on the causes of the banking crisis of 3 August 1931. He pointed out that 'the financing of the German economy and a portion of the financing of the public sector was conducted before the war in such a manner that first short-term credits were taken from the banks for the projected investments as was required by their progress and, afterwards, when the investments had progressed sufficiently and when the market offered special opportunity, these short-term credits were transformed into long-term loans'. The bank credits based on foreign cash of the 1924–9 period were nothing more or less than a continuation of traditional practice: 'The idea which lay behind these short-term loans was the same as in the financing of the pre-war period.'[53] What had changed, of course, was the capital base on which the banks rested after the war and inflation, which made past practice a very risky business, and the domestic and international situation, which compounded the risks.

At the same time, Schäffer's analysis poses serious questions about the degree of significance to be attached to the criticisms of the banks by both contemporaries and historians. If the banks had directed their lending towards 'sunrise' rather than 'sunset' industries, would this have made much difference given the unsound credit structure? It certainly would not have silenced the criticisms of medium-sized and small industry about the insufficient support of the banks which, as Schäffer pointed out, exerted constant pressure for increased credit. It could also be argued, as Schäffer did, that the Reichsbank and the banks could not easily pull back from their credit giving without creating mass unemployment:

> The Reich government . . . which had already begun to suffer in its budgetary disposition from the deteriorating business conditions, also had to fear that a policy of holding back credit would create further difficulties. For reasons of economic and social policy, they wished to delay the recession to a time when a burdening of the labour market would be less fateful in its effect because of the reduced flow of employable workers.[54]

If this was the case, then the banks had in fact acted as they had been asked to act in 1921, namely, to provide credit for counter-cyclical purposes. It is possible to argue that they had been priming the wrong pumps, but then one must also show what the right pumps were and that priming them under the conditions of Weimar's so-called good years would have made a difference.

NOTES

1 The most important work in the older literature is P. B. Whale, *Joint Stock Banking in Germany: A Study of the German Creditbanks Before and After the War* (London, 1930). For the newer literature, useful material is to be found in the general works of M. Pohl, *Konzentration im Deutschen Bankwesen 1848–1980* (Frankfurt, 1980);

K. E. Born, *International Banking in the 19th and 20th Centuries* (New York, 1983). On Weimar banking in particular, see H. James, *The German Slump. Politics and Economics 1924–1926* (Oxford, 1986), especially chs. 4 and 8; G. Schulz, *Deutschland am Vorabend der grossen Krise* (Berlin and New York, 1987), especially ch. 3; G. Hardach, 'Banking and industry in Germany in the interwar period 1919–1939', *Journal of Economic History*, 13 (Fall 1984), 203–34.

2 *Untersuchung des Bankwesens 1933*, 2 vols. (Berlin, 1933), vol. I, esp. chs. 1–3, 8–11, II, p. 3.

3 M. Nussbaum, *Wirtschaft & Staat in Deutschland. Bd. 2. Weimarer Republik* (Berlin, 1978), pp. 307ff.

4 Hardach, 'Banking and industry', p. 215.

5 C.-L. Holtfrerich, 'Das Eigenkapital der Kreditinstitute als historisches und aktuelles Problem', *Bankhistorisches Archiv. Zeitschrift für Bankengeschichte*, Beiheft 5 (April 1981), pp. 14–29; 'Zur Entwicklung der deutschen Bankenstruktur', Deutscher Sparkassen- und Giroverband, *Standortbestimmung. Entwicklungslinien der deutschen Kreditwirtschaft* (Stuttgart, 1984), pp. 13–42; 'Auswirkungen der Inflation auf die Struktur des deutschen Kreditgewerbes', in G. D. Feldman (ed.), *Die Nachwirkungen der Inflation auf die deutsche Geschichte* (Munich, 1985), pp. 187–209.

6 K. Borchardt, ' "Das hat historische Gründe." Zu Determinanten der Struktur des deutschen Kreditwesens unter besonderer Berücksichtigung der Rolle der Sparkassen', in H. Henning, D. Lindenlaub and E. Wandel (eds.), *Wirtschafts- und sozialgeschichtliche Forschungen und Probleme* (St Katharinen, 1987), pp. 270–87, quote on p. 279.

7 James, *German Slump*, p. 295.

8 This is based on research in progress on a biography of Hugo Stinnes.

9 James, *German Slump*, ch. 4.

10 Much of the general discussion here as well as certain matters of detail are based on my forthcoming study, *The Great Disorder: Politics and Society in the German Inflation, 1914–1923* (Oxford, 1991). Further background is provided in a paper 'Banks and banking in Germany after the First World War: strategies of defence', to be published in a forthcoming volume on banking history to be edited by Youssef Cassis. The best economic history of the inflation is C.-L. Holtfrerich, *The German Inflation 1914–1923. Causes and Effects in International Perspective* (Berlin and New York, 1986).

11 Meeting of the Sub-Committee for Production Credit of the Reich Economic Council, Zentrales Staatsarchiv Potsdam (ZSAP), Reichswirtschaftsrat (RWR), Meeting of 10 Oct. 1920, Nr. 459, Bd. 1, Bl. 9ff.

12 Meeting of 28 Oct. 1920, *ibid.*, Bd. 1, Bl. 111.

13 *Plutus*, 24 March 1920.

14 Reich Cabinet meeting of 19 Sept. 1919, A. Golecki (ed.), *Das Kabinett Bauer, 21. Juni 1919 bis 27. März 1920. Akten der Reichskanzlei. Weimarer Republik* (Boppard am Rhein, 1980), p. 264.

15 *Ibid.*, p. 569 n. 4. The memorandum was reprinted in the 10 March 1920 issue of *Plutus*.

16 *Kabinett Bauer*, pp. 569ff.

17 *Plutus*, 20 March 1920.

18 *Ibid.*

19 *Ibid.*, p. 88.

20 ZSAP, Reichsfinanzministerium, Nr. 2800, Bl. 191.

78   Gerald D. Feldman

21 See his remarks at a meeting on 1 Oct. 1920 in Zentrales Staatsarchiv Merseburg, Rep. 120 AX Nr. 34, Bl. 43.
22 See reports in the *Berliner Tageblatt* of 10 Aug. and 11 Sept. 1920, *ibid.*, Bl. 1–3 and Hamburg Chamber of Commerce to Reich Finance Ministry, Bl. 5–11.
23 For a copy, see *ibid.*, Bl. 15.
24 Meeting of 1 Oct. 1920, *ibid.*, Bl. 38–50, quote on Bl. 45.
25 *Ibid.*, Bl. 45.
26 *Ibid.*, Bl. 50.
27 On the relative stabilization, see G. D. Feldman, 'The political economy of Germany's relative stabilisation during the 1920/21 world depression', in G. D. Feldman *et al.*, *Die Deutsche Inflation. Eine Zwischenbilanz* (Berlin and New York, 1982), pp. 180–206.
28 The complete protocols of the Ausschuss zur Prüfung von Massnahmen gegen die finanzielle Not der produktiven Stände are to be found in ZSAP, RWR, Nr. 459–60. The discussion which follows is based on these protocols, but only the quotations will be cited.
29 Expert testimony of Heinmann, 28 Oct. 1920, *ibid.*, Nr. 459, Bd. 1, Bl. 82f.
30 Statement by Neustadt, meeting of 28 Jan. 1921, *ibid.*, Bd. 2, Bl. 313.
31 *Ibid.*, Bl. 282ff.
32 Meeting of 11 Feb. 1921, *ibid.*, Nr. 460, Bd. 2, Bl. 185.
33 Meeting of 29 Jan. 1921, *ibid.*, Nr. 459, Bd. 1, Bl. 130ff.
34 Meeting of 11 Feb. 1921, *ibid.*, Nr. 460, Bd. 1, Bl. 179.
35 *Ibid.*, Bl. 186–93.
36 For the Reichsbank memorandum, see Zentrales Staatsarchiv Merseburg, Rep. 120, AX Nr. 43, Bl. 78–101.
37 Meeting of 16 Nov. 1920, ZSAP, RWR, Nr. 459, Bd. 1, Bl. 152ff.
38 Meeting of 29 Jan. 1921, *ibid.*, Nr. 460, Bd. 2, Bl. 41ff.
39 *Ausschuss zur Untersuchung der Erzeugungs- und Absatzbedingungen der deutschen Wirtschaft. Der Bankkredit* (Berlin, 1930), p. 40. See also R. H. Tilly, 'Gemeinde-finanzen und Sparkassen in Westfalen in der Inflation, 1918–1923', in K. Düwell and W. Kollmann (eds.), *Rheinland und Westfalen im Industriezeitalter, Bd. 2. Von der Reichsgründung bis zur Weimarer Republik* (Wuppertal, 1984), pp. 398–411.
40 Meeting of 11 Oct. 1920, ZSAP, RWR, Nr. 364, Bl. 174.
41 *Ibid.*, Bl. 199.
42 Oscar Schlitter to Siegen Bank for Industry and Commerce, 27 April 1921 and Essener Bank to Bergassessor Schleifenbauer, 30 April 1921, Deutsche Bank Archiv. On the Siegen Memorandum, see the report by Maurice Parmele of 28 May 1921 on 'Concentration and combination in German industry and finance', US National Archives, 862.60/38, pp. 45ff. See also Pohl, *Konzentration im deutschen Bankwesen*, pp. 3ff., 211. The Siegen Bank for Commerce and Industry finally was taken over by the Deutsche Bank in 1925.
43 Meeting of 11 Feb. 1921, ZSAP, Nr. 460, Bd. 1, Bl. 202.
44 Reichsbank memorandum of 8 Nov. 1920, ZStA Merseburg, Rep. 120, AX, Nr. 43, Bl. 97.
45 Meetings of 29 Jan. and 11 Feb. 1921, ZSAP I, RWR, Nr. 460, Bd. 2, Bl. 98ff., 272ff.
46 *Bank-Archiv*, 20 (1 Nov. 1920), pp. 33ff.
47 *FZ*, 11 Oct. 1920. This is in some contrast to Hahn's later views. See Carl-Ludwig Holtfrerich, 'Zur Entwicklung der monetären Konjunkturtheorien: Wicksell, Schumpeter, Hahn, Mises und Hayek', *Schriften des Vereins für Sozialpolitik*,

Gesellschaft für Wirtschafts- und Sozialwissenschaften, Neue Folge Band 115/VIII. Studien zur Entwicklung der ökonomischen Theorie, 8 (1989), 103–40, esp. pp. 116–24.

48 There is a good collection of gravamina in Bundesarchiv Koblenz, R 2, Nr. 2424.

49 See P. Beusch, *Währungszerfall und Währungsstabilisierung* (Berlin, 1928), pp. 166–9 and Max Warburg's unpublished memoirs, 1923, p. 64.

50 Borchardt in Henning *et al.*, *Wirtschafts- und sozialgeschichtliche Forschungen*, pp. 285ff.

51 James, *German Collapse*, pp. 418ff.

52 Bendix at meeting of 29 Jan. 1921, ZSAP, Nr. 460, Bd. 2, Bl. 70. More generally, see R. H. Tilly, 'German banking, 1850–1914: development assistance for the strong', *Journal of European Economic History*, 15 (Spring 1986), 113–52.

53 In I. Maurer and U. Wengst, *Politik und Wirtschaft in der Krise 1930–1932. Quellen zur Ära Brüning. Quellen zur Geschichte des Parlamentarismus und der politischen Parteien. Dritte Reihe. Die Weimarer Republik*, 2 vols. (Düsseldorf, 1980), vol. I, p. 817.

54 *Ibid.*, p. 819.

7 State, banks and industry in Sweden, with some reference to the Scandinavian countries

MATS LARSSON

What is a banking system?

An important aspect in defining a banking system is the relationships between banks and their customers. Fundamentally these relationships are determined by the connections between several actors. The market situation influences the banks' activities through competition and price mechanism. Banks can also function as entrepreneurs in the guidance of the economy as a whole. The right of the banks to issue banknotes and to hold and transfer monetary deposits of the public is also a distinctive mark of the banking system.[1]

The financial system, however, has also another dimension, in which the institutional setting has a profound influence. In all countries the financial markets are more regulated by public and governmental measures than other markets. This involvement is also of vital importance when we are looking at the establishment of the banking system in Sweden in the nineteenth century – the choice between deposit banking and universal banking.

In this paper I take as my starting-point the governmental view of the credit market and those actions taken in order to guide and control the financial system in certain directions. During the interwar period these governmental measures mostly took the form of banking legislation, with – in Sweden and the other Scandinavian countries – the Bank Inspection Board to exercise control. Besides legal regulations monetary policy was important in specifying the banking system. Both the government and the Bank of Sweden, 'Riksbanken', were able to actively participate in these kinds of activities. In this way the relationships between banks and industry can in part be regarded as a result of changes in the relations between the government and the commercial banks. Changes in financial policy can for example be seen in deposits and lending, as well as in the bank's ownership in industrial companies. The banks and their customers have also in their turn influenced public policy so that both banking legislation and monetary policy have become a response to the actual development.

I will in this chapter focus on changes in Swedish banking during the interwar period concerning the relationships between government, banks and industrial companies. In order to stress the comparative aspect both in specific and in general trends some reference will be made to the development in the other Scandinavian countries during the interwar period. An important question is whether governmental activities – such as the establishment of Bank Inspection Boards – helped the banks to overcome the financial crisis in the 1920s and 1930s.

Roots and traditions

An analysis of the Swedish banking system in the interwar period cannot be undertaken without considering the development, especially during the latter part of the nineteenth century. In this historical development the choice of banking system and the growing demand for long-term capital in the industrialization process played a major role in the shaping of the banking structure and the development of banking activities.

As in several other European countries poised on the edge of industrialization, a regionally oriented banking system developed in the decades around the 1850s. The ownership in these private banks – 'enskilda banker' – was solidary, with the owners being liable, one for all and all for one, for the bank's obligations. Since the possibility of attracting deposits was limited – because of poverty and low savings – the banks' capital base originated from their right to issue banknotes.[2]

It was not until the establishment of Stockholms Enskilda Bank in 1856 that deposits came to play a major role in the development of banking. Although this bank was given the right to issue banknotes, it represented a new way of thinking concerning the mobilization of deposits from companies as well as private persons.[3] During the latter part of the nineteenth century several banks gave depositing a higher priority than before. At the same time an extensive clearing system developed, which made it possible to build up a nation-wide network of commercial banks, where regions with either an excess or shortage of capital could be brought together.[4]

This development created the conditions needed for the banks to compete with private financiers and trading houses in financing the industrial expansions. From the 1860s, the banking system was also strengthened by the creation of Swedish joint-stock banks with limited liability. These banks were not given the right to issue their own bank-notes; instead they had to increase their capital base through higher deposits. The rise of bank corporations with limited liability and a new banking situation due to larger industrial credits led, during the latter part of the nineteenth century, to discussion of the role of the banks.

Swedish banking was traditionally oriented towards short-term lending and depositing – retail banking. But developments on the European continent, and especially in Germany, showed the advantages of closer contacts between banks and industrial companies. Long-term lending, in combination with short-term lending, was profitable both for the banks and for industrial development.

Although Swedish commercial banks continued to be deposit banks even towards the end of the nineteenth century, the size of lending to industry increased. The contacts between banks and industrial companies underwent a particular boom during the period of high business activity in the beginning of the 1870s. The following long depression, however, resulted in liquidity problems for many banks.[5]

The immediate effect of this was a growing public interest in the development of the commercial banks. A special section of the Department of Finance was established as early as 1877, to control the activities of the commercial banks and protect the depositor's money.[6]

In the banking legislation of the 1880s speculative activities among commercial banks were prohibited. This meant that banks were not allowed to own and trade shares on their own account.[7] In spite of this public support for deposit banking, many commercial banks continued to finance and otherwise engage themselves in industrial development.

Swedish banking also underwent other changes during the last decades of the nineteenth century. Several new banks were founded and the number of offices increased so that bank services were no longer reserved for urban areas. Most of these eighty-three bank companies, which had had their charters accepted by 1908, were however only of local or regional importance.

The rapid development of Swedish banking and industrial demands for credits led to an increased discussion of what a bank should and should not do. Looking to the German universal banks, influential political groups in Sweden started to reconsider their traditional banking policy.

The right of private banks to issue banknotes was repealed in 1904 and in 1907 the control of commercial banks was transferred to a special civil service department – the Swedish Bank Inspection Board. At the same time, a total review of both banking legislation and the regulations for joint-stock companies started.[8]

One question of special importance was how banks should be involved in the financing of industrial development. A step towards universal banking was also taken in 1909 when – according to a new legislation – special share-issuing banks were permitted.[9] But the discussion of banking continued and in 1911 new legislation for joint-stock banks with both limited and unlimited liability was presented.

The banking legislation of 1911 was in many respects completely new for Swedish conditions. The larger commercial banks – with an equity higher than 6 million Sw. crowns – were thus allowed to acquire shares in industrial and other companies in relation to the banks' equity.[10] This regulation, however, was not accepted without discussion. In the Riksdag (Parliament) and among banks and other organizations, arguments were put forward supporting, as well as rejecting, this change in the commercial banks' activities.[11]

This change in the banking legislation allowed the banks to participate more actively in the industrial development. The limitation of shareholdings in relation to equity restricted the banks' activities. In order to circumvent this regulation, affiliated investment companies with the purpose of administering and trading with shares were founded. Commercial banks' involvement in industrial companies thus became much larger than originally intended in the legislation. At the same time the need for special share-issuing banks permitted under the law of 1909 was limited.[12]

During the first decade of the twentieth century commercial banks had been criticized for not participating sufficiently in the mobilization of capital for industrial development. The legislation of 1909 as well as 1911 can therefore be seen as a public reaction to this criticism.[13]

The development of the commercial banks' involvement in industry as well as other activities which did not always correspond to the legislative regulation shows that the Bank Inspection Board's right to govern the banks was limited. However, the existence of the Bank Inspectorate probably encouraged several banks to strengthen their internal control in order to fulfil the fundamental requests which had been put forward in the Banking Law of 1911.

Developments during the First World War

The immediate effects of the banking legislation of 1911 could already be seen during the First World War, when both the banks and the banking system underwent extensive changes.

The number of commercial banks in Sweden had peaked in 1908, but the regulations accepted in the legislation of 1911 were an additional incentive for the concentration of Swedish banking. The minimum size of a bank's equity was thus increased under the new legislation, which meant that many small banks that could not increase their equity were forced to merge with other bank companies or liquidate.[14] Small locally oriented joint-stock banks with limited liability were especially hard hit by this structural change.

The governmental control over the establishment of new banks, which had been incorporated into the Banking Law of 1911, also favoured a concentration of Swedish banking.

In spite of these regulations, there was a strong tendency towards the new establishment of firms during the period of high business activity after the outbreak of the First World War. This development, however, was counteracted by an even stronger merger movement. In 1914 there was a total of 75 commercial banks in business, while in 1918 the number was down to 50. The number of bank offices developed in the opposite direction. In 1914 there were 659 offices, and in 1918 the number was nearly doubled to 1,319 offices.[15] Thus the competition between the banks increased during the war, as an effect of rising profits and the inflation which from 1915 struck the Swedish economy.

The rapid inflation also meant that the joint-stock banks had increasing difficulties in keeping deposits within the legal limitation –

20 per cent of deposits to be covered by the banks' equity. The stipulation was changed, but only for the large banks, which from May 1917 only had to cover 12.5 per cent of their deposits by their equity. Since the stricter limitation was kept for smaller banks, this change in the banking legislation encouraged a further concentration of banking.[16]

The increased role of the Swedish Bank Inspection Board which was taken into the Banking Law of 1911, meant that the Board was obliged to control each bank individually. Since there were about seventy commercial banks, control was both difficult and time-consuming. This was also a reason why the state easily could accept a concentration of banking. The Bank Inspection Board would then have fewer banks to supervise, 'sounder' banking practice could more easily be enforced, and the financial strength of banks in relation to the fast-growing industrial firms would be increased. The economic risks connected with banking would, it was felt, also be diminished if the number of big banks increased.[17]

Another major tendency in the development of Swedish banking during the war was the increasing lending to industrial companies and private persons against shares as collateral. Thus the involvement of banks in industry was both direct through shareholdings and indirect through lending on shares owned by industrial firms of bank-affiliated companies. This dangerous behaviour was dependent on a continuous inflation, since an increased value of money would lead to problems in repaying the advances made by the banks.

From bank crisis to consolidation – Swedish banking during the 1920s

The causes of the Swedish bank crisis in 1922–3 had thus been established during the war, with high inflation and lending on bad collateral. Already in 1918, however, some banks began to become aware of the danger connected with lending on shares. In spite of a somewhat more restrictive policy this lending did not culminate until January 1920.[18]

The industrial credits are believed to have been about 43 per cent of the total lending from commercial banks in 1921. The largest borrowers were found in heavy industry with iron, metal, engineering and wood industry as the largest customers. Credits to private persons – of which a great deal probably indirectly accrued to industrial companies

– corresponded to about 23 per cent of the total credits. Bank-affiliated investment companies accounted for about 14 per cent of the total lending from commercial banks.[19]

The bulk of the credits to private persons and holding companies had shares, bonds, goods or other real estate as collateral. Industrial credits were secured in about the same proportion by business mortgage, shares, bonds and other real estate and bills. Credits to heavy industry had often been secured with property.[20]

The biggest risks in the banks' lending were to be found in credits with shares as collateral. This lending had often been given against a background of highly inflated prices on shares. Favourable valuation of the securities – with small margins between market and loan values – were also a weapon in the competition between banks.[21]

When a rapid deflation started during the summer of 1920, it soon became clear that credits given against shares as collateral no longer could be paid off, and that the banks had to take the shares as claims against default. This development is best illustrated by the changes in the collateral value. In February 1919 the average value for all shares corresponded to 64 per cent of the total value of the shares on the stock exchange. However, in March 1922, when the deflation had culminated, the stock exchange value was only 57 per cent of the col-lateral value. This development was also similar to the changes in wholesale prices, which fell from an index value of 362 in September 1920 (1 July 1913–30 June 1914 = 100) to 169 in September 1921.[22]

The early deflation crisis was speeded up by the governmental monetary policy with high interest rates, which aimed at a quick return to the gold standard and more stable rates of exchange. The way company taxation was organized, involving profit taxes from the inflation years that were paid with a time-lag, made things still worse.[23]

The first signs of a banking crisis were seen as early as in 1919, when AB Privatbanken was liquidated after a number of illegal affairs by the managing director. During the spring of 1920, the 'socialistic' AB Nya Banken was also liquidated after large losses on trade credits given to Russia. These liquidations, however, were mostly related to low risk spreading and cannot be blamed on early crisis tendencies in the economy.[24]

The commercial banks were not hit by the crisis in the first wave. The economic sector that was stricken first and hardest by the crisis was instead heavy industry. Several industries had been forced to buy raw materials and other goods at inflated prices and, since the time for production and delivery to the customer was long, the deflation had already reduced profits. Products were often sold at a loss. This meant that the value of a company's real estate or shares could be reduced relatively soon. In order to secure their credits the banks were thus forced to take over the collateral, which – if the loan was secured by shares – could mean that the banks entered as the major owner of the company. This resulted in substantial changes in ownership, and during 1921/2 the commercial banks emerged as the largest shareholders in Swedish industry. Among those industrial sectors most affected by this development were the important Swedish export industries – the iron, steel, wood and pulp industries. The deflation crisis affected light industry less, since credits given during the inflationary period were considerably smaller than those given to heavy industry.[25]

The commercial banks' credits to the industrial sector were augmented by the loans given by bank-affiliated investment companies which had acquired a lot of shares during the war. The deflation, however, meant that these companies – which had small equities in relation to pledged shares – soon were forced to liquidate.

This increased industrial engagement on the part of the banks was in most cases probably unintentional. But especially larger banks also had an interest in connecting major industrial companies closer to the bank, and this could be one way to achieve it.

Larger bank involvement in industrial development, however, also resulted in economic problems for several banks, and from 1922 there was a general banking crisis, due to losses on the credits given to industry. These losses were primarily to be covered by funds voluntarily built up during earlier years. However, if the losses were larger, even venture capital might be used. The share capital was not allowed to be reduced by more than 10 per cent. If the reduction was higher, the shareholders were supposed to increase the firm's share capital or else liquidate the bank.[26]

Thus the banks could, for a limited period, carry fairly large losses. But as the prices of shares did not rise until December 1922 – while they started to increase as early as during the spring of 1922 in Paris and London – the financial situation for the banks got worse.[27]

During 1921 and 1922 four and five commercial banks respectively were forced to liquidate. Their business was, however, taken over by one or several other joint-stock banks. The effects of the banking crisis continued also in the following years. During the period 1921–5 a total of fourteen commercial banks were liquidated.[28]

Financial problems mostly hit smaller banks, which in their lending had low risk spreading. Banks founded as joint-stock banks with limited liability were also more often liquidated than banks with unlimited liability, probably owing to higher risks and therefore larger losses. These liquidations did not, however, mean that the depositor's money was lost. The business of the liquidated banks was taken over by larger banks through mergers. There were also examples of financial reconstructions, where the remaining venture capital from a liquidated bank, together with additional payments of capital from shareholders, resulted in the establishment of a new bank. These reconstructions were done with both governmental aid and financial support from other commercial banks.[29]

Even if financial difficulties were a greater problem for the smaller banks, losses on lending also affected the four largest banks. One example is the financial consolidation of Svenska Handelsbanken, the largest bank in Sweden. As early as the First World War this company had difficulties in keeping its liquidity at the stipulated level. The actions taken to restore the liquidity were not, however, very successful.[30] The situation with regard to both liquidity and solvency instead deteriorated during the deflationary crisis, owing to an extensive lending to bank-affiliated companies. Even if the bank in the legal sense was not directly approaching liquidation, public confidence in the bank was reduced. This was shown for example in the falling prices of the bank's shares, and supporting purchase of the shares by a special bank-oriented syndicate was needed.

Large depreciations on losses were undertaken in 1921 and 1922, from existing funds and profits. This resulted, however, in a reduction of venture capital and since the bank's equity no longer covered 12.5 per cent of the deposits, as was required by the banking law, the deposits had to be reduced or equity increased. The weak position of the bank on the stock market made an issue of new shares impossible. In order to keep up the level of deposits, the bank therefore issued a debenture loan for 40 million Sw. crowns due in fifteen years, with the hope that this capital would be allowed to be included in the equity. With the assistance of the Bank Inspection Board, a provisional law was passed in May 1923 which provided the banking companies with the possibility of considering capital brought into the bank by loans of debentures as part of the equity. This exemption from the original legislation was brought about by special circumstances during the deflation. Together with other state activities, this was an example of a pragmatic governmental policy. The commercial banks could also periodically circumvent the regulations of solvency and liquidity without any action from the Bank Inspection Board.[31]

Governmental activities during the deflation also included an interest in forming a public commercial bank – either through a new establishment or through the take-over of an already existing bank, which also would mean a large public ownership in Swedish industry. Proposals concerning a governmental partnership were put forward to the two largest banks – Svenska Handelsbanken in 1922 and Skandinaviska Banken in 1923 – but were turned down by the banks' boards of directors.[32]

More important was the governmental support in saving Swedish commercial banks in crisis. Through the establishment of AB Kreditkassan the government could transfer capital to the banks in basically three ways: through guarantees for issues of shares in new banks, established to take over the activities of old banks; through lending on shares – to the par level – when banks issued new shares; and through taking over granted credits or other engagements from banks in crisis.

Even if public financial support was only about 15 per cent of the open depreciations on loans done by the commercial banks in the period 1920–4, the importance of this governmental support was fundamental. It probably prevented losses of the depositors' money in at least four of the commercial banks which were liquidated during the period.[33]

The disturbing development of the relations between banks and industry in the beginning of the 1920s also had other effects on governmental policy. A Banking Committee appointed in 1924 was thus instructed to pay special attention to banking influence in industry and trade and the right for banks to acquire shares.

Already in 1921 a law prohibiting banks from acquiring shares in companies whose main activity consisted of administering or trading shares or real property was passed. This new regulation, however, was introduced when the problems with credits to affiliated companies had already passed the peak.[34]

The final report from the Banking Committee proposed a total repeal of the right for banks to acquire shares. This was justified not only because of the danger that the banks would become masters of industry rather than servants, but also because of the risk that owning shares could endanger the banks' liquidity and their depositors' money. The Banking Committee also stressed the importance of adequate collateral.[35]

When this proposal was presented in 1927 the economic situation had stabilized compared to the begining of the 1920s. Such restrictive regulations were therefore not regarded as necessary. However, by providing banks with the right to issue preference shares – not ordinary shares – short-term capital requirements could be covered.[36]

The government thus avoided a stricter regulation of banking activities and – concerning the right to acquire shares – a return to the situation before the Banking Law of 1911. The government instead preferred to guide the banks' activities via the official discount rate. Owing to improved liquidity within the commercial banks, this however turned out to be a blunted governmental tool.[37]

Another reason for the unsuccessful official discount rate policy during the 1920s lay in the close contacts which had been established between banks and industrial companies in the beginning of the decade, and the need for capital in order to restructure industrial production. It was not until the 1930s that the bank rates more closely followed the official discount rate.

During the latter part of the 1920s several of the commercial banks' shareholdings in industrial firms were sold to other companies or to other financial groups – one of these being the Kreuger group of companies. This was made possible by a quick financial recovery especially in the export sector, which reduced the need for bank credits.[38]

Increased governmental activity in banking during the 1920s followed from changes in the political situation in Sweden. The Social Democratic Party had at their congress in 1920 adopted a new programme supporting socialization of trade and industry. After a successful election in September 1921 the Social Democratic Party was able from a governmental position to begin to carry through this policy. The government's position was not, however, very strong and more radical changes of the Swedish economy were not enforced. Political activity instead focused on reducing the effects of the deflation crisis especially for the working class. The introduction of

governmental activities in banking such as AB Kreditkassan and proposals for a governmental partnership in some of the largest commercial banks, should be seen as part of the social democratic policy
during the period 1921–3. In 1923–4 governmental power went over
to the conservatives. The new government, however, continued the
pragmatic policy already adopted by the Social Democrats and the
activities in saving commercial banks – through AB Kreditkassan –
continued. When the Social Democrats gained power again in
September 1924 the economic as well as the political situation had
changed and a broad nationalization of trade and industry was no
longer of current interest.

The Kreuger crash and a new banking policy – Swedish banking during the 1930s

At the beginning of the world depression 1929–33, the Swedish economy performed comparatively well. Both investments and production
were kept at a surprisingly high level. This was to a certain extent due
to an increasing building activity, which supported rising investments
in spite of stagnating private consumption in other sectors and a drop
in export demand.[39]

The strong confidence in the Swedish economy also resulted in a
large capital inflow during 1930 and the beginning of 1931. Although
interest rates were falling, a large part of these capital flows were
deposited in the commercial banks. This development, however, was
interrupted when the international financial crisis started in the
summer of 1931. The foreign exchange reserves were then within
three months (30 June–30 September) reduced by two-thirds or by
300 million Sw. crowns, while at the same time deposits for about 237
million crowns were withdrawn from the Swedish commercial banks.
The financial situation did not stabilize until Sweden had left the gold
standard on 27 September 1931.[40]

The result of the financial crisis and the lower business activity
could, for most of the banks, not be seen until 1932. In this year sixteen
banks were forced to depreciate loans, which affected their equity.
These depreciations were mostly related to credits given to the
Kreuger concern. There was also a substantial decrease in the
depreciations during the following year. The losses in 1932, however,
forced one bank to liquidate during 1933, and in 1935 there was also a

merger due to the bad financial situation.[41] As a whole, however, the effects of the crisis in the 1930s were of much less importance for the banking industry than the crisis in the 1920s, when fourteen commercial banks were liquidated. This might be seen as a result of stricter control of banks by the Bank Inspection Board, during the 1920s. However, financial consolidation within industry itself and governmental support in other economic sectors also had an impact.

Depreciations on loans and structural changes in banking affected the development of banking especially after the Kreuger crash. The solvency and liquidity of the commercial banks had been strengthened in comparison with the crisis in the 1920s, and the resistance against financial problems was therefore better.

The relations between banks and industrial firms were also not as close as at the beginning of the 1920s. Several bank loans had been paid off in the restructuring of Swedish industry. From the latter half of the 1920s credits were granted against better securities – real estate – than during the First World War when shares frequently were used as collateral. The commercial banks' indirect involvement in industry through affiliated investment companies was also of less importance in 1929 than in 1920.[42] The banks' financial problems and the increasing governmental interest in banking in the 1930s can therefore be regarded as primarily a result of the Kreuger concern's financial manipulations and the Kreuger crash.

The extensive international business of the Kreuger concern had already towards the end of the 1920s created a state of confusion in the commercial banks' lending, as well as in the Swedish balance of payments. It was not until a few years after Ivar Kreuger's death in 1932 that the companies' financial activities could be surveyed. The financial crisis created by the Kreuger crash, however, had different implications for different banks, mainly because of the size of the credits given to Kreuger.

At the beginning of 1932 credits at a total of 830 million Sw. crowns – about 20 per cent of total advances from commercial banks – had been given to Kreuger. This heavy engagement was mostly related to Skandinaviska Banken – at this time the second largest commercial bank in Sweden – which contributed about half of these credits. The largest bank, Svenska Handelsbanken, contributed 23 per cent, while the Wallenberg-dominated bank Stockholms Enskilda Bank 'only' had advances corresponding to about 7 per cent of total credits.[43]

In 1931 and 1932 not only the commercial banks, but also the Bank of Sweden 'Riksbanken', was engaged in actions taken to save the Kreuger empire. It was obvious that the poor liquidity of the Kreuger concern made it impossible to pay off the loans which were due. Both the government and the national bank regarded the existence of the Kreuger concern as a question of national importance. Therefore they recommended the three large banks – Svenska Handelsbanken, Skandinaviska Banken and Stockholms Enskilda Bank – to give further credits to Kreuger. The Wallenberg-dominated Stockholms Enskilda Bank, however, refused to take part in this rescuing action, because the securities were regarded as too poor. After the Kreuger crash, this refusal made the bank look especially far-seeing compared to the other larger banks and it probably strengthened the Wallenbergs both as financiers and industrial owners.[44]

Skandinaviska Banken, which had given the largest credits to Kreuger, not only lost the money, but public confidence in the bank was also badly damaged. An immediate governmental liquidity support (through the 'Riksgäldskontor', the National Debt Office), at a total of 100 million Sw. crowns, and deposits from other commercial banks at 40 million crowns, however, helped both the bank and the financial system to regain public confidence.[45]

In spite of the large transactions made by the Kreuger concern and the actions taken after the crash to restore the financial system, the effect of the Kreuger concern's activities were in the long run relatively small. Those companies which Kreuger had acquired from the banks in the 1920s were once again taken over by the banks after the crash as securities.

Several banks, however, did suffer for a couple of years. In four banks equity had to be used in order to write off loans, and in three of these banks a reconstruction involving an issue of new shares was needed in order to keep up the level of deposits.[46]

The importance of the Kreuger crash was also stressed by the government, and as early as 1932 a Parliamentary Investigation was appointed. Based on the proposals put forward by the Banking Committee of 1924 the experts were to examine the right of banks to acquire shares and the question of collateral for lending. Special attention was also to be paid to the role of the Bank Inspection Board.[47]

On most questions the result of this investigation was in accordance with the proposals given by the Banking Committee of 1924. The major difference was that the proposed regulations in 1933 really were incorporated into the banking law.

From 1934 commercial banks were thus deprived of their right to acquire shares – except as securities against claims in default. The new regulation also contained requirements regarding adequate security for credits. In order to raise a loan on shares, there should be a reasonable margin between loan and market value – the credit given was at no time to exceed the market value. These regulations were no more detailed than the requirements actually practised before. The most important effect of the new legislation was probably psychological, since the banks also in the future were to decide what was to be regarded as adequate securities.[48]

The role of the Bank Inspection Board in the financial system was, however, strengthened by these new regulations. The prospects for a detailed control were enlarged as new fields of the banks' activities were opened to inspection. The Parliamentary Investigation also stressed the importance of frequent analyses of the banks' financial situation.[49]

The new legislation adopted in 1933 was a departure from the more corporate finance-aiming bank policy of the Banking Law of 1911. The traditional types of deposit banking and short-term lending were thus once again the model for the Swedish banking system, as during the nineteenth century.

This new policy, however, also became a problem for those banks that for the last twenty years had built up close relations with industrial firms. Shares in companies, acquired in accordance with the Banking Law of 1911, according to the new regulation had to be sold before the end of 1938 – if this could be done without losses. This additional regulation meant that many shares were kept by the banks well into the 1950s. For most banks, however, this regulation resulted in the establishment of a new type of relationship between banks and industrial firms. With the exception of Göteborgs Bank, the larger commercial banks tried to dispose of their share holdings to affiliated organizations or companies, especially to investment companies.[50]

Skandinaviska Banken thus in 1937 started to transfer its share holdings to a newly founded investment company, 'Custos'. With the priority for the shareholders of the bank to acquire shares in Custos and through a gradation of the voting value of different shares, the bank's control over the investment company and their industrial shareholding was guaranteed. Svenska Handelsbanken carried through a similar transfer of shares when an affiliated investment company 'Industrivärden' was founded in 1943.[51]

Stockholms Enskilda Bank had become highly involved in the industrial development as early as the nineteenth century, and already in the 1910s some industrial shareholdings had been transferred to its investment company 'Investor'. Together with its sister-company 'Providentia', from the 1940s Investor became the basis for the industrial shareholdings of the Wallenbergs.[52]

The changes in the banking legislation in 1933 thus did not mean that the close contacts between bank and industry were broken off. The framework for these contacts changed, but the mutual dependence between banks and industrial companies continued in spite of governmental involvement.

Banking in Sweden – a comparative outlook

The development of the Swedish banking system during the interwar period was far-reaching. Many changes had their roots in the inflation during the First World War, with higher deposits and increasing lending. An extensive inflation also hit the Danish and Norwegian economies. As a consequence the commercial banks in all three Scandinavian countries therefore experienced financial difficulties during the deflation period at the beginning of the 1920s, when advances to industrial companies against shares as collateral no longer could be amortized.[53]

A second important tendency in Sweden during the First World War was the accelerating concentration of banking. High profits in banking during the war encouraged the establishment of new commercial banks, but the tendency towards concentration through mergers and take-overs was stronger. This development was also hastened by the Banking Law of 1911 which promoted big banks.

In contrast to Sweden the number of commercial banks in Denmark and Norway continued to increase during the 1910s. In Denmark there was a total of 207 commercial banks and in Norway 195 banks in 1920. Despite its larger credit market the number of commercial banks in Sweden was only 41. The decentralized banking system in Denmark and Norway was to some extent a result of banking being an unregulated market – Norway had its first banking law in 1924, while Denmark's first banking law came in 1919 – but it was also an effect of the demand side of the market. The economies of Denmark and Norway were – compared to Sweden – directed towards agriculture and fishing.[54]

The decentralization of banking and the poor control of credits also contributed to the financial crisis in the 1920s, which especially in Norway had serious effects. At the beginning of the crisis both the governments and the national banks tried to avoid involvement in the commercial banks' financial problems. With the prospects of liquidation of several banks and losses of both venture capital and deposits, however, the governments were forced to act in order to save the banking system. The reluctance of governments to become involved at the beginning of the crisis is evidenced in the deflationary policy with high interest rates, which the governments in all three countries urged in order to return to the gold standard.[55]

The Swedish commercial banks initially tried to solve their economic problems through depreciations on granted credits and reconstructions of the banks' activities with the assistance of other banks. As the situation deteriorated after 1922, however, even the government was forced to participate in the reconstructions of liquidated banks. Through the establishment of a special joint-stock company – AB Kreditkassan – the government could transfer capital to the banks in basically three ways: (1) as guarantees for issues of shares in new banks, established to take over the activities of old banks; (2) lending on shares – at par – when banks issued new shares; (3) taking over granted credits or other engagements from banks in crisis.

The Norwegian banks were also stricken by losses, not only through credits granted to industrial companies – especially the nickel industry – but also through advances to the fishing industry during the war and credits to local governments. In spite of a stable liquidity and solvency – which had been built up without any legal regulation – the banks were forced to undertake large depreciations on credits granted. In order to relieve the effects of these depreciations the banks were allowed to rediscount advances at the Norwegian National Bank. Mergers in order to increase the capital base and support the banks' economies were also, as in Sweden, undertaken by the Norwegian commercial banks.[56]

However, public confidence in the banking system in Norway

decreased. As depreciations were carried out and in order to avoid losses, depositors began to withdraw their holdings. Banks were then forced to suspend their payments and the financial crisis accelerated. The government did not, however, choose only to contribute capital for reconstruction, they also participated in the administration of the commercial banks. Through a special regulation banks suspending their payments were supposed to be put under public management. During the serious crisis of 1923–8 a total of forty-seven commercial banks, among these several big banks, were administered according to this regulation. By the end of 1927 a total of 46.7 per cent of the commercial banks' capital was administered by the government. To prevent these banks from taking over the deposits from other, 'non-governmental' banks, the banking law had to be revised. A regulation concerning the winding up of the governmental involvement was included in the legislation. Only six of those forty-seven banks put under governmental administration, however, managed to reconstruct within the following ten years, while forty-one banks were liquidated. As in the liquidations of other commercial banks, the loss of depositors' money could not be avoided.[57]

The financial crisis in Denmark in the 1920s did not develop in the same way as in Norway. It is true that big commercial banks in Denmark also experienced losses and liquidations, but it was primarily the smaller banks with a local capital base that were hit by the financial crisis. Danish banks, like Swedish banks, had often granted credits against shares while at the same time the banks' ownership in trade and industry had increased through an extensive acquisition of shares. When these firms from 1921 could no longer make payments, the banks were forced to write off loans. A total of thirty-two commercial banks were forced to liquidate during the 1920s with large losses for depositors, while sixteen banks on the brink of liquidation were taken over by other banks. Apart from these rescue actions private capital from other parts of the banking system was used in order to prevent the financial crisis from developing. The government tried to avoid involvement in the crisis, but in the case of the liquidation of 'Landmandsbanken' – one of the largest banks in Denmark – the government in 1922 was forced to guarantee the banks' activities.[58]

The development of banking in Denmark and Norway in the 1920s also meant a beginning of concentration of banking in these countries. This development was in some cases painful with losses for shareholders as well as depositors. In Sweden this concentration had already started in the 1910s when the financial stability due to high profits made take-overs possible. This stability as well as governmental support meant that depositors only in some cases suffered losses of their capital.[59]

Of special importance for the concentration of banking and for the financial stability in Sweden was the extensive development of banking legislation and public control of commercial banks. In Denmark the first banking legislation was adopted in 1919, and compared to the Swedish legislation, this regulation was fairly liberal. It is true that the Danish banking legislation also contained a control of the establishment of banks, but the requirement of a minimum size of share capital was not as extensive as in the Swedish legislation. The regulations concerning a bank's activities were not as restricted as in Sweden, which meant that Danish commercial banks could freely act as universal banks with share-issuing activities. Also the regulation concerning solidity and liquidity (the size of the cash reserve) was not as restrictive in the Danish legislation as in the Swedish regulation.[60]

With large losses in the banking system during the crisis of the 1920s a revision of the legislation was presented in 1923. This new banking legislation, however, was not accepted until 1930 and did not mean any fundamental change of banking in Denmark. In the light of low risk spreading concerning granted credits in the 1920s, a regulation of lending was taken into the new banking law. This meant that a bank's advances to one customer were not to exceed 35 per cent of the sum of the bank's share capital and its funds. The new legislation also contained a regulation of collateral and control of credits given to bank-affiliated private persons. In order to secure the banks' solvency, the minimum size of the share capital was also raised for banks to be established.[61]

The purge of commercial banks in the Danish financial system during the 1920s had affected large as well as small banks. During the 1930s the concentration, however, mostly hit local and regional banks. In contrast to the 1920s the continuing concentration in banking was mostly a result of rationalization and not due to financial problems. Of a total of nineteen commercial banks liquidated during the 1930s, fifteen banks were taken over by other banks. In the remaining four banks liquidations could be undertaken without losses for the depositors. As in Sweden the financial situation among Danish industrial companies during the 1930s was improved compared to the 1920s. Thus the commercial banks did not experience the same large losses on industrial credits as during the crisis of the 1920s.[62]

As a result of the financial development during the First World War and the crisis at the beginning of the 1920s the Norwegian banking system was the object of a public investigation. The committee work preceding the banking legislation of 1924 rejected a state monopoly for banking, which otherwise easily could have been carried through considering the large governmental administration of banks. In the new banking legislation the establishment of commercial banks was regulated in the same way as in Sweden and Denmark. Thus the law contained a minimum value of share capital for the establishment of a commercial bank.[63]

The regulation concerning solvency and liquidity was on the whole the same as in Denmark, i.e. more liberal than the Swedish legislation. As in the Danish legislation of 1930, but in contrast to Swedish regulation, the Norwegian banking laws also contained restrictions in the size of lending. Advances to one customer were not to exceed 25 per cent of the sum of the bank's share capital and funds. Norwegian commercial banks were not allowed to trade with shares on their own account or take shares as payments on loans. However, 20 per cent of the banks' equity could be invested in shares, which gave the banks limited possibilities to take part in the direct development of industrial companies. This opportunity was not, as in Sweden and Denmark, used for activities connected with universal banking. In the Norwegian as in the Danish legislation (1919), a special Bank Inspection Board was created to control the financial development of the commercial banks. In Norway this type of control had already since 1887 been carried out for savings banks.[64]

In several respects 1924 came to be a turning-point in the development of Norwegian banking. As the new legislation was introduced the financial situation improved for both banks and industrial companies and even if there were liquidations among the commercial banks, these could be done in a more controlled way than during the earlier crisis. The governmental involvement in the banking sector was, from the middle of the 1920s, more concentrating towards the strengthening of savings banks. These banks made large losses as a result of lending to local government and agriculture, and during the period 1929–33 direct governmental financial support was needed.

In 1931, however, commercial banks in Norway once again suffered financial difficulties. Two of the largest banks encountered problems with liquidity owing to large losses on advances to industrial companies and to the shipping industry as the volume of deposits decreased. The reconstruction of these banks also included governmental financial support. By means of a moratorium for three months and guarantees of the banks' liquidity from the national bank, these banks were able to reconstruct their business.[65]

During the following years the Norwegian commercial banks experienced some problems with liquidity and solidity too, but from 1933 there was a general improvement in the financial situation. As in Sweden, business activities changed for the better. Owing to these developments deposits increased, originating from private companies and public organizations and institutions, and the liquidity of commercial banks was strengthened.[66]

The deflationary crisis which hit the Scandinavian economies from 1920 thus had similar consequences for banking in Sweden and in Denmark and Norway. The relative stability of Swedish commercial banks was based on the banking legislation of 1911, while in Denmark and especially Norway the 1920s banking crisis led to dramatic steps designed to save the banking system. More strict regulations concerning banking were adopted in all three countries during the 1920s and 30s. In Denmark and Norway these regulations were – to a greater degree than in Sweden – aimed towards a regulation of the structure of lending and strengthening of liquidity. The focus in Swedish legislation was from the end of the 1910s rather the relationship between banks and industry. The discussion of an abolition of the banks' right to acquire shares and a strict regulation of lending against shares dominated the politics of Swedish banking until 1934, when a new law was introduced.

The serious consequences of the crisis of the early 1920s in Denmark, Norway and Sweden probably led to a consolidation of banking towards the end of the decade. This, in turn, helped the commercial banks to overcome the international crisis of the 1930s with comparative ease.

NOTES

1 R. Cameron, *Banking and Economic Development* (London, 1972), pp. 5ff.
2 M. Larsson and H. Lindgren, 'Risktagandets gränser', in L. Engwall and C. G. Thunman (eds.), *Finansmarknader i förvandling* (forthcoming).
3 G. B. Nilsson, *Banker i brytningstid, A. O. Wallenberg i svensk bankpolitik 1850–1856* (Stockholm, 1981), pp. 325ff.
4 I. Nygren, *Från Stockholms Banco till Citibank* (Stockholm, 1985), p. 47.
5 Larsson and Lindgren, 'Risktagandets gränser', pp. 46ff.
6 Nygren, *Från Stockholms Banco*, p. 53.
7 Larsson and Lindgren, 'Risktagandets gränser', p. 7.
8 M. Larsson, 'Public control of commercial banks and their activities', in Uppsala Papers in Economic History, Working Paper no. 2 (1989), *Banking and Bank Legislation in Europe 1880–1970*, pp. 40ff.
9 SFS 1909: 64.
10 The size of these acquisitions varied in relation to the reserve fund which, according to the banking law, was to be set aside each year. This reserve fund was also included in the equity. The restrictive right to acquire shares, however, was fundamentally overthrown by the establishment of bank-affiliated companies. Through credits to these companies, the commercial banks more or less performed activities of a universal bank, while still being deposits banks.
11 S. Fritz, 'Frågan om affärsbankernas aktieförvärvsrätt under 1900-talets första decennium', in *Från vid fält. Festskrift till Rolf Adamsson 25.10.1967* (Stockholm, 1987), pp. 65ff.
12 No share-issuing bank was ever founded according to the law of 1909. This was mainly due to the existence of the bank-affiliated companies, 'emissionsbolag'. Trading of shares through these companies made it possible for the bank to avoid control by the Bank Inspection Board. The question of share-issuing banks and the banks' right to acquire shares is closely examined by S. Fritz in 'Frågan om affärsbankernas aktieförvärvsrätt under 1900-talets första decennium'.
13 Statens Offentliga Utredningar (SOU), 1927: 11, pp. 54ff.
14 The minimum size of the equity was, in the Banking Law of 1911, raised from 200,000 Sw. crowns to 500,000 crowns.
15 The concentration of the Swedish banking industry continued also in the 1920s. In 1920 the number of banks was 41 and in 1925 it was reduced to 31. The concentration then slowed down and in 1935 the number was still as high as 28. See: *Sveriges Officiella Statistik* (SOS), *Uppgifter om bankerna 1914–1935*.
16 Larsson, 'Public control of commercial banks', pp. 48ff.
17 Larsson and Lindgren, 'Risktagandets gränser'.
18 A. Östlind, *Svensk samhällsekonomi 1914–1922* (Stockholm, 1945), pp. 301ff., 595ff.
19 *Ibid.*, p. 597.
20 *Ibid.*, pp. 597ff.
21 SOU 1927: 11, pp. 103ff.
22 SOU 1927: 11, pp. 56ff., 106ff.
23 Larsson, 'Public control of commercial banks', pp. 54ff.
24 Östlind, *Svensk samhällsekonomi 1914–1922*, pp. 602ff.
25 SOU 1927: 11, pp. 56ff.
26 Banking Law of 1911, § 93.
27 Östlind, *Svensk samhällsekonomi 1914–1922*, p. 605.
28 SOS, *Uppgifter om bankerna 1921–1925*.

29 Those banking companies which were taken over by newly founded banks were AB
    Köpmannabanken in 1921, AB Mälarprovinsernas bank and Sydsvenska Kredit-
    aktiebolaget in 1922, Svenska Lantmännens bank in 1923, AB Nordiska Handels-
    banken in 1925. These financial reconstructions were rather successful as four of
    these five banks were still in existence even in 1934. See SOS, *Uppgifter om bankerna
    1921–1934*, and M. Larsson, 'Public support or internal restructuring – Swedish
    commercial banks during the crisis of the 1920s', paper for the International
    Workshop on 'Bank–Industry Relations in Interwar Europe: Austria, Hungary and
    Sweden', Uppsala, 10–12 September 1989.
30 According to the Banking Law of 1911 commercial banks were supposed to have
    a cash reserve of 25 per cent of the commitments the company was obliged to
    honour on demand. Concerning the financial problems of Svenska Handels-
    banken during the deflation crisis see K. G. Hildebrand, *I omvandlingens tjänst,
    Svenska Handelsbanken 1871–1955* (Stockholm, 1971).
31 Apart from Svenska Handelsbanken, Wermlands Enskilda Bank also used loans of
    debenture to increase the companies' capital and restore the banks' solidity. See
    Hildebrand, *I omvandlingens tjänst,* pp. 166ff.; Larsson, 'Public support or internal
    restructuring'.
32 Larsson, 'Public support or internal restructuring'.
33 *Ibid.*
34 SOU 1927: 11, pp. 86ff.; E. Söderlund, *Skandinaviska banken 1914–1939* (Uppsala,
    1978), p. 21.
35 SOU 1927: 11, pp. 74ff.
36 SOU 1927: 11, pp. 134ff.
37 Nygren, *Från Stockholms Banco,* pp. 70ff.; Larsson and Lindgren, 'Risktagandets
    gränser'.
38 The commercial banks' engagement in the restructuring of different industrial
    sectors is described in, for example, Hildebrand, *I omvandlingens tjänst,* and in
    H. Lindgren, *Bank, Investmentbolag, Bankirfirma, Stockholms Enskilda Bank
    1924–1945* (Stockholm, 1988).
39 K. Kock, *Kreditmarknad och räntepolitik 1924–1956,* part I (Uppsala, 1961), pp. 53ff.
40 *Ibid.*
41 SOS, *Uppgifter om bankerna 1931–1935.*
42 SOS, *Uppgifter om bankerna 1919–1935.* The commercial banks' credit to industrial
    companies is traditionally said to have decreased during the 1930s, as an effect of
    larger self-financing. This conclusion, however, has been based on credits given to
    larger industrial companies from individual banks. Later research based on total
    advances (each individual credit larger than 50,000 Sw. crowns per year) reported
    to the Swedish Bank Inspection Board shows that this may be wrong and that
    credits to the industry did not decrease until the beginning of the 1940s. See
    H. Sjögren, 'Credit connections in the interwar period, the advances of Swedish
    commercial banks and their distribution according to economic sectors and geo-
    graphical regions', Paper for the International Workshop on 'Bank–Industry
    Relations in Interwar Europe: Austria, Hungary and Sweden', Uppsala, 10–12
    September 1989.
43 Lindgren, *Bank, Investmentbolag, Bankirfirma,* pp. 439 ff.
44 Söderlund, *Skandinaviska banken 1914–1939,* pp. 475ff.; Lindgren, *Bank, Invest-
    mentbolag, Bankirfirma,* pp. 439ff.
45 Söderlund, *Skandinaviska banken 1914–1939,* pp. 492ff.
46 Reconstructed banks were Uplands Enskilda Bank, Göteborgs Handelsbank and

Östergötlands Enskilda Bank, while Sydsvenska Banken reorganized its business activities after a reduction of the equity. See: Söderlund, *Skandinaviska banken 1914–1939*, pp. 496 ff. and SOS, *Uppgifter om bankerna 1932–1937*.

47 SOU 1932: 30, pp. 37ff.
48 SOU 1932: 30, pp. 55ff.; Larsson, 'Public control of commercial banks', pp. 58ff.
49 SOU 1932: 30, pp. 80, 86ff.
50 Göteborgs Bank sold its share holdings to buyers detached from the bank: Larsson and Lindgren, 'Risktagandets gränser', pp. 21ff.
51 Söderlund, *Skandinaviska banken 1914–1939*, pp. 538ff.; Hildebrand, *I omvandlingens tjänst*, pp. 336ff.
52 Lindgren, *Bank, Investmentbolag, Bankirfirma*, pp. 305ff.
53 P. Winding, *Det danske kapitalmarked* (Copenhagen, 1958), pp. 319ff.; E. Engebretsen, *Norsk bankvesen, saerlig efter verdenskrigen* (Oslo, 1939), pp. 26ff.
54 P. Winding, *Tavlehefte till det danska kapitalmarked* (Copenhagen, 1958), p. 314; S. A. Hansen, *Okonomisk vaekst i Danmark, bind II, 1914–1983* (Copenhagen, 1983), pp. 31ff.; Engebretsen, *Norsk bankvesen*, pp. 36ff.
55 Hansen, *Okonomisk vaekst i Danmark*, pp. 41ff.; N. Rygg, *Norges bank i mellomkrigstiden* (Oslo, 1950), pp. 3ff.
56 Engbretsen, *Norsk bankvesen*, pp. 51ff.
57 *Ibid.*, pp. 72ff.; E. Hoffstad, *Det norske Privatbankvaesens historie* (Oslo, 1928), pp. 201ff.
58 Winding, *Det danske kapitalmarked*, pp. 319ff.
59 The government tried to avoid losses for depositors when commercial banks liquidated. In the case of Privatbanken (1919), however, about 23 per cent (670,000 Sw. crowns) of the depositors' money were lost as the government, owing to illegal activities of the bank, would not support the bank. See Östlind, *Svensk samhällsekonomi 1914–1933*, pp. 602ff.
60 Swedish commercial banks were restricted to have a cash reserve corresponding to 25 per cent of the commitments the company was obliged to honour upon demand, while the share in Denmark was 15 per cent and in Norway 20 per cent. Lov om banker 4 oktober 1919, § 2–7 och § 11; SOU 1927: 11, pp. 217ff.
61 Winding, *Det danske kapitalmarked*, pp. 324ff.
62 In 1930 there was a total of 179 commercial banks in Denmark, while in 1940 the number was reduced to 162. See Winding, *Det danske kapitalmarked*, pp. 321ff.
  The Danish banking system was able at the beginning of the 1930s to avoid losses through a governmental support for agriculture. During the latter part of the 1930s the official priority was more towards the industrial development through, for example, trade policy. The governmental involvement in the Danish economy did also increase in other respects during the 1930s compared to the previous decade. See Hansen, *Okonomisk vaekst i Danmark*, pp. 48ff.
63 SOU 1927: 11, pp. 221ff.; Engebretsen, *Norsk bankvesen*, pp. 113ff.
64 SOU 1927: 11, pp. 225ff.; Engebretsen, *Norsk bankvesen*, pp. 113ff.
65 Rygg, *Norges bank i mellomkrigstiden*, pp. 444ff.
66 Engebretsen, *Norsk bankvesen*, pp. 170ff.

8   State, banks and industry in Belgium and The Netherlands, 1919–1939

GUY VANTHEMSCHE

It is mainly for reasons of geographic proximity that the banking systems of Belgium and The Netherlands can be studied under one and the same heading.* Indeed, their historical tradition, structure and performance during the period under consideration show many contrasts. That is not to say that both systems radically differed in every respect, for while there were many divergences, there were also many similarities. Thus, a comparative study, such as the present one, will have to take various nuances into account. The final result will be a rather complex picture.

However, these considerations have an impact on our treatment of the topic in such a short space. A general overview of the problem seems preferable to a detailed analysis of the action of one or two large individual institutions. While the latter, more painstaking method can indeed provide greater insight in the long run, the former, more fragile and provisory approach seems preferable here since the banking history of both small West European countries is not very well known outside the Belgian and Dutch national boundaries. Of course, it is impossible to give an overview of the banking activity in its entirety. We can do no more than furnish a very broad outline of the most important points, mainly those mentioned in the title: the relationship between the banking system, industry and the state.

The uneven development of mixed banking in Belgium and The Netherlands in the 1920s

Belgian banking is not altogether unknown in international historical literature. Belgium is in fact relatively well known for its very early

104

development of mixed banking. The activity of the two largest banking institutions, the Société Générale de Belgique and the Banque de Belgique, largely antedated similar developments in other countries. The early industrial development in Belgium was largely sustained by the action of the banking system. This has already been treated in different studies.[1]

Between 1895 and 1914, the Belgian banking system was already vigorously expanding, but after the First World War, two features dominated the Belgian banking system. The first was an increasing trend towards concentration.[2] The 1920s were marked by a number of important mergers and take-overs leading to a banking structure where two groups, centred around the Société Générale de Belgique and the Banque de Bruxelles, cumulated in 1930 not less than 52 per cent of the total paid-up capital and reserves of all Belgian banks, and 55 per cent of the total value of the share portfolio.[3] The second feature of the evolution of Belgian banks was the reinforcement of the already existing industrial involvement. Belgian industry had been badly damaged during the war and was to be reconstructed; the Belgian mixed banks fully responded to this need. They supplied large amounts of capital on the occasion of the creation of new societies or the enlargement of existing ones; they kept large amounts of industrial shares in portfolio. An evaluation of the assets of eighteen of the most important banking institutions showed that they held 550 million Belgian francs in private securities in 1919, as against 1.450 million in public securities; in 1929 these items respectively amounted to 3.085 and 340 million.[4] Another important symptom of the banks' growing industrial involvement is the huge development of current account-credits (30 per cent of the balance sheet total of all Belgian banks in 1913, 46 per cent in 1929).[5] On the other hand, the item 'commercial paper' became relatively less important. The ratio of this item to the current accounts was 60 per cent in 1913, but fell back to only 25 per cent in 1926.[6] Some estimates show that these current account-advances mainly consisted of credits to industrial enterprises.[7]

So, after the First World War, the Belgian banking system reinforced its mixed character without any hesitation. The nexus was especially strong in the large-scale basic industries. It has been estimated that in the early 1930s the single Société Générale group controlled 25 to 30 per cent of the coal-mining sector, 48 per cent of the iron and steel sector, 60 to 75 per cent of the zinc industry, 40 per cent of the glass sector, etc.[8] A handful of large banks thus formed the nerve centre of the industrial core in Belgium; it is important to stress the will of the banks to control and orientate the industrial structure of the country. Banks stimulated the concentration, the rationalization or the cartelization of enterprises in the sectors they controlled. Thus, the 1920s might well be termed the climax of mixed banking in Belgium.

Recent studies have pointed to the negative effect of this dominating position in the long run. The mixed banks (and, later, the holding societies that developed from them) seem to have contributed to a growing rigidity and obsolescence of Belgian industrial structure. They clung to the basic, heavy industries, and did not stimulate the creation or development of younger, more innovative sectors, such as the consumer goods industries.[9] But this was not to become evident until after the Second World War, so that, for the moment, the public criticism of the banks was of a more general nature. When the banking concentration had come to a climax at the end of the 1920s, the banks were being criticized for their overwhelming domination of industry mainly by the socialists. At the same time, the discontented lower middle-class producers accused the banks of completely ignoring their specific credit needs, and concentrating exclusively on the large-scale basic industries.[10]

If the developments in Belgium were, on the whole, the logical extension of an already existing pre-war tendency, the Dutch banking evolution, in contrast, was marked by far more drastic changes. This cannot be understood without reference to the general economic context. It is a well-known fact that the Dutch 'industrial revolution' occurred with some time-lag in comparison with the neighbouring countries. Industrialization did not accelerate until after 1895. Small-scale enterprises were more important than in Belgium.[11] This basic situation helps to explain the particular relationship of Dutch banks with industry. All authors agree that in the nineteenth century, Dutch industrialization owed very little to the banks.[12] Till the beginning of the twentieth century the banking system itself could be characterized as a 'rather passive sector of the Dutch economy';[13] it was small-scale and of a local character. This was to change when, in the first years of this century, Dutch industrialization quickened and large-scale enterprise became more important. The parallelism between these changes and the changes then taking place in the banking structure has already been stressed.[14] In the older literature on Dutch banking, the year 1911 is often presented as the starting-point of an important movement towards concentration and modernization of the banking structure. That year, the Rotterdamsche Bank fused with the Deposito -en Administratiebank in order to form a larger institution, the Rotterdamsche Bankvereeniging (called Robaver). This move was followed by accelerated changes in the whole of the country's banking structure. In 1920, one author went so far as to say that 'A whole new spirit took possession of the banking system after 1911.'[15] Recent historical literature has taken a more critical look at the importance of this watershed, and stressed the anticipatory evolution of the preceding ten or fifteen years, though it was perhaps not as rapid as that of the following decade.[16] For our purpose, it suffices to say that during and immediately after the First World War, these new trends gained enormous momentum and led to a completely new stature of the banks and, in particular, to their new relationship with industry, even if links between banks and industry were not altogether absent before this breakthrough (the Twentsche Bank, for instance, traditionally supported textile enterprises).

Just as in Belgium, we note a strong tendency towards concentration and a scaling-up of the banking institutions, notwithstanding a rise in the total number of banks.[17] The local character of the banks gave way to the creation of nation-wide banking networks, either through the establishment of offices of a mother bank, or, mainly, through the take-over of local institutions by a large institution; the former either continued to exist nominally, or were incorporated into a large unit.[18] A handful of large institutions stood out against the mass of small ones: the Dutch 'Big Five' dominating the banking landscape of the 1920s and 1930s were the Nederlandsche Handel-Maatschappij, the Robaver, the Amsterdamsche Bank, the Twentsche Bank, the Incasso Bank. In 1918 they constituted 70.2 per cent of the balance sheet total of the general commercial banks, in 1928 67.5 per cent.[19] It is important to underline the strengthening of the banks. Capital and reserves of the big five expanded at an amazing pace, mainly during and immediately after the war. This trend paralleled other drastic changes, in the first place a new relationship with the public. Before the war, the Dutch banking system was known for its 'Depositenarmut';[20] its foreign resources were rather limited because the public preferred to channel its available cash into the stock exchange. The circumstances of the war were about to change this state of affairs. The temporary closure of the stock exchange and the growth of the monetary mass brought large disposable assets into the banking system. On the other hand, as The Netherlands remained neutral during the First World War, Dutch industry did not fare too badly during this crucial period. Indeed, it even showed some tendencies towards development, and experienced a general expansionist trend once the conflict was over.[21] The resulting industrial demand for credit could now be met by the sturdier banking system – and indeed it was. During and immediately after the war, the Dutch banking system made a decisive move towards mixed banking, granting advances and supplying capital to industry. The increasing willingness of the banks to grant credit is directly visible in the balance sheets of the big five, where the item 'debtors' accounts for 44 per cent of the total in 1914, and 55 per cent in 1920.[22] It is difficult to give precise quantitative evidence of this growing industrial involvement, but all studies agree that the overall application of the new banking policy was far from cautious and, on the contrary, often rather daring.[23]

This became fairly obvious when the international recession hit The Netherlands at the end of the year 1920. Several Dutch banks met with serious difficulties and some of them paid a heavy toll for their imprudent industrial policy. A bank that was rapidly reaching the bracket of top-ranking institutions, the Marx en C° Bank, was forced to close down in 1922; another recently formed but already fairly important enterprise, the Bank-Associatie, had to undergo drastic reorganization. More important still were the troubles of the Rotterdamsche Bankvereeniging, one of the big five. In 1924 the public authorities had to intervene in order to save this important bank from failure.[24] Indeed, it has been noted that the afflicted institutions were in fact the most 'expansionist' ones;[25] the Rotterdamsche Bankvereeniging was especially aggressive in its policy of industrial support. Its difficulties were, among other things, attributable to large and unilateral credits to Müller en C°, a concern with interests in shipping and mining that ran into serious trouble in the early 1920s.

Again, it is very difficult to provide precise data documenting the resulting reorientation, but it seems fairly certain that the banking crisis changed the attitude and mentality of the main banking leaders. They became far more prudent in their investment policy. The banks did not sever all ties with industry; they continued to participate in the floating of securities[26] and to grant short-term credits. But they were not at all keen on furnishing enterprises with longer-term advances, nor on building up a permanent dominating position in industry, contrary to what happened in Belgium. One of the interesting symptoms of the changing and, by now, far more cautious attitude of the bankers is the declining number of directorships held by top-ranking bankers in other financial, commercial and industrial enterprises: rising from 229 in 1910 to 412 in 1923, this number declines to 157 in 1931.[27] In the 1920s, the Dutch banking system was characterized by a special mix of its own, by a peculiar intermediary position between English pure deposit banking and German (or Belgian) mixed banking, 'with the consequence', as one author noted, '... that nobody is really satisfied'.[28] Indeed, towards the end of the decade, the role of the banks in the economy became the subject of prolonged public debate. The plea of a top-ranking Dutch industrialist, Fentener Van Vlissingen, for a more active support of industry by the banks was a striking aspect of this controversy. The Netherlands had to intensify their industrialization, he said, but existing and future enterprises did not get enough financial support from the banks. Consequently, he proposed the creation of an 'Industriebank', supported by the main banks and industries, in order to undertake a real collaboration between the two sectors. The bankers' point of view in this debate was that their institutions did in fact already support industry, but that they first had to take into account their own liquidity. Nothing would be gained by forcing a collaboration between banks and industry, a situation that could develop only slowly.[29]

Nevertheless, it is not yet very clear which type of industry was dissatisfied with the banks' 'passivity'. If some large industrialists, like the one just cited, raised their voices, others expressed their satisfaction with the existing situation; many documents seem to indicate that it was mostly the small and middle-scale enterprises that suffered from the lack of banking credit.[30] Some detailed regional studies demonstrate that the small, independent local banks were more disposed to sustain (equally small and local) enterprises, while the ever-growing national banking networks just mentioned were less willing to do so.[31] Moreover, it is extremely important to note that, notwithstanding the 'discrete' attitude of the banks in the Dutch economy, The Netherlands were extremely successful in the development of new activities of international standing, such as the electrical industries, artificial textiles, food industries, aeroplane construction. The present state of historical research limits us to the mere assertion that the Belgian industrial structure, dominated by the banks, had not developed such new dynamic activities, whereas the Dutch one, notoriously independent of the banks, effectively did so. Future studies possibly will make clear whether or not the varying impact of the banking system constitutes a real causal factor in this contrasting evolution.

The different vicissitudes of the Belgian and Dutch banking systems in the 1930s

The impact of the crisis of the 1930s was to be extremely important, especially in Belgium.[32] The great Belgian banks were indeed aware of the dangers inherent in mixed banking. They tried to adapt their balance sheets to the threat posed by the growing crisis of the early 1930s. Even before the beginning of the economic difficulties, the banks corrected a dangerous imbalance in the ratio between paid-up capital plus reserves and the securities portfolio. This ratio fluctuated between 44 and 71 per cent in the years 1920–6, climbing to 88, 110, 131 and 121 per cent in 1927–30, only to recede to 93, 92 and 97 per cent in 1931–3.[33] Once the crisis set in, the Belgian banks tried to augment their liquid assets; they raised cash holdings from about 10 per cent of the balance sheet total in 1926–31 to 17 and 20 per cent in 1932 and 1933. On the other hand, the advances in current account fell back from 46 per cent in 1929 and 1931 to 36 per cent in 1933.[34] Precisely this item posed serious problems to the Belgian banking system and was at the core of the hardship it was soon to experience. Large amounts of advances to industrial enterprises turned out to be frozen. Cutting back on these advances was very difficult or even impossible and could endanger the survival of the productive units. Some of these frozen long-term advances were converted into participations, a factor contributing to the growth of the share of the security portfolio in the total balance sheets of all Belgian banks (15, 15 and 16 per cent in 1928–29–30; 20, 22 and 28 per cent in 1931–32–33).[35]

Thus the Belgian banks were quickly drawn into an unpleasant dilemma: they had to look after their liquidity (deposits falling from 4,774 million gold francs in 1930 to 3,636 in 1933) while at the same time having to sustain the industrial enterprises with which they had built up a close relationship. Some of them managed to handle this delicate situation quite well, particularly the Société Générale, the *most important bank. It succeeded in maintaining or even expanding its credits to industry while being able to preserve a secure position.*[36] But in 1934, the latent difficulties materialized for two middle-sized banks, the Banque Belge du Travail and the Algemeene Bankvereeniging.[37] Their bankruptcy obliged the (conservative Catholic-Liberal) government to support them financially, in order to prevent the spreading of panic amongst the public and to avoid a possible run on other, already shaky banks. Meanwhile, the government took another step that was far more wide-ranging. In August 1934 a mechanism was installed whereby a public credit institution, the Société Nationale de Crédit à l'Industrie, helped the private banks in mobilizing their frozen advances to industry. Simultaneously, but by another Royal Decree, the government, in a few laconic lines, ordered the end of mixed banking in Belgium.[38] The existing institutions had to split into deposit banks on the one hand and holding companies on the other. Henceforth, the former were to have a minimum capital and were forbidden to hold industrial and commercial securities in portfolio. Why this drastic, sudden and unexpected measure?

Monocausal explanations are deficient. Only a complex combination of reasons can explain this drastic measure. First, it must be noted that the banking reform did not arouse loud protest from the banks themselves; on the contrary, the inspiration for reform seems to have come from the highest banking circles. In part, the governmental decree aimed to restore the public's dangerously waning confidence in the solidity of the banking system. In addition, the government showed the public that it was capable of acting effectively. Thus, it did not hesitate to intervene in the banking sector, in order to compensate for the somewhat negative impression attached to the above-mentioned credit mobilization operation, which was interpreted as a 'gift' to the banks. Finally, the official end of mixed banking in Belgium has to be seen in the context of a broader evolution of the financial institutions themselves. Already in the 1920s, a trend had set in whereby the mixed banks created separate holding societies ('sociétés de participation'), in charge of managing part of the enormous share portfolios the mixed banks held before. Without giving up their industrial participations altogether, the banks themselves thus tended towards a greater measure of specialization. The Société Générale created several holding societies, each one specialized in the management of the Société's interests in one particular field (i.e. colonial, maritime, electrical, glass-producing sector, etc.). The Banque de Bruxelles went even further and set up a single large society, the Compagnie Belge pour l'Industrie (1928), centralizing the bank's participations in very diverse Belgian industries.[39] Seen from this point of view, the Royal Decree of 22 August 1934 rather continued and intensified an already existing tendency towards financial specialization. The decree nevertheless reversed the relationship of dependency between bank and holding. Previously, the holding society was dependent on the (mixed) bank; the 1934 reform, splitting the mixed bank, led to the transformation of the latter into a holding, controlling the newly formed deposit bank. Finally, it has also been argued that this complex institutional reform was inspired by the will of the banks to hide substantial losses and make large inevitable amortizements less visible.

As can be seen, the year 1934 was a troubled one for the Belgian banks, but more difficulties were to come. Belgium was a member of the gold bloc and firmly rejected any monetary manipulation. The ensuing policy of deflation soon became intolerable for the country's economy. At the end of 1934 and in the first months of 1935, the lack of confidence in the Belgian franc reached a climax and capital outflow assumed worrying proportions.[40] Coupled with the public's growing lack of confidence in the liquidity of banking itself (the cited failure of the Algemeene Bankvereeniging took place at this time), this factor led to a heavy withdrawal of deposits. Now the survival of the banking system in its entirety seemed to be at stake. The government was forced to grant a special credit to the Banque de Bruxelles, to save the country's second largest bank from collapse. The speculation against the franc could have been broken by drastic credit restrictions, but at the same time this would have meant the closing down of the banking system. The political authorities did not want to provoke a banking moratorium: 'A country such as ours cannot live without the banks', as the new Prime Minister told Parliament.

The alternative, a devaluation of the Belgian franc (March 1935), brought about substantial changes. It facilitated Belgian exports, thereby considerably stimulating the performance of the Belgian economy. Capital flowed back into the country. All these factors tended to ease the pressure on the banks, which subsequently emerged from their perilous position. But the monetary crisis had also led to political changes, which were to have a major impact on the relation between the banks and the state. The demand for 'banking control' (even if it was a rather vague one) was mentioned for the first time in a 1931 programme of the Socialist Party, in the wake of the already mentioned growing criticism of the huge power the banks wielded in Belgian society. The same party's much more precise (and famous) 1933 'Plan du Travail' (drawn up under the guidance of Henri de Man, the father of socialist 'planism') had asked for the out-right 'nationalization' of the credit sector. The Socialist Party now joined the Catholic and Liberal parties in a government of 'national union', a younger generation of politicians taking over the leading posts. One of the key elements in the 'renovation' of economic policy that the new government wanted to realize was the establishment of banking control. The Royal Decree of 9 July 1935 instituted a legis-lative framework that was to regulate Belgian banking for several decades.[41] Contrary to the laconic text of the 1934 decree, this new act was far more detailed and proved to be a real 'charter' of banking busi-ness. The notion 'bank' itself was defined very clearly and financial institutions had to fulfil certain conditions before they could call themselves 'banks'. They were required to observe certain precise rules, for example, not to hold an industrial and commercial share portfolio; the splitting of the mixed bank was thus maintained in this second decree. In addition, a 'Banking Commission' was established to supervise the working of the banking system, while within the banks themselves sworn 'revisors' now controlled the actions of the individ-ual institutions. The Banking Commission was also empowered to impose certain ratios between balance items. As with the first decree, this one was not imposed upon a reluctant banking community either. In fact, top-ranking bankers participated very actively in the elabor-ation of the legislation and inspired several measures. The threat of state control of the holding societies, a socialist demand, could be avoided by the bankers (the socialists themselves having abandoned the demand for nationalization earlier) and the control system, including the Banking Commission, worked in a collective, consen-sual spirit and not at all in an authoritarian one.

Thus, the 1930s were an important transitional period for the Belgian banks: they experienced serious difficulties and their relation-ship with industry and with the state was profoundly altered. Again, the evolution of the banking system in The Netherlands was different, although some parallels can be found with the Belgian situation. The Dutch banks had just experienced some very bad years; precisely this had made them cautious in their relations with industry and had kept them from heading towards a fully developed mixed banking system. However, this also preserved them from serious difficulties during the 1930s. Of course, these years were by no means free of problems, and hardship was indeed felt. One great bank, the Nederlandsche Handel-Maatschappij, had to be thoroughly reorganized in 1934, its capital and reserves being reduced drastically. But this resulted mainly from losses in her colonial activities in the Dutch East Indies. Most banks registered losses due to the crisis of the international financial system, more precisely to the abandonment of the gold standard by Great Britain and to the difficulties in Central Europe.[42] Another characteristic feature of the Dutch banking evolution was its notable liquidity, which even expanded. The most liquid assets (cash, call money, etc.) constituted 4.3 per cent of the balance sheet total of all Dutch general banks in 1928, 14.1 per cent in 1933 and 20.8 per cent in 1938.[43]

Indeed, the Dutch financial institutions were able to sustain an important contraction of the banking activity. The balance sheet total of all Dutch general banks fell from 2,435 million guilders to 1,596 million in 1940. Foreign means dwindled: the cumulative deposits of the six leading banks, for instance, fell from 1,355 million guilders in 1929 to 755 million in 1935. On the other hand, the credit-granting function to the private sector also receded. For the same banks, on the same dates, the advances in current account, for instance, fell from 582 to 375 million.[44] Obviously, the Dutch bankers were not saddled with the problem of frozen credits to home enterprises in the same measure as their Belgian colleagues were. Studies of the Dutch banking evolution often stress the lack of demand for credit on part of the economy.[45] The lack of remunerative investments posed important profitability problems to the banks. During the 1930s, they increasingly used their means to finance the public authorities. All general banks held 122 million guilders of Dutch treasury paper in 1933 (7.2 per cent of their balance sheet total); in 1938 their holdings had increased to 244 million (13.7 per cent).[46] One might note, incidentally, that after the suppression of the mixed banks, the Belgian (deposit) banks also became large and increasing purveyors of credit to the state, to the detriment of the private sector.[47]

On the whole, the 1930s were a far less difficult period for the Dutch banks than for the Belgian ones. Nevertheless, just as in Belgium, Dutch banks were the object of intense public discussion, resulting in a changing relationship between the state and the banking sector. But, given the different context, it comes as no surprise that this change had different manifestations in each country. The already ongoing debate concerning the lack of support of industrial enterprises by the banks continued during the 1930s. A supplementary effort in favour of Dutch industrialization was, in the eyes of many, made necessary by economic stagnation and unemployment. In order to obviate the hesitation or lack of enthusiasm of the private banks to grant long-term credits to industry, the suggestion was made to call upon the public authorities to fill the gap left by the private financial sector. This idea was favoured mainly in the ranks of the Catholic Party (which took part in the government) and, of course, also in the Socialist Party (which was in opposition). After a long and complex political process which we cannot go into here,[48] some steps were taken, such as the creation of a regional institution in 1935, the 'Industriebank' of the province Limburg, and the foundation, in 1936, of a national institution, the 'NV Maatschappij voor Industriefinanciering' (Mavif), of which the state had nearly all the shares. From the onset, the Mavif was reduced to a 'limited' and 'suppletory' role; its means were extremely small. As a result, its activity was almost negligible.[49] It did not fundamentally (or even marginally) alter either the working of the existing credit-granting mechanisms or the specific role of private banks herein.

Even if this form of public intervention remained very limited, it was totally out of the question in Belgium in the 1930s. The overwhelming position of the private banking sector did not leave any (political or economic) space for the creation of a public body of credit-granting to large industry in this period.[50] But, on the other hand, the form of public intervention that was realized in Belgium, namely banking control, never came about in The Netherlands before the Second World War. The paradox is that this topic was publicly discussed in the latter country before it seriously was in the former one. The question had already come up for discussion in the 1920s, in the context of the recent banking crisis. The subject was even raised in Parliament.[51] At the beginning of the 1930s, several parties, most notably the Catholic and Socialist ones, declared themselves in favour of some sort of banking control.[52] But the fear for the safety of the public's holdings in the banks was incapable of stimulating legislative action, because of the extraordinary liquidity of these financial institutions. Moreover, the importance of banking control as an instrument in the management business cycle had not yet become a generally accepted notion.[53] The problem of state control over the banking system went no further than the establishment, in 1937, of an official commission to study the problem; its proceedings were still under way when the war broke out.[54]

Nevertheless, though a formal system of banking control failed to materialize in The Netherlands, some sort of closer link between the public and private sphere began to take shape. At the beginning of the 1930s, a system of closer but informal and voluntary co-operation developed; The Netherlands also being a member of the gold bloc, a hard struggle had to be fought to maintain the parity of the guilder.[55] The private banks agreed to help the central bank in its anti-devaluation struggle: they regularly communicated figures relating to their gold-holdings to the central bank, De Nederlandsche Bank. On a more general scale, the banks also agreed regularly to transmit detailed figures on their situation and activity to the central bank; the Nederlandsche Bank stressed the fact that 'any control over the private banking system is out of the question',[56] but the central bank could keep an eye on the development of the private institutions; dangerous evolutions could be avoided or averted by consultation between the private banks and the central one. The crash of the Mendelssohn bank in Amsterdam in 1939 demonstrated, however, that this system of voluntary co-operation had its limits: some large banks, such as the Nederlandsche Handel-Maatschappij, had tied up relatively large sums in this single debtor.[57] Just before war broke out, the Nederlandsche Bank took the initiative of tightening the 'voluntary co-operation' between the central bank and the private banks.[58] Although the Dutch public regulation of the banking system was far behind the Belgian one, the complete liberty of financial business was waning in The Netherlands too.

Conclusion

As we said in the introduction, any comparison of the Dutch and Belgian banking structures and their relationship with industry and state must be a nuanced one. Converging and diverging tendencies were at work simultaneously. Nevertheless, if we examine the Dutch and Belgian banking systems at the end of the nineteenth century and on the eve of the Second World War, it cannot be denied that, on the whole, they had become increasingly similar by the end of this period. The interwar years were years of thorough change for both national variants of banking, but both rhythm and direction of change were different in the neighbouring countries. A marked tendency towards concentration and scaling-up was discernible in both systems and Belgian banks, as well as Dutch ones, played an expanding role in the economy and, more particularly, in industry. But whereas this was the reinforcement of an already strong tradition and practice in Belgium, it was a fairly new move for The Netherlands. The full development of mixed banking was, nevertheless, soon broken off in the latter country, as a somewhat daring application of this system had led to a painful crisis in the first half of the 1920s. Without severing all ties with industrial enterprises, Dutch banks became extremely cautious from the second half of the 1920s onwards. As a result, the Belgian mixed banks extended their hold on the main industrial sectors and, more than ever before, came to dominate the essential parts of the Belgian economy. Never did the Dutch banks play such a role and, indeed, they did not want to. Consequently, the criticism each banking system had to endure was of a different nature: while the Belgian banks were accused of exerting an excessive influence on Belgian society as a whole, their Dutch counterparts were being admonished for extreme timidity.

Owing to their different role in society, each banking system felt the impact of the crisis of the 1930s differently. Compared with the dramatic trials the Belgian banks endured in that period, the hardship felt by their northern counterparts was only slight. The ensuing evolution is almost a mirror image of the evolution that had taken place in the previous decade, for now it was the Belgian banking system that underwent a severe crisis, leading up to a reorientation of the structure and practice of banking. The prohibition of mixed banks meant that the Belgian banks now came to resemble more closely the Dutch ones because contacts with industry were markedly diminished. The Dutch banks, for their part, did not alter their structure or practice fundamentally. Of course, Belgian industry inherited a specific feature from its particular historical tradition, i.e. the holding companies continued to hold the centralizing and dominating position in the entrepreneurial structure that was previously held by the mixed banks – a feature that knew no real equivalent in Dutch industry. An intriguing and crucial aspect of our subject is the impact of the banks on the industrial orientation of the national economy. Much more research is needed here, but a possible hypothesis points to the fact that the dominating position of the banks in Belgium slowed down the process of transformation and renewal of this country's industrial structure; this contrasts with the industrial dynamism and diversification in The Netherlands, where the banks did not play a leading role in the economy.

An important element in this contrasting evolution was, of course, the diverging manner in which the state was implicated in the banking debate: Belgium left the group of countries with a wholly unregulated banking business, whereas The Netherlands remained one of the few ones where the state did not (formally) impose a legislative framework on the private banking sector. Nevertheless, though the pressure of circumstances was less hard in this country, an irreversible tendency set in, leading to the post-war legislation providing formal public control over private banking activity. Looking back over the entirety of the banking evolution in these troubled decades, one can say that the global trend in this financial sector confirms the conclusion that has already been made for the Benelux economies on the whole: in the course of the twentieth century, the economies of these small West European countries displayed an increasingly pronounced uniformity.[59]

NOTES

* I would like to thank Prof. Joh. de Vries and Prof. Herman Van der Wee for reading my text and commenting on it and also for permitting the consultation of the unpublished text mentioned in note 59. I am also grateful to Dr William L. Chew III who corrected this text linguistically.

1 Bibliography in H. Van der Wee, 'La stratégie d'investissement des entreprises belges et son influence sur le développement économique de l'Europe', *Revue Internationale d'Histoire de la Banque*, 22–3 (1981), 1–22.

2 B. S. Chlepner, 'Les finances', in E. Mahaim (ed.), *La Belgique restaurée* (Brussels, 1926), pp. 495–8.

3 *Bulletin d'Information et de Documentation de la Banque Nationale de Belgique*, VI-2 (25 Sept. 1931), p. 208 (hereafter quoted as *Bull. BNB*). A good sketch of Belgian banking evolution is R. L. Hogg, *Structural Rigidities and Policy Inertia in Interwar Belgium* (Brussels, 1986).

4 B. S. Chlepner, *Le marché financier belge depuis cent ans* (Brussels, 1930), p. 131.

5 *Bull. BNB*, VI-1 (25 Sept. 1930), p. 216.

6 M. Gernaert, *Le financement des entreprises industrielles et son évolution* (Brussels, 1939), p. 149.

7 R. Durviaux, *La banque mixte* (Brussels, 1947), p. 177.

8 H. M. H. A. Van der Valk, *De betrekkingen tussen banken en industrie in België* (Haarlem, 1932), p. 123.

9 Hogg, *Structural Rigidities, passim,* and Van der Wee, 'La stratégie', 13–22.

10 R. J. Lemoine, 'Banques de classes et de groupes sociaux', *Revue de l'Institut de Sociologie,* 42 (April–June 1936), 345–71.

11 J. A. De Jonge, *De industrialisatie in Nederland tussen 1850 en 1914,* 2nd edn (Nijmegen, 1976), pp. 232, 237.

12 An excellent overview of Dutch banking history from 1910 to 1931 is J. de Vries, *De geschiedenis van de Nederlandsche Bank. Vijfde deel De Nederlandsche Bank van 1914 tot 1948. Visserings tijdvak 1914–1931* (Amsterdam, 1989). The role of banks in Dutch industrialization is treated in e.g. P. W. Klein, 'Het bankwezen en de moderniser- ing van de Nederlandse volkshuishouding tijdens de tweede helft van de 19e eeuw', *Economisch- en Sociaal-Historische Jaarboek,* 36 (1973), 142–3; R. Bos, 'Kapitaal en industrialisatie in Nederland tijdens de 19e eeuw', *AAG-Bijdragen,* 22 (1971), 89–105; De Jonge, *De industrialisatie,* p. 302.

13 W. M. Zappey, 'Bankgeheimen. Enkele opmerkingen over Nederlandse bankgeschiedenis', in *Bedrijf en samenleving* (Alphen, 1967), p. 307.

14 J. de Vries, *The Netherlands Economy in the Twentieth Century* (Assen, 1978), p. 25.

15 W. M. Westerman, *De concentratie in het bankwezen* (The Hague, 1920), p. 120.

16 J. de Vries, *Een eeuw vol effecten* (n.p., 1976), p. 90.

17 *Financiële instellingen in Nederland 1900–1985* (Amsterdam, De Nederlandsche Bank, 1987), p. 15; W. Boeschoten, 'Commercial banks in The Netherlands 1900–1985', *De Nederlandsche Bank Quarterly Bulletin* (1986-3), p. 3.

18 D. C. J. Van der Werf, *De Bond, de banken en de beurs* (Amsterdam, 1988), pp. 49ff.

19 *Financiële instellingen,* pp. 38 and 40.

20 C. Eisfeld, *Das niederländische Bankwesen* (The Hague, 1916), pp. 269–70.

21 de Vries, *The Netherlands Economy,* pp. 43–4.

22 *Financiële instellingen,* p. 42. See also R. Van Seenus, *Bankpolitiek en conjunctuur* (Amsterdam, 1945), p. 119.

23 G. M. Verrijn Stuart, *Geld, crediet en bankwezen. Deel II. Bankpolitiek* (Wassenaar, 1941), pp. 174, 259.

24 See de Vries, *De geschiedenis,* pp. 203–67.

25 R. Brandes de Roos, *Industrie, Kapitalmarkt und industrielle Effekten in den Nieder- landen* (The Hague, 1928), pp. 92–3.

26 D. C. Renooij, *De Nederlandse emissiemarkt van 1904–1939* (Amsterdam, 1951), p. 201.

27 de Vries, *De geschiedenis,* p. 222.

28 W. Posthumus Meyjes, *Bankpolitik* (Haarlem, 1931), p. 45.

29 P. E. de Hen, *Actieve en re-actieve industriepolitiek in Nederland* (Amsterdam, 1980), pp. 130–9.

30 See e.g. Archives of De Nederlandsche Bank, Amsterdam (ADNB), Directie Prof. De Jong (DDJ), n° 80F, 'Stukken . . . enquête' and 'Rapport . . . enquête', June 1938.

31 H. F. J. M. Van Den Eerenbeemt, *Industrieel ondernemerschap en mentaal kilmaat 1914–1940* (Tilburg, 1979), pp. 85–8, and idem, 'Handels- en industriële banken in Noord-Brabant vóór 1900', in idem (ed.), *Bankieren in Brabant in de loop der eeuwen* (Tilburg, 1987), pp. 250, 253, 254.

32 H. Van der Wee and K. Tavernier, *La Banque Nationale de Belgique et l'histoire monétaire entre les deux guerres* (Brussels, 1975), pp. 253–68.
33 Shares not put on record at current market values.
34 *Bull. BNB*, IX-2 (15 Oct. 1934), pp. 242ff.
35 *Bull. BNB, passim*, and Durviaux, *La banque mixte*, p. 176. The global banking statistics did not make the difference between public securities and industrial shares.
36 Durviaux, *La banque mixte*, pp. 157–8; Hogg, *Structural Rigidities*, p. 138.
37 See resp. G. Vanthemsche, 'De lange weg van regionale spaarkassen naar Coop-Dépôts 1900–1940', in *Samen sparen. De geschiedenis van het socialistisch spaarwezen in België* (Brussels, 1989), pp. 171–293, and H. Van der Wee and M. Verbreyt, *Mensen maken geschiedenis. De Kredietbank . . . 1935–1985* (Tielt, 1985).
38 G. Vanthemsche, 'De politieke en economische context van de Belgische bankwetgevingen van 1934 en 1935', *Revue de la Banque*, 44 (Sept. 1980), 31–50.
39 Durviaux, *La banque mixte*, pp. 126ff., and Van der Valk, *De betrekkingen*, pp. 126ff.
40 Van der Wee, *La Banque Nationale*, pp. 268ff.; V. Janssens, *Le Franc Belge. Un siècle et demi d'histoire monétaire* (Brussels, 1976), pp. 233ff.; R. L. Hogg, 'Belgium, France, Switzerland and the end of the gold standard', in R. T. Griffiths (ed.), *The Netherlands and the Gold Standard 1931–1936* (Amsterdam, 1987), pp. 195–203.
41 G. Vanthemsche, 'L'élaboration de l'Arrêté Royal sur le contrôle bancaire (1935)', *Revue Belge d'Histoire Contemporaine*, 11 (1980-3), 389–437.
42 Van Seenus, *Bankpolitiek*, pp. 153 and 160.
43 *Financiële instellingen*, p. 38.
44 *Money and Banking 1938/1939. Vol. II. Commercial and Central Banks* (Geneva: League of Nations, 1939), p. 132.
45 F. de Roos and W. J. Wieringa, *Een halve eeuw rente in Nederland* (Schiedam, 1953), p. 179.
46 C. D. Jongman, *De Nederlandse geldmarkt* (Leiden, 1960), pp. 230ff.
47 Durviaux, *La banque mixte*, p. 206.
48 See de Hen, *Actieve industriepolitiek*, pp. 139–89.
49 *Ibid.*, pp. 185 and 235–48.
50 A 'Société National de Crédit à l'Industrie' (SNCI), created in 1919, never fully developed.
51 H. M. Hirschfeld, *Nieuwe stroomingen in het Nederlandse bankwezen* (Roermond, 1925), pp. 24ff.; J. de Vries, 'Opportuniteitsbeginsel en algemeen economisch belang in Nederland in de jaren 1920', in *Bewogen en bewegen. Liber amicorum Prof. Van Den Eerenheemt* (Tilburg, 1986), p. 215.
52 H. W. J. Bosman, *De wet toezicht kredietwezen* (Leiden, 1958), pp. 27–37.
53 Bosman, *De wet*, pp. 17–23; P. Bergsma, *Das niederländische Bankwesen* (Gelnhausen, 1939), pp. 103–18; ADNB, DDJ, n° 80A, 'Aide-Mémoire', 27 April 1938; ADNB, Studiedienst, President Trip, file 33, note 'Bezwaren tegen wettelijke reglementering van het bankwezen', 16 June 1938.
54 Documents in ADNB, DDJ, n° 80A–80L.
55 R. T. Griffiths (ed.), *The Netherlands and the Gold Standard 1931–1936* (Amsterdam, 1987).
56 *De Nederlandsche Bank 1931–1932. Verslag* (Amsterdam, 1932), p. 22. See also Bosman, *De wet*, pp. 18–21.
57 ADNB, DDJ, n° 80D, proceedings Staatscommissie, 18 Oct. and 17 Nov. 1939.
58 *De Nederlandsche Bank 1939–1940. Verslag* (Amsterdam, 1940), pp. 7–8. See also ADNB, DDJ, n° 80B, 'Memorandum omtrent de betrekkingen tussen De Nederlandsche Bank en de particuliere banken', 6 Jan. 1938, 12pp.

59 J. de Vries, 'Benelux 1920–1970', in C. M. Cippola (ed.), *The Fontana Economic History of Europe. Vol. 6-1* (Glasgow, 1976), pp. 4–11; H. Van der Wee, 'Convergente en divergente bewegingen in de economische ontwikkeling van Nederland en België 19e en 20e eeuw', unpublished MS.

9 Investment behaviour of industrial joint-stock companies and industrial shareholding by the Österreichische Credit-Anstalt: inducement or obstacle to renewal and change in industry in interwar Austria

ALOIS MOSSER and ALICE TEICHOVA

Introduction*

This chapter consists of two parts. The first part, 'Investment behaviour of Austrian industrial joint-stock companies in the interwar period' (written by Alois Mosser), is based on the analysis of annual totals of joint-stock companies' balance sheets in individual branches of industry, and in the industrial sector as a whole, of the Austrian interwar economy. It examines the question of the failure of Austrian industry to make the necessary investments in order to pursue new strategies and technical solutions and to adapt to the changed market situation after the break-up of the Habsburg Monarchy.

The second part, 'Shareholding in and credit-financing of joint-stock companies in the Austrian manufacturing industry by the Öster-reichische Credit-Anstalt für Handel und Gewerbe (CA) (from the early 1920s to 1932)' (written by Alice Teichova), is based on material in the Finanzarchiv, Vienna, and on an analysis of advances by the CA to industrial enterprises belonging to the sphere of influence of this largest bank of interwar Austria. For evidence, material from the CA-archive was also used, mainly fortnightly minutes of meetings of the Board of Directors between 1918 and 1932.

Our presentation is intended as an attempt, first, to elucidate the relationship between the share-owning bank and the provision of advances to its industrial clients who were in varying degrees dependent on the supply of credits; and, secondly, to examine the role of the

122

bank in determining the investment behaviour of industrial joint-stock companies. In this way the conclusions of Alois Mosser in the first part of the paper can, to some extent, be tested by empirical evidence.

Investment behaviour of Austrian industrial joint-stock companies in the interwar period

It is widely agreed that Austria's economy, which belonged to the category of highly industrialized countries,[1] stagnated between the two world wars. But it is less widely known that the industrial sector was mainly responsible for this lack of economic growth. Its contribution to the Gross National Product (GNP) decreased absolutely and relatively.[2] Not until 1950 did the industrial sector regain the significant place in the creation of the national product that it occupied in 1913. Thus the years between 1918 and 1938 appear as a period of deviations from the long-term trend of economic development, i.e. from the general pattern of modernization.

At first sight the 'failure' of Austrian industry seems surprising because, in spite of the break-up of the Habsburg Monarchy and the resulting structural disruption, Austria inherited a high proportion of industrial plant and resources.[3] The question thus arises why industry was not able to undertake the necessary structural adjustments and to utilize the considerable capacities inherited from the Austro-Hungarian Empire as a basis for post-war economic reconstruction. What prevented enterprises from adapting to the new market situation by directing investments to necessary objectives and by adopting new strategies and technical solutions?

The following considerations are designed to explore the investment behaviour of Austrian industrial enterprises during the interwar period and, at the same time, the relations between industry and banking will be discussed. How did these relations shape the volume, financing and motives of industrial investments?

Unfortunately, no quantitative information exists about the volume of investment in Austria's industrial sector, neither have any estimates been attempted so far.[4] Only joint-stock companies were under the legal obligation to publish their annual balance sheets and this allows a certain insight into the state of their assets, their capital structure and economic performance. If consecutive annual balances are compared, changes in the value of capital goods can be ascertained. However, even the total of industrial joint-stock companies cannot be examined because not all joint-stock companies provided the legally required information. From the information the *Bundesamt für Statistik* gathered it endeavoured to combine the annually registered balances into a total statistical survey. For the years from 1919 to 1936 annual balances are thus available which contain data about fixed and current assets, and also about equity and reserves (*Eigenkapital*), on the one hand, and outside capital (*Fremdkapital*), on the other, comprising between 70 and 90 per cent of all existing Austrian industrial joint-stock companies.[5] Since, according to contemporary estimates, the equity of these joint-stock companies amounted to one-third of total industrial capital,[6] results obtained from the available material can be characterized as fairly representative.

By comparing annual total values of fixed assets, increases and decreases of net investments and net disinvestments can be calculated. In these calculations of a time series one has to take as a basis the 'average industrial enterprise' in order to avoid errors which arise from the fact that the number of reporting joint-stock companies changes year by year. Also the years of the inflation from the end of the war until the end of 1922 have to be excluded because not only is it difficult to determine the real value of the highly inflated expenditure on investments but also because data for the years 1919 and 1921 are lacking (cf. table 9.1). My analysis shows that the highest increases in the value of capital assets took place in the years 1924 and 1925.[7] But these values were influenced by the legally required revaluation in the so-called gold-balances,[8] and the precise evaluation of this process remains an open question. Until 1930 the figures show a discontinuous, erratic growth of the gross capital stock, but an extensive stagnation in the following years.

Changes in the volume and average value of capital equipment have been influenced by the process of concentration of enterprises. Between 1920 and 1925 the number of industrial joint-stock companies rose from 374 to 812 but thereafter until 1935 it fell to 469.[9] This decrease was chiefly the result of the difference between liquidations and new foundations of companies but a notable number disappeared as a result of mergers. In calculations of averages the increasing amalgamation of enterprises appears as an increase in capital assets. Thus the growth of gross capital stock which appears up

Table 9.1. *Fixed assets of industrial joint-stock companies (JSC) in Austria,*
1923–35

Year	Reporting companies		Book value of fixed assets in 000 AS	
	No.	in % of all JSCs	average	change in %
1923	583	80	227	—
1924	554	68	523	130.4
1925	414	51	2,745	424.8
1926	515	69	2,612	−4.8
1927	522	74	2,818	7.9
1928	540	81	2,781	−1.3
1929	525	82	2,927	5.2
1930	470	84	3,341	14.1
1931	452	83	3,288	−1.6
1932	455	87	3,458	5.2
1933	431	84	3,357	−2.9
1934	429	88	3,265	−2.7
1935	398	85	3,315	1.5

AS = Austrian Schilling
Source: *Statistisches Handbuch für die Republik Österreich*, Bundesamt für Statistik, 4 (1924) to 16 (1936).

to 1930 has to be seen also in connection with the process of concentration. In the following years between 1930 and 1935 on the average no increase in plant and equipment had taken place at the same time as the number of industrial joint-stock companies decreased by a fifth of the total. This can, to a large part, be explained by the legally enforced depreciation[10] which led to an overdue correction of artificially boosted company assets in Austria.

In contradistinction to this concentration movement a process of deconcentration can be observed on the level of establishments the volume of which, unfortunately, cannot be specified because sources are not available. Some more concrete information can, however, be gained by observing the changes in the size of industrial establishments: in 1926 there were in Austria 124 establishments employing more than 500 persons, which contained 22.3 per cent of the total number of employees; while in 1936 there existed only 67 establishments in this category, employing 14.4 per cent of all employees.[11]

Here it must be pointed out that the changes in the gross capital stock of joint-stock companies which are calculated from company balance sheets allow only for the assessment of net-increases or net-decreases of book values; they do not disclose the extent to which companies decreased their assets through depreciation. If companies omitted depreciations in their balance sheets, for whatever reason, then their capital investments appear as increases in their net assets although, perhaps, real losses may have existed. Thus in any judgement about their investment behaviour the question about the intensity of depreciations has to be posed.

With regard to the amounts of depreciation the balance sheet totals for individual branches of industry referred to in this contribution do not provide any information, neither are there any statistical accounts nor estimates available. This can only be gleaned from annual balance sheets published by certain individual joint-stock companies. With Wolfgang Kemmetmüller I attempted an analysis of the financial accounts of thirty-four industrial joint-stock companies selected from four branches of producer and consumer goods industries which gave results as follows.

The figures calculated for depreciations between 1919 and 1924 fluctuated so violently that they cannot have corresponded to real wear and tear and outdated equipment. If inflationary increases in the value of capital equipment are taken into account one can hardly speak of a net increase in capital investment during that period. Friedrich Hertz wrote in 1929 with regard to this period that capital goods had 'for a long time been exposed to a ruinous consumption (*raubbauartigen Aufzehrung*)'.[12]

In the years of economic growth following the introduction of the Schilling currency between 1925 and 1929 the majority of industrial joint-stock companies calculated a depreciation quota of plus/minus 10 per cent. The resulting increase in the capital stock can therefore largely be regarded as representing a net increase.

During the economic crisis of 1929 to 1933 – and in a smaller measure also in the following years – many enterprises tried to improve their bad business situation optically by neglecting to include depreciations into their annual balance sheets. Not a few ceased to calculate a decrease in the value of their assets for a large number of years. Thus in the 1920s, especially in 1931 and 1932, balance sheets show increases in the value of capital stock which, in reality, denote an appreciable shrinkage of substance. This is borne out by the repeated observation made in the process of reconstruction of insolvent indus-

Table 9.2. *The profitability of industrial joint-stock companies (JSC), 1918–35*

Year	Number of companies total	reporting JSCs	Average profits/ losses (−)[a]
1918	344	205	51
1919	?	?	?
1920	374	255	31
1921	?	?	?
1922	581	467	51
1923	718	583	85
1924	811	554	32
1925	812	414	126
1926	752	515	86
1927	705	522	114
1928	667	540	123
1929	637	525	23
1930	563	470	24
1931	545	452	−42
1932	526	455	−148
1933	516	431	40
1934	489	429	58
1935	469	398	96

[a] Data for 1918 to 1922 in 000 Austrian Crowns (deflated according to the cost of living index), data for 1923 to 1935 in 000 Austrian Schillings (AS).
Source: Statistisches Handbuch für die Republik Österreich, Bundesamt für Statistik, 1 (1920) to 16 (1936).

trial joint-stock companies which was conducted by credit institutions (mainly by banks) that plant and equipment of those companies were strongly overvalued in their balances.

Any attempt to estimate the volume of investment must necessarily take account of the availability of finance to companies. Obviously, the planning and realization of investments depend on the existing possibilities to finance them. In turn the financing of investments depends upon the internal capital formation and/or the external procurement of capital. Within an enterprise its capital formation draws from retained profits, depreciation and from capital transfers. External sources of capital can be obtained by share issues or by taking up credits.

Also for the reconstruction of these sources of financing of industrial companies their annual balance sheets provide important information. Let us first pose the question of the internal financial strength of joint-stock companies by measuring the development of net profits (table 9.2), turnovers (table 9.3) and cash flow.

If average profit is measured, the often cited 'post-war and inflation boom' appears very modest indeed; net profits – assuming purchasing power to remain equal – did not reach even one-third of the pre-war level. Equally, the often mentioned 'stabilization crisis' seems to have been, in my view, overcome already by 1924. Between 1925 and 1928 the companies consolidated and, at the same time, increased their earning power but in 1929 – although undisputedly the peak of the boom – profits fell to one-sixth of the previous year. This situation remained unchanged through 1930 after which the profit and loss balances sank into deficit for the next two years. Earning capacity improved relatively fast in 1933.

A valuable complement to these figures can be gleaned by comparing annual turnovers as they developed in accordance with the rise and fall of profits (table 9.3). Only between 1929 and 1933 a contrary course appeared: at the peak of the boom turnover totals rose while profits declined as a result of falling prices. At the trough of the crisis in 1933 stabilization of prices led to an increase in profits while total turnovers still moved downward.

The movement of profits and turnovers give the impression of a slow recovery of the earning power of enterprises after the First World War but a rapidly rising profitability between 1924 and 1928 which fell significantly in 1929 and declined further during the economic crisis. From 1934 the upward trend is demonstrated in the more rapid rise of profits in comparison with turnover figures.

The development of the cash flow (the sum of retained profits, reserves and depreciation) cannot be ascertained from the above-mentioned annual balance sheet totals of whole branches of industry. Also in this case only annual balances of individual industrial joint-stock companies can be taken into account for this purpose. On the basis of the above-cited sample of thirty-four companies the following conclusions about the financial strength of enterprises can be drawn:

In general the cash flow moved in accordance with profits but often overtook them. Until the currency stabilization (1924/5) one can observe a very cautious improvement followed by a rapid strengthening of financial power up to 1928; 1929 can already be regarded as belonging to the crisis years in this respect, inclusive of 1933 during which the majority of enterprises lost all their disposable funds. In the

Table 9.3. *Changing proportions of annual average turnovers of industrial joint-stock companies, 1926–36*

Year	Changes in %
1926	−0.5
1927	+13.3
1928	+21.7
1929	+4.9
1930	−11.6
1931	−15.4
1932	−21.1
1933	−4.6
1934	+8.2
1935	+6.6
1936	+3.5

Note: For the individual years the census comprises one-third to one-half of all industrial joint-stock companies. The changing proportions are calculated on the basis of an equal number of companies.
Source: Statistisches Jahrbuch für die Republik Österreich, 14 (1933); *Wirtschaftsstatistisches Jahrbuch,* 1928–1931/2.

years 1931 and 1932 losses exceeded profits in the total balance of industrial joint-stock companies, and depreciation fell to the lowest level since the First World War, so that cash flow often appeared as a negative quantity. Also after 1934 all items which had registered losses managed to show only marginal gains and, therefore, the ability to finance the business of enterprises remained on a very low level.

Between cash flow and intensity of investment there appears a far-reaching parallelism which signifies that companies utilized internal capital formation when they embarked on the financing of larger investments. This behaviour is particularly evident in the years when earning power and the cyclical fluctuations took a contrary course, as for instance in 1929. Although, as was emphasized above, turnover rose, profits fell back and the firms reacted by immediately decreasing expenditure on investments.

If increases in the value of fixed assets are compared with the financial strength of industrial joint-stock companies it seems very likely that in the period 1923–7 and in a somewhat smaller measure also in 1922 and 1928–9 the money capital they expended on producer goods exceeded the volume they obtained by internal capital formation. Also after the economic crisis had been overcome companies must have taken greater recourse to external sources of finance.

The question arises as to how the procurement of capital from external sources developed. Fundamentally, enterprises pursued their investment aims in accordance with their own earning power so that recourse to external financing was considered opportune only under certain conditions. On the basis of the available sources it appears that the majority of industrial joint-stock companies – most probably more than four-fifths of the total number – covered the necessary expenditure for investments which exceeded their own financial power by issuing shares. Against this method of financing, long-term credits played a subordinate role. It is remarkable that in the interwar period conditions prevailed similar to those before the First World War.[13] At that time, as during the twenties, investments were financed frequently with short-term credits until such time as the increase in the value of fixed assets justified an increase in equity.

During the crisis of the 1930s this method of giving preference to self-financing rather than using external credit seems to have been strategically justified. This, doubtless, saved the industry from even greater bankruptcies and liquidations. Although the total losses during 1930–3 devoured the greater part of equity and reserves – these amounted in 1932 to only three-quarters of the total value of fixed assets – and although the value of shares fell dramatically, the same course of financing investments continued to be followed. Companies sought to cope with this situation by devaluation and new issues of shares which, to a considerable extent, remained in the safes of the issuing banks.

The insufficient propensity to invest by Austrian industry during the interwar period as well as the subordinate role played above all by long-term credits create the impression of an inadequate supply of capital. But this certainly was not the case. Banks willingly accepted the issue and placing of shares and, for reasons of maintaining their business connections, they took pains to expand rather than contract their services to industry. Causes for the relatively poor investment activity can more likely be seen in the predominant forms of provision of credits and the conditions attached to them.[14] Thus banks connected with the extension of credit to industry had certain profitable expectations which they hoped to realize by charging high interest rates. In their endeavour to secure high returns the banks supplied industrial enterprises with short-term credits which were designed for long-term investments. During the years of the Great Depression banks held on to this strategy in order to minimize their losses; however, they made their services available at the cost of extensive intervention into the organization and management of enterprises.

Another reason for companies' preference for self-financing of investments can be found in the Austrian tax system which rendered certain forms of credits unprofitable as, for instance, the issue of bonds because interest as well as dividends emanating from them were taxed. Altogether, credit-financing from external sources was dearer than self-financing. Especially in economically insecure times many enterprises tried to avoid the burden of fixed interest payments; self-financing is in any case more adaptable and in extreme cases there is always the possibility of suspending payments of dividends or directors' fees or managers' commissions.

In trying to answer the question whether there existed a sufficient supply of credit, the influence of cyclical fluctuations was included in my argument. Further, if one considers that in the second half of the 1920s there occurred an increase in the demand for loan capital at the same time as the bank rate fell and that during the economic crisis both the interest rate and the demand for capital decreased, it seems obvious that the relatively poor intensity of investment was not caused by a lack of financial resources but rather by a lack of profitable possibilities for investments. In these circumstances entrepreneurs preferred – for the above-mentioned reasons – to draw on internal sources of capital; also in the years of recovery they maintained this posture which can certainly be interpreted as a result of the widespread mistrust in the solidity of economic growth.

It may seem, judging from the above insights into the investment behaviour of industrial joint-stock companies, that there existed no promising investment opportunities at all in Austria. Such an interpretation would be mistaken. A closer look at the cost–benefit structure leads one to the conclusion that this element was able to change investment behaviour substantially. In the following I want to examine this problem further although this can be done only in a limited sense since, on the one hand, statistical material is scarce and, on the other, the evaluation of such sources as there are is still in progress.

A Commission of Inquiry into the prevailing economic difficulties set up by the Austrian government in 1930 found that the low propensity to invest stemmed, above all, from the high costs of production.[15] In the first place it mentioned the rising pressure of taxation which, in large measure, hit producers and thus increased their costs. Compared with 1913 the *per capita* tax burden was 56 per cent higher in 1929; if only the years of economic growth after 1925 are taken into account the tax burden was 32 per cent higher. Further, the Commission stated that the employers' contributions to social insurance (health, accident, pensions and unemployment insurance) rose in the same period (1925–9) by 52 per cent. Similar pressures on production costs were exerted by the movement of wages. According to calculations by the Chamber of Workers and Employees and the Chamber of Commerce, Trade and Industry, wages in Vienna rose in the same period by 24 per cent. Also the increase in rates for goods transport on Austrian railways contributed to rising costs. High freightage brought about changes in production localities and was a hindrance to the concentration of establishments.

How did these factors influence the amount and the composition of real production costs? Based on the rather sparse information from enterprises, the following tendency seems to emerge: the proportion of expenditure on personnel remained, except for short-term fluctuations, stable; companies succeeded in controlling rising wages by reducing employment. Increasingly, however, the burden of compulsory and voluntary social expenditure grew. In the interwar period the proportion of depreciation in overall costs was smaller than before the First World War. Also the procurement of raw and auxiliary materials – although with great variations between the branches of industry – took up a decreasing proportion of total production costs. But taxes and duties experienced absolutely as well as relatively the highest rise in expenditure.

Companies sought to align their investment aims by reducing their costs (above all, wages, social expenditure, taxes and duties). Contemporary estimates of the 1920s calculate that rationalization reduced workplaces by 50,000, which accounted for 5 per cent of all persons employed in the secondary sector.[16] Investments made in the course of rationalization concerned not only the area of production but equally organization and sales networks. Until the second half of the 1920s investments were aimed chiefly at rationalization. In the period of the economic upswing until 1929 the motivation for investments

Table 9.4. *Industrial production in Austria and Germany, 1923–35*

	Total production		Producer goods		Consumer goods	
Period	Austria	Germany	Austria[a]	Germany	Austria[b]	Germany
1923–9	48	117	25	137	106	70
1925–9	27	24	13	27	30	14
1929–35	−20	−4	−30	−3	−29	−6

[a] Turnovers.
[b] Turnovers without food, shoes and household goods.
Sources: Austria: *Monatsberichte des Österreichischen Institutes für Konjunkturforschung*, 1 (1927) to 11 (1937). Germany: Werner Abelshauser and Dietmar Petzina, 'Krise und Rekonstruktion. Zur Interpretation der gesamtwirtschaftlichen Entwicklung Deutschlands im 20. Jahrhundert', in Wilhelm H. Schröder (ed.), *Historische Konjunkturforschung* (Stuttgart, 1980), p. 86.

seems increasingly to have turned to the expansion of capacities. However, in 1930 this development ended abruptly. During the crisis investments did not even cover the decreasing value of production goods. Even from 1934, when the period of slow recovery began, the value of productive assets rose only in a few branches of the extractive, energy and engineering industries. If the interwar period is viewed as a whole those investments which furthered rationalization and productivity exceeded investments directed towards expansion of productive capacities.[17]

The index of production for Austria during the interwar period reflects the small measure of growth-inducing investments; above all, the composition of producer and consumer goods shows this significantly (table 9.4). Total industrial production increased by not quite 50 per cent between 1923 and 1929, and from 1925 to 1929 by somewhat more than 25 per cent. Comparing producer goods for the same periods the figures are 25 and 13 per cent respectively, while consumer goods rose by 106 and 30 per cent respectively. But in the falling value of industrial production by 20 per cent between 1929 and 1935 producer and consumer goods had equal shares.

Therefore, the causes of the stagnation during the 1930s must also be traced to the structural weaknesses inherent in the previous period of economic growth. This appears more clearly if Austria is compared for instance with Germany which, after the economic crisis, developed a particularly forceful drive to economic growth. In Germany the index of industrial production rose by 117 per cent between 1923 and 1929, the proportion of producer goods was 137 per cent while consumer goods reached a 70 per cent increase; by 1933 the index was four points lower than in 1929 – the trough had been passed in 1932 – and also in that period the output of producer goods took a more favourable course than that of consumer goods.

From whatever aspects one views the above analysis one has to conclude that Austria's industry was unable to utilize her relatively overproportionate industrial inheritance from the Habsburg Monarchy; that is, she was unable to build upon it by undertaking the necessary structural changes. Or, expressed in a different way, the existing potential productive forces could not effectively develop because of the paucity of investment. The investment behaviour of joint-stock companies itself was a true reflection of the greatly fluctuating and largely unsatisfactory (only in a minimal number of years satisfactory) profitability. The short-term bursts of investment alone disclose that enterprises had little trust in the solidity of economic growth and, at the same time, they signify the lack of growth strategies. This led to an increasing proneness to crises, indeed, in a sense, to the anticipation of economic crises.

Shareholding in and credit-financing of joint-stock companies in the Austrian manufacturing industry by the Österreichische Credit-Anstalt für Handel und Gewerbe (CA) (from the early 1920s to 1932)

By now it is a well-researched theme in the economic history of Central Europe which establishes that on the eve of the First World War the big Viennese universal banks had secured strategic positions in almost all branches of industry throughout the Habsburg Monarchy.[18] When after the end of the Great War the League of Nations examined the shattered Austrian financial system the role of the Vienna banks in the pre-1918 period was described thus:

> They served every relatively important operation in all areas: share issues, formation of syndicates, placing of loans or any larger industrial credit. Relations with international finance concentrated in Vienna – here foreign credits were taken up and administered for the entire Empire . . . [19]

Table 9.5. *Annual balances of the CA in comparison with total balances of the big Viennese banks, 1925–30 (in million Austrian Schillings – AS)*

Year	No.	Balance total all	CA	%	Debtors all	CA	%	Securities all	CA	%
1925	9	2,221	608	28	1,609	484	30	106	39	37
1926	8	2,597	927	36	1,867	742	39	110	43	39
1927	7	3,039	1,064	35	2,150	838	39	103	45	44
1928	7	3,266	2,045	62	2,265	1,499	65	121	99	82
1929	6	2,673	1,399	52	1,932	1,073	56	96	72	75
1930	6	3,223	1,885	59	2,273	1,382	60	96	71	74

Source: Compiled from *Monatsberichte des Wiener Institutes für Wirtschafts- und Konjunkturforschung*, 12 (1938), p. 138; *Wirtschaftsstatistisches Jahrbuch* (1927, 1930/1, 1931/2) and CA balances in *Geschäfts-Bericht des Verwaltungsrates der Oesterreichischen Credit-Anstalt für Handel und Gewerbe*, 1925, 1926, 1930, 1931–2.

The Austrian banking system performed the usual functions of accumulating and mobilizing capital like that of other developed countries but it played a much greater active role in employing resources in industry and trade. Banks not only provided advances but they conducted an extensive business of promotion of industrial enterprise; they secured their credits by acquiring equity preferably in the largest and soundest enterprises, mainly in those they had changed into public companies and in those whose comparatively frequent share issues they organized; they strengthened their supervision through interlocking directorships, and they were initiators or mediators of mergers. The leader in this field was the Austrian Credit-Anstalt (CA). By 1913 it held a dominating position:[20] its total balance amounted to 19 per cent of the total balances of the ten biggest Viennese banks in 1913,[21] and after an unprecedented period of fusions between 1925 and 1930 the CA's leading place was undisputed – its total balance reached around 60 per cent of the remaining six largest Vienna banks in the Austrian Republic (cf. table 9.5).

In the case of Austria-Hungary not only internal but, above all, external conditions determined the specific closeness of banks and industry. Industrial joint-stock companies in their quest for capital tried to avoid long-term credit and chose rather the path of repeated new share issues through banks because taxation and company law thwarted the development of the capital market at least until the turn of the century.[22] Consequently, the big banks to a large extent carried out the functions of a capital market.

According to Alois Mosser's work on company balance sheet analyses covering the period 1880 to 1914 in the Austrian half of the Dual Monarchy, the majority of joint-stock companies drew on capital in two ways: first, from their own resources, and, secondly, by taking up short-term credit from banks and, eventually, repaying them by new share issues. He continued his research by carrying his balance sheet analyses forward into the economy of the Austrian Republic and found, as he shows in the first part of this paper, that a similar policy of capital procurement was pursued by Austrian industrial firms also during the inflation- and crisis-ridden interwar period. However, chiefly because of the unfavourable economic climate, joint-stock companies needed to take increasing recourse to their banks. What form this took is the theme of the considerations which follow concerning the capital and credit ties of the leading Vienna bank, the CA, with Austrian industrial joint-stock companies. How very close these ties were is incisively, though with a certain element of exasperation, expressed by its Director Van Hengel who, as the appointee of the foreign creditors after the CA's insolvency, reported in November 1932:

> It must be understood that the Credit-Anstalt is not a bank. It still carries on a larger banking business than any other bank in Austria, but this, compared to its total business, is relatively small, and has contracted with the decrease in banking turnover all the world over. The Credit-Anstalt is chiefly a holding company, most of whose holdings are industrial and in a very weak state.[23]

As one of the central questions of our research project is the relationship between banking and industry, the amount, conditions and purpose of advances provided by banks to their industrial customers need to be ascertained. For the fulfilment of this aim it would have been ideal to get an insight into accounts of industrial clients of the big universal banks of Vienna. As far as we are aware no such convenient material is available. But the *Protokolle* (Minutes of Directors' Meetings) of the CA give information about credits granted to industrial client firms.

Thus one line of the research the author of this part of the paper has been conducting since the mid-eighties consisted of the painstaking and time-consuming reconstruction of accounts which industrial enterprises held in the CA between 1912 and 1938. The fullest records in this respect pertain to the decade from 1919 to 1929. During this period 2,348 Austrian and 666 foreign-based industrial, commercial and financial firms were granted advances. The great majority of these belonged to branches of the manufacturing industry; listed in descending order of the number of client joint-stock companies they belonged to the following industries: engineering and metalworking, textiles, chemicals including mineral oil, mining and metallurgy, paper, wood, brewing, building, electricals and leather. (Cf. also table 9.6 which refers exclusively to industrial joint-stock companies dependent either through capital or credit participations on the CA.)

Financing of industrial enterprises as a major component of business policy of the big universal banks of Vienna took off in the 1890s when the banks expanded their network of industrial subsidiaries and consolidated their concerns. Also in this area the CA was leading by 1914 when its concern was estimated to include direct participations in the share capital of 102 industrial joint-stock companies amounting to at least 20 per cent of the total direct industrial capital participations of the big Vienna banks.[24] There was no legal limit imposed on the banks' ownership of shares which increased greatly during the inflation of the 1920s when banks were hoarding shares of domestic and foreign companies, thereby 'fleeing into substance' (*Flucht in Sachwerte*) in order to prevent losses. Also in the years of the only relative boom of the interwar Austrian economy between 1925 and 1929, the banks' industrial share ownership rose – in the case of the CA by at least 15 per cent (cf. table 9.6, col. C).

During the brief life of the First Austrian Republic the CA's leading position in relation to the other big banks became unassailable, and after amalgamating with other banks, it held 70 to 80 per cent of the total securities shown in the balance sheets of the remaining big Vienna banks. At the same time as the total of its shareholdings had increased far beyond its equity and reserves[25] the sum of its debtors had doubled between 1926 and 1930, placing the bank with 60 per cent of the total indebtedness to the six big commercial banks in Vienna (cf. table 9.5) in a most precarious position at the onset of the world economic crisis.

According to the general director's reports to the annual meetings of shareholders of the CA, a recurring theme of the 1920s is that its main business remained credit provision to its industrial customers which also constituted the main source of income. The bank, therefore, expanded its clientele to keep up profits by larger turnovers but, although the bank rate fell, interest rates and provisions had to be kept high enough to enable the bank to maintain acceptable profit margins. Bank loans for productive investments were confined to a small number of large enterprises, such as electric power stations, modernization in engineering and chemical works, beer-brewing and paper production; however, such investments took place in a very limited period of relative economic growth, i.e. mainly from 1925 to 1927.[26]

During the first post-war decade the CA prided itself on providing its industrial clients, above all its subsidiary companies, with working capital not only by giving them direct advances but also by mediating credits from abroad.[27] It was one of the hallmarks of this internationally respected institute to channel capital from both its highly prestigious shareholders, who by 1931 participated in about 47 per cent of its capital, and its sound creditors – mainly in Britain, France, Holland, Belgium, Switzerland and the USA – to Austria and to other Central and South-east European countries.[28] Remarking aptly on the situation of the CA at the end of the 1920s Dieter Stiefel wrote that the bank had excellent creditors but bad debtors.[29] Only with hindsight was it admitted in the directors' report of 4 August 1931 that the debts of Austrian industry had substantially increased since the inflation of the 1920s and even more so during the business crash of 1930, although it had been gravely indebted already before that. This had been exacerbated by short-term advances which had obviously been used for long-term purposes and by unduly high interest charges on loans, quite apart from many wrong decisions concerning investments.[30]

With hindsight the bank's management has been accused of negligence, although there was general agreement in the contemporary press that it was both the task and the duty of the great Viennese banks to provide industry with capital. Regarding the CA all advances were approved by the board of directors in their fortnightly meetings. At the same time they, in most cases, set limits to credit facilities provided for their clients, more often than not increasing the credit limit with every new advance and allowing their debt balance to roll over (*Fortbelassung des bisherigen Kredits*). Following a long-established practice individual directors proposed advances to enterprises which had been allocated to them and for whose creditworthiness they were responsible to the management of the bank.[31] After the currency reform and the introduction of the Schilling (AS – Austrian Schilling) as legal means of payment at the end of 1924 the board of directors accepted proposals of advances up to AS30,000 simply by listing them, while larger credits were to have been vetted and granted on the basis of unanimity.[32] However, judging from the recorded minutes of board meetings until 1930, hardly any of the larger advances to industrial enterprises proposed by directors was seriously questioned or rejected. Thus there is no evidence of any reluctance on the part of the CA to grant credits to industrial clients, although there is evidence that the Industrial Department of the CA kept a check on the accounts of large debtors between 1925 and 1931. The largest consisted of ten industrial groups belonging to the concern of the CA of which three were foreign oil companies, two foreign textile firms, three domestic engineering works, one a domestic shipping company and one a domestic wool trading enterprise.[33] But records show that, in spite of the apparent anxiety of the *Industrie Inspektorat,* up to the reconstruction of the CA apparently no serious credit restrictions were applied to industrial clients held to be dubious debtors.

As shown above, among the largest debtor groups foreign companies were conspicuously represented. The overwhelming majority of the foreign industrial client enterprises had their seats in the successor states, the territory of which formerly either wholly or partially belonged to the Austro-Hungarian Empire (Czechoslovakia, Hungary, Italy, Poland, Romania and Yugoslavia), but also firms from France, Germany and the USA were represented. In addition, holding companies belonging to the bank-industrial concern of the CA were situated in The Netherlands and in Switzerland.[34] The significance of these foreign industrial, trading and financial firms as subsidiary companies and debtors of the CA will be examined closely later during the research project in progress since blame has been apportioned to the Vienna banks that they credit-financed foreign industrial firms (mainly in South-east Europe) substantially more than domestic companies and that such investment behaviour harmed the growth prospects of the interwar Austrian economy. While certainly significant the foreign engagement of the CA during the 1920s most probably did not exceed one-third: it was estimated that the ratio of foreign to total credits granted by the CA remained almost stable around

30 per cent,[35] and that about one-third of the CA's total direct capital participations were held in foreign joint-stock companies.[36] My count of business clients receiving advances from the CA seems to corroborate these figures, as the number of foreign firms came to 22 per cent of the total number of industrial, commercial and financial firms which had taken up credits between 1919 and 1929.

In this chapter we are concerned with the aspect of the bank, i.e. the CA, as shareholder and creditor of domestic enterprises. Thus only *Austrian* joint-stock companies have been examined and the following three criteria for selection of firms were applied: (1) All industrial joint-stock companies which were before and after 1931 clients of the CA were included, (2) in whose share capital the CA participated; also (3) such companies whose debts to the CA were nearly equal to or exceeded their own total equity. In these cases the CA might have been, but need not have been, a shareholder.

Various estimates of shareownership by the CA have been put forward purporting to show the strength and power,[37] or even the comparative weakness,[38] of the bank's influence on the country's industry. It is, of course, entirely legitimate to try to measure the amount of a bank's stake in industrial companies *as a first step* towards ascertaining whether as a shareholder and/or as a main creditor the bank exercised control. And this is also our purpose here, but in comparison with previous guesses we believe that our sources enable us to present a more precise picture.

According to the investigations conducted by the Austrian Ministry of Finance between 1930 and 1932 the following overall figures seem to be as near to historical reality as one can possibly get:[39] at the end of 1929, that is before the great mergers of the big Viennese banks with the CA, 163 Austrian joint-stock companies with a total nominal share capital of AS1,141,593,450 were held to be dependent on the CA. This figure includes not only industrial but also transport, trading and insurance companies as well as joint-stock financial institutions. The overall total number of joint-stock companies in Austria at the end of 1929 was 871 with a total share capital of AS1,661,065,000. Thus the companies held to be in the sphere of influence of the CA represented 18.6 per cent of the total number but 68.75 per cent of the total capital of Austrian joint-stock companies.

The number of dependent companies had increased by the end of 1931 when the CA was by way of fusions to become by far the largest universal bank of Austria[40] – this process was completed with the CA's merger with the Wiener Bankverein.[41] According to the list of Austrian companies dependent on the CA, dated 31 May 1932 but containing investigations for the years 1930 and 1931, two results on two different dates were given. The first on 7 August 1931, considered by the Ministry of Finance to be 'a conservative estimate', states that the CA participated in 216 joint-stock companies whose total nominal capital was AS700 million, representing 24.75 per cent of the total number and 42.33 per cent of the total capital of joint-stock companies in Austria.[42] The third and last available list was constructed by the Ministry of Finance as to 31 May 1932 during its investigation of the insolvency of the CA which shook the international financial system in late spring 1931. According to this very full list of debtors held to be dependent on the CA, 281 joint-stock companies were counted.[43]

The concept of dependency as applied by the Ministry of Finance at that time is open to question as it is a blanket definition. Closer scrutiny of the individual cases shows that the degree of dependency obviously varied from company to company. The author examined each of the 281 joint-stock companies which were included in the official inquiry of the Austrian Ministry of Finance and established the following categories in relation to the CA:

> 11.7 per cent were found to have only capital participations of the CA;
> 40.6 per cent were found to have both capital and credit participations of the CA; and
> 47.7 per cent were found to have credit participations of the CA only.

Further, out of the 281 Austrian joint-stock companies 32 per cent had taken up credits from the CA in excess of their own equity (cf. table 9.7 for details). This refers to the state of shareownership and credit participation of the CA after it had absorbed the second biggest universal bank, the Allgemeine Österreichische Boden-Credit-Anstalt, and, as pointed out above, includes not only industrial but all joint-stock companies. Thus the results of the official inquiry distort the picture we wish to give of the relationship of the CA with the industrial joint-stock companies in which it owned shares and to which it was tied with large credits over a longer period.

Therefore, applying the three criteria mentioned above, only

Table 9.6. *Austrian joint-stock companies dependent on CA as a percentage of the total number and total equity of joint-stock companies in ten main branches of manufacturing industry, 1926/7 and 1929/30*

		A		B	C		D	
					Cos. dependent on CA[b]		(Ca) & (Cb) as % of	
		No. of cos.		Total nominal capital of A2	(a) No.	(b) Total equity		
Industry	Year	1[a]	2	in AS 000		in AS 000	A2	& B
Beer-brewing	1926	19	18	75,825	8	55,150	44	73
	1929	12	11	87,975	7	86,875	58	98
Building	1927	38	23	13,306	5	5,746	22	43
	1930	34	25	16,262	6	7,341	24	45
Chemical	1926	63	43	50,482	15	20,694	35	41
Industry	1930	50	48	91,149	16	29,660	33	33
Electrical	1927	27	24	64,952	6	17,850	25	27
Industry	1930	—	27	82,340	5	21,925	19	27
Engineering	1926	173	125	231,690	32	106,120	26	46
& Metalworking	1930	—	101	192,053	32	110,343	32	57
Mining &	1926	47	23	115,179	11	101,420	48	88
Metallurgy	1930	—	20	122,617	11	99,985	55	82
Leather &	1927	—	21	32,714	5	3,370	24	10
Shoes	1930	20	6	5,750	5	3,150	83	54
Paper	1927	29	26	64,396	9	28,759	35	45
	1930	28	28	72,609	11	37,259	39	51
Textile	1927	53	41	92,941	17	48,085	41	52
Industry	1930	50	44	109,820	18	50,885	41	46
Wood	1927	52	31	12,920	10	6,519	32	51
Industry	1930	37	32	15,883	10	6,044	31	38
10 industries	1926/7		375	754,405	118	393,713	31	52
total	1929/30		342	796,458	121	453,467	35	57

[a] A1 = total number of industrial joint-stock companies; A2 = number of reporting companies.
[b] Criteria for selection of companies: (a) companies in whose equity the CA participated, and (b) companies whose debts to CA exceeded their equity and reserves (cf. text).
Abbreviations: CA = Österreichische Credit-Anstalt für Handel und Gewerbs; cos. = companies; AS = Austrian Schillings.
Sources: Compiled from Finanzarchiv, Vienna: CA-Protokolle, *Compass-Oesterreich*, and *Statistisches Handbuch für die Republik Österreich*, relevant years.

Table 9.7. *Shareholding and credit participation of the CA in joint-stock companies of ten main branches of Austrian manufacturing industry, 31 December 1931*[a]

Name of company	Nominal capital in AS 000	Shareholding of CA in AS 000	%	Debt to CA AS 000
Beer-brewing				
Gösser Brauerei A.G. vormals Max Kober, Göss	9,600	2,644.8	27.55	3,900.4
Erste Grazer Aktienbrauerei, Graz-Puntigam	4,000	242.4	6.06	
Vereinigte Brauerein Schwechat	21,600	2,432.2	11.26	4,604
Brauerei Zipf A.G. v. Wm. Schaup, Zipf	4,000	546.4	13.66	2,717
Building				
Niederösterreichische Ziegel-und Tonwaren Fabriks A.G.	105			86
Brüder Redlich & Berger, Wien	770			4,905
Universale Bau A.G. Wien	1,100	491.5	44.68	86
Wienerberger Ziegelfabriks- und Baugesellschaft, Wien	4,665.6	578.1	12.3	9,799
Stuag, Strassenbau- unternehmung, A.G., Wien	1,250			192
Chemical industry				
'Allchemin' A.G., Wien	300			386
Danubia Mineralölindustrie A.G., Wien	100			2,324
Austria Petroleum Industrie A.G., Wien	100			3,213
A.G. für Mineralölindustrie v. Dav. Fanto & Co., Wien	1,200			5,087
A.G. für chemische Industrie Wien	3,150			1,189
'Akalit' Kunsthornwerke A.G., Brunn A.G.	600	131.1	21.85	638
Chemische Industrie Wagemann, Seybel & Co. A.G., Wien	1,000			1,904
Chemosan Union Fritz Petzold A.G. Wien	2,375	1,045	43.54	3,718

Table 9.7 (*cont.*)

Name of company	Nominal capital in AS 000	Shareholding of CA in AS 000	%	Debt to CA AS 000
Chemical industry (cont.)				
Gimberg & Zifferer A.G., Wien	125			170
Pulverfabrik Skodawerke-Wetzler A.G., Wien	7,000	3,376.8	48.24	6,282
KAMIG Österr. Kaolin & Montanindustrie A.G.	1,060	828.2	75.29	755
Spiritus A.G., Wien	1,250	242.8	19.42	
Vereinigte Fettwarenindustrie Josef Estermann A.G., Wien	750			96
Wiener Oelwerke A.G., Wien	500	464	92.8	2,645
Franz Wilhelm & Co., A.G., Wien	100			835
Electrical industry				
AEG Union Elektrizitäts-Ges., Wien	7,200	358.6	4.98	
Elin A.G. für elektrische Industrie, Wien	8,750	913.5	10.44	571
Ericsson Österreichische Elektrizitäts-A.G., vorm. Deckert & Homolka, Wien	2,500	364.3	14.57	133
Paul Schiff & Co. A.G., Wien	300	300	100	1,231
S. Schön A.G. für Elektrotechnik, Wien	100	61.7	61.7	992
Engineering (mechanical and metalworking)				
Friedrich Siemens Werke A.G., Wien	100	70	70	4,243
A.G. der Locomotivfabriken v. G. Sigl, Wr. Neustadt	7,500	3,552	7.36	
Berndorfer Metallfabrik Arthur Krupp A.G.	18,000	8,517.6	47.32	45,601
Brüder Eisert, Wien	600	199.2	33.2	351
Enzesfelder Metallwerke A.G.	2,500			155
Hirtenberger Patronon- Zünd-hütchen- und Metallwarenfabrik	4,200	3,775.5	80.37	2,073
Maschinenfabriks-A.G. N. Heid, Stockerau	3,600	1,597.3	44.87	9,511

Table 9.7 (*cont.*)

Name of company	Nominal capital in AS 000	Shareholding of CA in AS 000	%	Debt to CA AS 000
Engineering (cont.)				
Wiener Automobilfabrik A.G. vorm. Gräf & Stift, Wien	2,000	413.4	20.67	3,802
Feinstahlwerke Traisen A.G., vorm Fischer, Wien	900			148
Austro-Daimler-Puchwerke A.G.,Wien	3,800	1,330	35	13,825
Automobilfabrik, Perl A.G., Wien	1,000	734	73.4	19,581
Bahnindustrie A.G. für Bahn- & Industriebedarf, Wien	100	57.5	57.5	469
Blech- und Eisenwerke Styria A.G., Wien	2,000	681	34.05	1,182
Climax Motorenwerk & Schiffswerft, Linz	1,750	834.8	47.7	22,066
Eisenwarenfabriken, Lapp Finze, Graz	5,400	3,139	58.13	
Grazer Waggon & Maschinen- fabriks A.G., Wien	2,500	358.8	14.35	49
Köllensperger Eisenindustrie & Handels A.G., Innsbruck	300			68
KROMAG A.G. für Werkzeug & Metallindustrie, Hirtenberg	1,200			698
Leobersdorfer Maschinen- fabriks-A.G., Leobersdorf	2,625			86.2
Maschinen-und Waggonbau- Fabriks-A.G. vorm. H.D. Schmid, Wien	6,400	185.6	2.9	
Maschinenfabrik A.G. Richard Herz, Wien	150			1,638
Metall- und Erz A.G., Wien	100	18	18	161
Österreichische Automobil- Fabriks-A.G. 'Austro-Fiat', Wien	5,400	2,305.8	42.7	
Patronenfabrik A.G. Lichten- wörth, Wr. Neustadt	500	255	51	76
Phoebuswerke A.G., Wien	400	119.6	29.9	
Rottenmanner Eisenwerke A.G. vorm. Brüder Lapp, Rottenmann	1,000	515	51.5	929

Table 9.7 (*cont.*)

Name of company	Nominal capital in AS 000	Shareholding of CA in AS 000	%	Debt to CA AS 000
Engineering (cont.)				
C. Schember & Söhne, Brückenwagen und Maschinen- fabriken A.G., Wien-Atzgersdorf	600	213.6	35.6	2,774
Schrauben- und Schmiedewaren A.G. Brevillier & Co. und A. Urban & Söhne, Wien	14,400			2,743
Steyr Werke A.G., Wien	15,120	12,255.2	81.16	69,221
Vereinigte Metallwerke A.G., Wien	7,590	4,628.4	60.9	11,220
Weicheisen-Stahlguss-und Hammerwerke A.G.	1,000	335	33.5	699
Wiener Armaturen-und Maschinenbau A.G., Wien	1,000	685	68.5	
Wiener Brückenbau- und Eisenkonstruktions-A.G., Wien	500	324.8	64.96	
Mining and metallurgy Allgemeine Montanbank A.G., Wien	1,000	326	32.6	222
Österreichisch-Alpine Montan- gesellschaft, Wien	60,000	534	0.89	
Bleiberger Bergwerks-Union, Klagenfurt	7,500			975
Mitterberger Kupfer A.G., Berndorf	5,000	1,303.5	26.07	18,021
Eisenwerke A.G., Krieglach	1,350	112.5	8.33	367
Grünbacher Steinkohlenwerke A.G., Grünbach	1,800	427.5	23.75	1,176.3
Montana A.G. für Bergbau, Industrie und Handel, Wien	2,000	970	48.5	259
Schoeller-Bleckmann Stahl- werke A.G., Wien	6,835.2	2,006.1	29.35	7,969
Steirische Gusstahlwerke A.G., Wien	1,755	1,755	100	3,652
Leather industry 'Aeterna' Schuhfabrik A.G., Atzgersdorf	840	168.8	20.1	3,296
Brüder Eisert, Wien	600	199.1	33.19	351

Table 9.7 (*cont.*)

Name of company	Nominal capital in AS 000	Shareholding of CA in AS 000	%	Debt to CA AS 000
Leather industry (cont.)				
Humanic, Leder & Schuh A.G., Graz	1,250			530
Union Lederwerke A.G., Schwechat	160	79.5	49.7	1,928
Paper industry				
Abadie Papier A.G., Wien	500	92.3	18.5	
Kleinzeller Papierfabrik A.G., Wien	100	51	51	245
Deutschlandsberger Papier-fabrik A.G., Wien	375			296
Geschäftsbücherfabrik A.G., vorm. J.C. König & Ebhardt, Wien	250	169.5	67.8	504
Lenzinger Papierfabrik A.G., Wien	5,000	2,655	53.1	2,202
Leykam-Josefsthal A.G. für Papier- und Druckindustrie, Wien	12,000	1,556.4	12.97	6,347
Natron Papierindustrie A.G., Wien	400			17
'Steyermühl' Papierfabriks- & Verlags-Gesellschaft, Wien	12,800	2,429.4	18.98	1,252
Vereinigte Papier-Industrie A.G., Wien	161.3	161.3	100	2,798
Zellulose-und Papierfabriken Brigl & Bergmeister A.G., Niklasdorf	4,000	462	11.56	26
Textile industry				
A.G. der Baumwoll-Spinnereien, Webereien, Bleiche, Appretur, Färberei und Druckerei Trumau und Marienthal, Wien	3,000			2,896
Awestem Band & Stoff-industrie, Wien	2,800	534.8	19.1	2,329
Bossi Hutfabriks A.G., Wien	800	280	35	3,448
Guntramsdorfer Druckfabrik A.G., Wien	1,400	627.2	44.2	8,064

Table 9.7 (*cont.*)

Name of company	Nominal capital in AS 000	Shareholding of CA in AS 000	%	Debt to CA AS 000
Textile industry (cont.)				
Hanf, Jute & Textilit Industrie A.G., Wien	11,718.8	2,158.8	18.42	8,224
A.G. der Kleinmünchner Baumwollspinnereien & mechanischen Weberei, Wien	6,000	1,668.6	27.81	
Knüpfteppichindustrie System Banyai A.G., Pottendorf	1,000	450	45	2,479.3
Pottendorfer Spinnerei und Felixdorfer Weberei A.G., Wien	6,166			19,243
Siag Textilindustrie A.G., Wien	2,000	820	41	2,312
Spinnerei & Wirkwaren- fabriken M. Honig A.G., Wien	2,500	1,032.5	41.3	2,143
Vereinigte Färbereien A.G., Wien	2,100	6.9	0.33	360
Vereinigte österreichische Textilindustrie A.G., Wien	2,500			2,860
Emil Wieselthier A.G., Wien	100	75	75	1,106
Wood industry				
A.G. für Mühlen & Holz- industrie, Wien	600	285.2	47.54	1,270
Allgemeine A.G. für Holz- verwertung, Wien	100	93.6	93.6	3,827
Alpenländische Holzverwer- tungs A.G., Wien	200			142
Klosterneuburger Wagenfabrik Gebr. Schwarzhuber A.G.	145	3.6	2.5	2,096
Silva Holz A.G., Wien	100	59	59	129
Staussziegel- & Rohrgewebe Industrie A.G., Wien	550			122
Steirische Holzverwertungs A.G., Leoben	100	90	90	931
Thurwieser Holzindustrie A.G. Kramsach, Wien	144	56.9	39.5	519

Summary of above table (in AS 000)

Industry	A Nominal capital	B Shares held by CA	B in % of A	Debt to CA in AS 000	%
Beer-brewing	39,200	5,865.8	15	11,221.4	2.8
Building	7,890.6	1,069.6	13.5	15,068	3.9
Chemical industry	19,610	6,087.8	31	29,242	7.3
Electrical industry	18,850	1,998.1	10.6	2,927	0.7
Engineering	114.235	46,701.1	40.9	213,369.2	53.5
Mining and metallurgy	87,240.2	7,434.6	8.5	42,641.3	10.7
Leather industry	2,850	447.4	15.7	6,105	1.5
Paper industry	35,086.3	7,577.3	21.3	13,687	3.4
Textile industry	42,084.8	7,653.8	18.2	55,464.3	13.9
Wood industry	1,939	588.3	31	9,036	2.3
Total of 10 industries	369,485.9	83,826.5	22.7	398,761.2	100

a Only joint-stock companies connected with the CA throughout the interwar period, i.e. before and after the banking crisis of 1931.
Source: as in previous table; data for shareholding of the CA and indebtedness to the CA extracted from Finanzarchiv, Vienna, 15-32757/32.

industrial joint-stock companies which had remained clients of the CA throughout the interwar period (i.e. before and after the crash of 1931) were selected: their total number in 1926/7 was 118 and their total equity AS393,713,000; and in 1929/30 their total number was 121 with a total equity of AS453,467,000 (cf. table 9.6). Their ties with the CA were cemented either through the bank's participation in their equity or through their continuously large indebtedness to the CA or through both, capital and credit participation by the CA. In this respect the investigated industrial companies can be described as being dependent on the bank. Tables 9.6 and 9.7 are the result of this effort.

Let us turn first to table 9.6. In order to obtain a more differentiated insight into actually existing bank–industry relationships than overall figures can provide, table 9.6 presents a survey of industrial enterprises, in which the CA was shareholder and creditor, divided into branches of industry. Also a certain, admittedly rather short-lived dynamic was attempted by taking into account the only two bench years which could be compared on the basis of the available source material, i.e. 1926/7, after the currency reform and the *Golderöffnungsbilanz* (legally enforced opening balances in Austrian Schillings by all

Austrian joint-stock companies), and 1929/30, the peak of the inter-war period on the eve of economic collapse. The results clearly show the substantial involvement of the bank in the ten most important branches of Austria's manufacturing industry. Its stake in those industries' total equity was in both years higher than 50 per cent if compared to the total share capital of the reporting companies (52 per cent in 1926/7 and 57 per cent in 1929/30, cf. table 9.6).

Particularly striking is the bank's heavy commitment in the traditional Austrian industries – mining and metallurgy, engineering and metalworking, textiles, wood and beer-brewing – whose origins go back to the second half of the nineteenth century, indeed to the bank's founding and promoting activities. This becomes even more evident from table 9.7 where the firms connected by shareownership and credits with the CA were identified as belonging to the oldest pioneers in those branches of manufacturing industries which by the 1930s had got into great difficulties, except for beer-brewing. These industries exhibited the strongest demand for advances. In addition to the breweries the companies in the building and electrical industries were less indebted to the CA and only a small percentage of their shares were in the possession of the bank. Another point of interest in connection with table 9.6 is that there was apparently little change in the number of dependent industrial companies belonging to the orbit of the CA, but that the total equity of these same companies had increased from AS393,713,000 to AS453,467,000. This rise can be observed in all examined industries except for mining and metallurgy, leather and wood, which corresponds to the comparative decline of these traditional and ailing branches of industry in the Austrian economy. The CA, sometimes alone and sometimes in collaboration with other banks (*Konsortium*),[44] was instrumental in these increases of equity by handling the issue of new shares for its dependent companies as a way of procuring long-term capital rather than proffering long-term loans. This method of capital procurement was also preferred by the joint-stock companies as it was less costly. More often than not such transactions included fusions of companies aiming at rationalization rather than modernization of their production technology.

The author's findings summarized in table 9.6 are reinforced by the content of table 9.7 which enumerates the CA's shareholdings in and credits to companies which belonged to the ten branches of industry listed in table 9.6. Most of the firms are well-known enterprises of which many have survived either from the times of the Habsburg Monarchy or from the early 1920s to this day. They were able to weather the crisis of the early 1930s by a radical reconstruction in which the CA played a leading part after 1932 and which showed clearly the great measure of control the bank was able to wield in order to enforce closures and reduction in production, as well as mergers, and to decide which company was to be rescued and which was to be liquidated. But that is a story which not only would go beyond the scope of this chapter, but which needs further thorough research.[45]

It remains to comment – as far as the material allows – on the character of the advances made by the CA to the industrial companies in its sphere of influence. The available sources to a large extent bear out the conclusions Alois Mosser drew from the analysis of annual balance sheet totals, namely that industrial joint-stock companies used new share issues rather than long-term bank loans for their investments, and this was encouraged by the banks which, as mentioned above in the case of the CA, handled these issues as part of their day-to-day business. The banks' charges for this service varied between 4 and 10 per cent between 1922 and 1932.[46] However, the advances the CA made to its industrial customers were, in most cases, only formally short-term credits. It was an accepted practice to adjust credit limits over and over again to the financial needs of the clients, especially if the bank owned shares in their companies. The cost of credits was very high between 1925 and 1932, not least because of the bank cartel (*Konditionenkartell*) which fixed the terms and conditions for deposits and set minimum levels for advances to first-time borrowers, thereby constructing a scale of interest rates from the highest to first-time clients to lower rates charged to enterprises within the banks' concerns. As the conditions of the cartel were kept secret it is difficult to measure the average cost of credit. According to the official publication by the Österreichische Institut für Konjunkturforschung the bank rate vacillated between 5 and 13 per cent from 1924 to 1932 and was increased for commercial loans by $1^{1}/2$ per cent plus a provision payment of 6 per cent in 1925, 4 per cent from 1926 to 1929, and $3^{1}/2$ per cent from mid-1929 to 1933, which brought total interest to be paid by borrowers on average from the highest rate of $20^{1}/2$ per cent in 1925 by a very slow and sticky decline to the lowest rate of 12 per cent by 1930.[47] Under these circumstances the material of the CA shows that the bank was not so much concerned with the ability of the companies to pay dividends – which many of them suspended for long periods – but mainly with the ability of the industrial clients to pay interest.

Another problem for industrial enterprises in their search for capital was posed by the severe collateral requirements of the banks. Thus the CA imposed a large range of collateral conditions, including participation in profits, option on shares and new issues of shares, foreclosures of shares and/or bonds, transfers of claims on invoices, pledges of assets, mortgages and liabilities of companies, partners or other guarantors, as well as contracting with the borrower that all his business will exclusively be conducted with the CA. In the real or imagined unfavourable economic climate in interwar Austria the way to the bank for credits was paved with difficulties, although the banks themselves were not unwilling to credit-finance industry. This is one of the conclusions to be made on the basis of the sources used in preparation of this paper.

Clients of the CA, especially those companies in which the CA owned shares, were able to draw on several accounts, such as a current account, a guarantee account, a bills of exchange account, an export account and an account for liabilities the bank had accepted as well as other special or separate accounts. In the only period which can be regarded as one of relative boom in the Austrian economy, i.e. from 1926 to 1929, the CA began an inspection of its largest debtors and took an active part in bringing about changes in the composition of managements, as for instance in the Maschinenfabriks A.G. Heid in 1929,[48] or in inducing changes in the financial policy, as in the case of the Wiener Automobilfabrik A.G. vorm. Gräf & Stift,[49] or in enforcing mergers, as for instance in the building industry,[50] or aiding in take-overs, of which the most spectacular development occurred in the brewing industry (whereas in the early 1920s twenty-four breweries belonged to the CA sphere of interest, by 1926 they were merged into eight and by 1930 into seven leading Austrian joint-stock brewing companies).[51]

The involvement of the CA in Austrian industry was undoubtedly great. As was shown in this first attempt to interpret a massive and scattered source material, the role of the CA was not confined to making advances to industrial companies but – always having in mind the ability of their industrial clients to meet commission and interest payments – it actively intervened in restructuring of companies, it organized fusions, it channelled capital to enterprises for various business operations, especially to enable export companies to fulfil orders. Evidence for the latter can be found in the extremely large number of guarantee credits to companies fulfilling export orders. Thus the bank serviced a capitalist market economy which only differed from others by the special conditions created by the outcome of the Great War and the collapse of the Austro-Hungarian Empire, an economic entity in which Vienna with its great universal banks had been the centre.

Conclusion

We hope that we have been able to convey the economic climate of the interwar period in which Austrian industrial joint-stock companies sought to procure capital. It appears that they had to take recourse to the banks, above all, to those universal banks which had either founded them or promoted their change into public companies. The examination of the connections between the CA and its industrial clients in whose companies the bank owned shares shows that these ties were crucial both to the bank and the enterprises. Their investments, their export business, their short-term capital as well as their day-to-day financial requirements – from payment of salaries and wages to petty cash – depended on the mutual ties between banking and industry. In this sense bank–industry relations in general are part and parcel of the capitalist market economy.

NOTES

 * In the course of their research the authors have received financial support for which they are very grateful to the funding institutions. Alois Mosser wants to thank the Volkswagen-Stiftung, and Alice Teichova's research has benefited from the academic encouragement and financial assistance of the British Academy, the Leverhulme Foundation and the promise of further support from the British Economic and Social Research Council for which she expresses her thanks.
   The authors wish to thank the following colleagues for their helpful comments: Bo Gustafsson, Håkan Lindgren, Ragnhild Lundström, Georg Péteri, Dieter Stiefel and Fritz Weber. For any errors or omissions the responsibility is their own.
1 Cf. *Industrialization and Foreign Trade*, League of Nations (1945), pp. 26–7.
 2 A. Klaussel, N. Németh and H. Seidel, *Österreichs Volkseinkommen 1913 bis 1963, Monatsberichte des Österreichischen Institutes für Wirtschaftsforschung*, 14th Sonderheft (Vienna, 1965), pp. 7, 38.

3 These complex problems were discussed by K. Bachinger, *Umbruch und Desintegration nach dem Ersten Weltkrieg. Österreichs wirtschaftliche und soziale Ausgangssituation in ihren Folgewirkungen auf die Erste Republik*, unpublished Habilitation, 2 vols. (Vienna, 1981).

4 A. Klausel *et al.* calculate in their national income statistics total figures for gross fixed investment in which industry plays an important role but its exact proportion has not been ascertained. See p. 17 n. 2.

5 The official statistics include only for 1925 about 50 per cent of all firms (in all other years the percentage of reporting firms was much higher). This obviously is connected with the introduction of the new Schilling currency and the impact this had on financial accounting of joint-stock companies.

6 F. Hertz, 'Kapitalbedarf, Kapitalbildung und Volkseinkommen in Österreich', in W. Lotz (ed.), *Kapitalbildung und Besteuerung* (Schriften des Vereins für Sozialpolitik, vol. 174, part 4) (Munich, Leipzig, 1929), p. 47.

7 Figures quoted here differ from those in my article 'Wachstumsstrategie oder Krisenmanagement? Vom Investitionsverhalten der Österreichischen Industrie in der Ersten Republik', in A. Kusternig (ed.), *Beiträge über die Krise der Industrie Niederösterreichs zwischen den beiden Weltkriegen* (Vienna, 1985), p. 107. This is due to printing errors which, for reasons beyond my control, I was unable to correct in the proofs.

8 Austrian joint-stock companies were required by law to publish their annual accounts in the stabilized Schilling currency by 1 January 1925 (Golderöffnungsbilanz).

9 *Statistisches Handbuch für die Republik Österreich*, Bundesamt für Statistik, 1 (1920) to 17 (1937), chapter 'Erwerbsgesellschaften und Genossenschaften: Aktiengesellschaften'.

10 Bundesgesetzblatt 1932, no. 213, *Bundesgesetz vom 28. Juli 1932 über die Herabsetzung des Grundkapitals von Aktiengesellschaften (Kommanditgesellschaften auf Aktien)*, pp. 667–9.

11 *Wirtschaftsstatistisches Jahrbuch* 1926 (1927), p. 119 and 1936 (1936), p. 419.

12 Hertz, 'Kapitalbedarf', p. 41.

13 A. Mosser, *Die Industrieaktiengesellschaft in Österreich 1880–1913*, Studien zur Geschichte der österreichisch-ungarischen Monarchie, vol. 18 (Vienna, 1980), pp. 142, 178.

14 Zur Entwicklung der Bankkonditionen: see 'Die Kreditwirtschaft in der Ostmark und im Altreich', in *Monatsberichte des Wiener Institutes für Wirtschafts- und Konjunkturforschung*, 12 (1938), esp. p. 140.

15 *Bericht über die Ursachen der wirtschaftlichen Schwierigkeiten Österreichs* (Vienna, 1931), pp. 9 and 83; cf. also W. Reik, *Die Beziehungen der österreichischen Großbanken zur Industrie* (Vienna, 1932), p. 36.

16 Hertz, 'Kapitalbedarf', p. 54.

17 A. Mosser, 'Industrielle Entwicklung und konjunkturelle Dynamik in Österreich 1920–1937', in *Christliche Demokratie Schriften des Karl v. Vogelsang-Institutes*, 3/4 (December 1935), 311–12.

18 Cf. E. März, *Österreichische Industrie- und Bankpolitik in der Zeit Franz Josephs I.* (Vienna, 1968); also A. Teichova, *Kleinstaaten im Spannungsfeld der Grossmächte. Wirtschaft und Politik in Mittel- und Südosteuropa in der Zwischenkriegszeit* (Vienna, 1988), p. 87.

19 W. Layton and C. Rist, *The Economic Situation of Austria*, Report presented to the Council of the League of Nations (Geneva, 1925).

20 E. März, *Österreichische Bankpolitik in der Zeit der grossen Wende 1913–1923. Am Beispiel der Creditanstalt für Handel und Gewerbe* (Vienna, 1981), pp. 54, 69.

21 D. Stiefel, *Finanzdiplomazie und Weltwirtschaftskrise. Die Krise der Credit-Anstalt für Handel und Gewerbe 1931* (Frankfurt on Main, 1989), p. 97.

22 Cf. H. Matis and K. Bachinger, 'Österreichs industrielle Entwicklung', in *Die Habsburgermonarchie 1848–1918. Die wirtschaftliche Entwicklung*, vol. I (Vienna, 1973), p. 216; see also Mosser, *Die Industrieaktiengesellschaft*, p. 184.

23 Cited by P. L. Cottrell, 'Aspects of Western equity investment in the banking systems of East Central Europe', in A. Teichova and P. L. Cottrell (eds.), *International Business and Central Europe, 1918–1939* (Leicester and New York, 1983), p. 334.

24 Stiefel, *Finanzdiplomatie*, p. 83; März, *Österreichische Bankpolitik*, p. 75.

25 Cf. H. Kernbauer and F. Weber, 'Multinational banking in the Danube basin: the business strategy of the Viennese banks after the collapse of the Habsburg monarchy', in A. Teichova, M. Lévy-Leboyer and H. Nussbaum (eds.), *Multinational Enterprise in Historical Perspective* (Cambridge and Paris, 1986), p. 190; also Stiefel, *Finanzdiplomatie*, p. 97.

26 *Geschäfts-Bericht des Verwaltungsrates der Oesterreichischen Credit-Anstalt für Handel und Gewerbe für das Jahr 1925*, presented on 30 June 1926, pp. 20–1; as to productive investments in companies tied to the CA the following received special mention in the report: in the mining and metallurgy industry a large-scale investment programme had taken place in the group controlled by the Allgemeine Montanbank A.G. belonging to the concern of the CA aimed at enabling production to meet future orders; in the engineering industry larger investments were made – financed by an increase in equity – in the group of the Maschinenfabriks-Aktiengesellschaft N. Heid to support its export programme of agricultural machinery; in the chemical industry the Pulverfabrik Skodawerke-Wetzler A.G. started manufacturing sulphuric acid and superphosphate in a newly built plant; substantial investments for the expansion of production were made in beer-brewing by the Gösser Brauerei Actien-Gesellschaft vormals Max Kober in Göss, and in paper production by the Leykam-Josefsthal Actien-Gesellschaft für Papier- und Druckindustrie. In both cases satisfaction was expressed that output in these two company groups had almost reached the pre-war level. Pp. 25, 28, 29, 32.

27 The same emphasis on meeting the demand for advances from an increased number of clients appeared in the report for 1926 presented on 27 May 1927 thus: 'Auch im abgelaufenen Jahre waren wir darauf bedacht, den Bedarf unseres so wesentlich erweiterten Klientenkreises an Betriebsmitteln sowohl durch direkte Gewährung von Krediten wie durch Vermittlung solcher Kredite aus dem Auslande zu decken.' *Geschäfts-Bericht des Verwaltungsrates der Oesterreichischen Credit-Anstalt für Handel und Gewerbe für das Jahr 1926*, p. 11.

28 The percentage of equity of the CA in possession of foreign shareholders is taken from a document entitled 'Foreign shareholders in the Credit Anstalt' drawn up by Sir Peter Bark for the Bank of England during his visit in Vienna in 1931. I am grateful to my colleague Phil Cottrell for allowing me to quote from it. This document is also used in Stiefel's *Finanzdiplomatie* but the figures in his table on p. 37 do not tally with some of those given in the Peter Bark paper.

29 Stiefel, *Finanzdiplomatie*, p. 99.

30 *Geschäfts-Bericht des Verwaltungsrates der Oesterreichischen Credit-Anstalt für Handel und Gewerbe für das Jahr 1930*, presented 4 August 1931, p. 10, and *Bericht an die 76. Ordentliche Generalversammlung der Aktionäre der Oesterreichischen Credit-Anstalt*

für Handel und Gewerbe vom 22. Juli 1933 which reports on the years 1931–2, p. 12.

31 According to the minutes of the directors' meeting on 1 June 1917, duties were allocated to bank directors on the principle that all important matters, particularly substantial credits as well as undertaking larger engagements in securities, foreign exchange or goods should be agreed collegially among all directors. Director Ludwig Neurath was entrusted among other duties with: 'Ueberwachung der industriellen Unternehmungen, deren Verwaltung anderen Direktoren angehören, deren Unterstützung bei der Ueberwachung'. CA Protokoll 12/1.6.1917.

32 CA Protokoll 11/23.7.1926. An entirely new division of duties was agreed upon at the directors' meeting on 5 August 1931 when 220 industrial companies of which 64 were foreign were allocated to ten directors for supervision and control of their advances: CA Protokoll 6/5.8.1931. But a thorough reconstruction of dependent companies started only after May 1932.

33 Based on a fragment from the CA-archive entitled: 'Verzeichnis der vorhandenen, im Industrie-Inspektorat der Credit-Anstalt erliegenden Revisionsberichte über nachstehende Firmen, bei welchen Verluste zu erwarten sind'. The list contains eighteen firms of which the ten largest debtors are extracted.

34 Cf. H. Kernbauer and F. Weber, 'Die Wiener Grossbanken in der Zeit der Kriegs- und Nachkriegsinflation (1914–1922)' in G. Feldman *et al.* (eds.), *Die Erfahrungen der Inflation im internationalen Zusammenhang und Vergleich* (Berlin, 1984), where they maintain that holding companies were founded in The Netherlands and in Switzerland to avoid the sale of Austrian enterprises to foreign firms (pp. 156–7).

35 Kernbauer and Weber, 'Multinational banking in the Danube basin', p. 195.

36 F. Weber, 'Die Österreichische Bankenkrise und ihre Auswirkungen auf die niederösterreichische Industrie', in A. Kusternig (ed.), *Beiträge über die Krise der Industrie Niederösterreichs zwischen den beiden Weltkriegen*, p. 124; also Stiefel, *Finanz- diplomatie*, p. 98.

37 Rudolf Nötel cites contemporary and later estimates in his article 'Money, banking and industry in interwar Austria and Hungary', *Journal of European Economic History*, 13, no. 2 (1984), p. 162.

38 D. Stiefel, 'The reconstruction of the Credit-Anstalt', in Teichova and Cottrell (eds.), *International Business*, p. 418.

39 The figures in the following text are calculated from files in the Finanzarchiv, Vienna: 1072/AP/1931, 55.142/1931, 32757/31 and 32.

40 A. Teichova, *Rivals and Partners: Banking and Industry in Europe in the First Decade of the Twentieth Century*, Uppsala Papers in Economic History, no. 1 (1988), p. 13.

41 Cottrell, 'Aspects of Western equity investment', p. 328.

42 Weber refers to the Finanzarchiv files 1072/AP/1931 and 55.142/32 in his article 'Die österreichische Bankenkrise', p. 128 n. 26.

43 Finanzarchiv, Vienna, 15-32757/32.

44 While many of the companies dependent on advances from the CA were required to bank exclusively with the CA, there was a number of very big groups – often as a result of fusions organized by banks – which were financed by two or more banks, i.e. a *Konsortium*. To those belonged, for instance, the Austro-Daimler-Puch A.G. which belonged to the *Konsortium* of the CA, the Wiener Bank-Verein, the Depositenbank and the Anglo-Austrian Bank, but after the big bank fusions by 1929 to the concern of the CA and the Wiener Bank-Verein (FA, Vienna, 47.197/34); or the Elin Aktiengellschaft für elektrische Industrie which had taken

up credits from a *Konsortium* of the CA, the Wiener Bank-Verein and the Oesterreichische Eisenbahn-Verkehrs-Anstalt (FA, Vienna, 22.204/36). Such examples of multi-banking were not isolated occurrences.

45 Fritz Weber is preparing a monograph which will include details of the reconstruction of the CA concern.
46 'Entwicklung der Bankkonditionen seit dem Jahre 1924', in *Österreichisches Institut für Konjunkturforschung, Monatsberichte*, 6 (June 1938), p. 140.
47 Exact information about interest rates to individual industrial clients is hard to come by. In the material I studied I found, for example, that the CA charged 4 per cent to Rohrböck's Söhne but 6–9 per cent to the Hirtenberger Patronen- und Metallwarenfabrik. In another case regarding the building industry the firm of Redlich & Berger agreed from 1927 onwards to the CA's 25 per cent participation in the net profits of the enterprise at home and abroad for the continuation of increases in its credit limits. The above information is extracted from CA Protokolle during my work on reconstruction of industrial customer accounts.
48 The CA insisted on changes in management in 1929 and introduced new organizational measures regarding the factory's production programme. Cf. FA, Vienna, 54646/33.
49 Pressure was exerted by the bank to induce the brothers Gräf to sell off part of their stores in order to reduce their debt to the bank. Cf. FA, Vienna, 94288/35.
50 Cf. FA Vienna, 84478/30, CA Protokoll 11/17.11.1933.
51 The CA was instrumental in the concentration movement of the brewing industry mainly through organizing the consolidation of shares, new share issues and providing bridging loans. This statement is based on the reconstruction of accounts of breweries with the CA from 1912 to 1938.

10   Financing of Hungarian industry by the Commercial Bank of Pest: a case study

ELIZABETH A. BOROSS

This case study of the Commercial Bank of Pest aims to provide empirical evidence of industrial financing policy as it was formulated and practised in the decade after the First World war.* It is also hoped that the quantitative evidence provided by the study will contribute to the ongoing debate regarding the mutual relations between banks and industrial enterprises.

The two most thoroughgoing works dealing with the pre-1914 period still influence largely the way in which macroeconomic assessments deal with the role of banks in Central-Eastern Europe (Hilferding, Gerschenkron): the question whether banks aided or hindered the industrialization process, whether the universal or mixed banks, due to scarcity of capital, were able to dominate industry as a result of capitalist development,[1] or whether this interdependence between banks and industry was restricted to some 'latecomer' industries suffering from limited investment resources which brought about the 'missionary' role of the banks during the pre-1914 period.[2] Development during the post-war decade appears to reinforce these influential theories as there was no break in the further concentration of industrial and finance capital in Hungary. Due to hyper-inflation and persistent economic crises interdependence, if anything, intensified. A welcome burst of empirical research activity is beginning to question and modify the above theoretical assumptions and to try to find quantitative evidence bearing out the role of the banks and examine the findings comparatively.

Although there had been rapid development of industry during the three-and-a-half decades prior to the First World War, Hungary

158

Table 10.1. *Assets of major banks based on 1913 balance sheets (in million K)*

	Share capital	Reserves	Total capital	Savings
PMKB	62.5	101.3	163.8	298.0
MAH	80.0	54.8	134.8	48.1
Magyar Jezálog-Hitelbank	40.0	32.4	72.4	—
Pesti Hazai Elsö Takarékpénztár	20.0	44.6	64.6	273.7
Magyar Leszámitoló & Pénzváltó Bank	50.0	12.3	62.3	163.8

remained a predominantly agricultural country. Nevertheless, great strides had been made as indicated by the fact that after 1867 Hungarian industry grew faster than Austrian industry. This cannot be claimed a spectacular achievement because she started from a much lower base, but resulted in lifting Hungarian industrial output rapidly. In 1841 Hungary's manufacturing produced 16 per cent of Austria's output which by the First World War came closer to 30 per cent.[3] Contemporary, mainly nationalist observers often claimed that Habsburg economic policy stifled Hungary's industrialization and that keeping her a primary and food producer hindered economic progress. This notion has since been successfully and conclusively challenged in recent historiography.[4] The Commercial Bank of Pest (Pesti Magyar Kereskedelmi Bank – PMKB) owes its origin to similar nationalistic aspirations, namely a desire for financial independence from the Viennese banking houses, and freedom to pursue policies perceived to be in the national interest. This study examines the way in which the Bank's industrial financing policy was formulated and carried out in the decade after the First World War when changed geopolitical circumstances, the collapse of the Austro-Hungarian Empire, ostensibly enabled it to pursue a more independent role in the industrial development of Hungary.

By 1913 the Commercial Bank of Pest had developed into a leading financial institute based on its capital, reserves and accumulated savings as table 10.1 indicates.[5] Nevertheless, in industrial financing the Hungarian General Credit Bank's (Magyar Általános Hitelbank – MAH) activity was far more extensive. As the name indicates, supporting commerce was PMKB's primary purpose, yet they too engaged in far-reaching industrial financing. The reason for choosing PMKB as case study was based on a very important consideration for an empirical study: this institute has the most complete and detailed primary source relating to credit extensions, which is simply not available for MAH. One may also assume that PMKB's credit policy was comparable to MAH's because being the two largest commercial banks they competed with one another and the former could equally attract nationally prominent industrial concerns as clients in mining, milling, electric and mechanical and chemical engineering, etc., occasionally sharing banking functions with MAH, presumably to co-ordinate policy and/or share risks.

The customer credit records have been analysed to establish PMKB's industrial financing policy and test the theoretical assumptions underlying the 'dominance', and/or the 'missionary' behaviour of the Bank during the 1920s. The task this study entailed was rewarding and frustrating at the same time as the Credit Register (Green Books; Z 34) contains all manner of loans recorded from 1907 to 1948 and has proved to be extremely revealing. However, the very minutiae of detail through which one has had to plough was so time consuming that analysis had to be restricted to one decade only.

The Green Books contain all domestic loans ranging from private individuals, to small business partnerships, to limited companies, to corporations and to other banks as well. It also records some foreign credit transactions negotiated for a client or groups of clients by the Bank. As the name of the Bank suggests, it concerned itself with a large number of small clients engaged in trade and commerce, one-man businesses, small and large retailers and wholesalers, as well as manufacturing enterprises of different kinds.

The PMKB was established on 14 October 1841 when Ferdinand V signed the charter, which provided – apart from licence to operate – twenty-five years of exemption from tax levy on income and mobile capital.[6] The establishment of the Bank was proposed by Moritz Ullmann, a wealthy merchant of Pest, and had been promoted by other merchants who felt obstructed in their commercial activity by the adverse credit conditions prevailing in the city. They felt that a specifically local financial institution would best serve local interests and would achieve the desired development of commerce in Hungary. This period was characterized by a heightened feeling of nationalist fervour, and desire to achieve independence from the Viennese banking houses was part of this process. The Bank's charter addressed the development and support of trade and industry and up to 1867 it founded various industrial enterprises.[7] After the *Ausgleich* its role became the continued support of existing commercial/industrial activity, rather than setting up enterprises. By the turn of the century its interest in mining and industry represented large-scale involvement in credit provision, emission of shares to raise capital, propositions of fusions to bring about rationalization in manufacturing and marketing.[8]

However, in 1896 the Bank's leading role in helping to develop new technology to meet new demands was evident when the Egger Electric Co. was set up as a limited liability company under the name of Egyesült Izzó (United Incandescent Lamp and Electric Ltd), which developed into a major concern during the interwar period with an injection of American capital.[9]

In the last decade of the nineteenth century PMKB drew into its sphere of interest[10] a major heavy industrial company, Rimamurány Salgótarján Iron Works Ltd, in order to ensure the continuous supply of iron rail for its district railway construction venture.

Several mining companies were brought under the umbrella of PMKB and the Wiener Bank-Verein (Hernádvölgy, Kalán) as well as the largest coal-mining company – Salgótarján Köszénbánya Rt. – at the end of the century. During the fifteen years of close association and support by the Bank, Salgó's total coal production output increased from 300,000 q to 24,000,000 q in 1914.[11] The other major mining company, the Hungarian General Coal Mine Ltd (MAK), refused PMKB's fusion/amalgamation proposals and entered into close business association with the competitor bank, the Hungarian General Credit Bank (MAH).[12]

In 1912 PMKB's machine engineering interest, Nicholson Machine Works, was set up through fusion with Schlick Shipbuilders as a limited company, called Schlick Nicholson Machine and Shipbuilding Ltd employing 2,600 workers.[13] The Bank's range of interest was evident in the agricultural industrial branches as well; in 1903 the First Budapest Steam Milling Ltd, Királmalom, Hedrich Strauss Ltd in the milling industry, Bácska (1911), Szolnok Sugar Refinery Ltd (1913) in food processing were set up to satisfy increasing domestic demand. Equally important in food processing, the PMKB supported Pig-Breeding and Meat Producing Ltd, which played a major role during the First World War in the public food supply.[14]

A further example of PMKB's progressive credit policy in

promoting technological advances is the chemical industry's Phylaxia Serum Producer Ltd which was sponsored by PMKB as early as 1914. In 1916 PMKB was also a founding member of the K27 million share capital venture to exploit natural gas at Kissármás (Magyar Föld Rt.) and was instrumental in financing the pipe system delivering the gas to Dicöszentmárton, which facilitated the establishment of the Hungarian Nitrogen Artificial Fertiliser Ltd. Together with MAH they provided K9 million share capital and extended large operational credits.[15] Also in 1916, PMKB purchased the First Hungarian Agricultural Machinery Ltd, its success accruing from producing the milling machinery which enjoyed strong demand on the Balkan markets.[16]

After the First World War, again anticipating modern development the Bank participated in the railway and road network reconstruction and extension, and expecting automobile transport to gain popularity it obtained Szobi Quarry Ltd, and later the Kissebes and Korlati Basalt Mines Ltd's share majority,[17] and with substantial investment extended their capacity to maximize their and the Bank's ability to profit from the country's road modernization programme.

As mentioned earlier, one of the original purposes behind setting up a domestic bank was to collect and mobilize domestic capital and to put it to a use which was deemed important for the nation's economic development. However, supporting the development of profitable enterprises thus furthering the modern industrial development of a predominantly agricultural country was only partially achieved by domestic banks. A large proportion of the investment venture capital still came from abroad, mainly from the Viennese banking houses during the pre-war period.[18] After 1918 the Bank's wide range of interest narrowed, but in 1925 it procured a foreign loan for forty-eight Hungarian cities ($10 million) which was to overcome the post-stabilization crisis.[19]

Table 10.2 indicates PMKB's participation in the manufacturing industry in 1947; most of these clients were already in the Bank's sphere of interest (through shareholding or founding and industrial financing) before or during the First World War.[20] During the post-war inflation years the Bank did everything in its power to save, rescue and support its client companies with share emissions, credit facility provisions and prolongation of the same.

The immediate post-war years were chaotic. The country reeled

Table 10.2. *PMKB's participation in the manufacturing industry in1947*

Budapest-Salgótarján Machine and Iron Works Ltd	88%
First Hungarian Mechanical Barrel Mfg Ltd	100%
Hydroxigen Ltd	37%
Királymalom, Hedrich & Strauss Ltd	40%
Hungarian Asphalt Ltd	66%
Hungarian Konfektio Works Ltd	18%
Hungarian Poszto Ltd (cloth mfg)	24%
Hungarian Food Transport and Goods Ltd	75%
Filial: Hungarian Game Export Ltd	
Mauthner Bros. & Co. (leather)	64%
Phylaxia Serum Producer Ltd	43%
Salgótarján Coal Mining Ltd	7%
Filial Cos.: Industrial Explosion Ltd	
Hungarian Electric Ltd	
Klotild, First Hung. Chemical Ind.	
Henrik Lapp Ltd	
Salgó Glass Ltd	
Szobi Quarry Ltd	44%
Szolnok Sugar Refinery Ltd	55%
Hunting Cartridge, Charge & Metal Works Ltd	33%
Zala County Basalt Mine Ltd	48%

Source: K. Jenei, *Pesti Magyar Kereskedelmi Bank és Beolvadt Vállalatai* (PMKB and Its Affiliated Companies) (Budapest, 1965, manuscript).

under the effects of a lost war, revolutions, undetermined reparation payments and territorial changes which disrupted the established financial, economic networks. One further crippling condition, a shortage of all manner of goods, resulting from the aforementioned disruptions, caused increasingly galloping inflation. Inflation wiped out the liquidity of the banks and savers, and thus venture capital was scarce for the better part of six years after the war.[21]

This was the period when the Hungarian banks had to fulfil a special role. As there was no alternative source of credit available, reconstruction of Hungary's economy depended on banks continuing a flexible credit policy towards productive enterprises which were to carry out the post-war reconstruction and restructuring to adjust to the changed geopolitical conditions.

Political reconstruction and stable social order depended on accommodating and employing returning soldiers; economic reconstruction depended on credit being available to begin the process, to establish sufficient confidence in the country's ability to function as a precondition for foreign capital to take a renewed interest in the disrupted region.

This is not to say that the banks consciously set about to create a new policy to aid national reconstruction. The policy evolved from existing preconditions and obligations. The banks had a large self-interest in saving/rescuing companies in their sphere of interest, partly because the banks may have had a shareholding in the company, or at least known them to have been reliable sources of revenue through conducting all their financial business with them ranging from commercial credit, to working capital provision, to share emissions. Initially they looked after their clients according to established, sound banking principles, lending on justifiable demand, expecting repayments according to agreed conditions. As, however, inflation increased pressure on providing larger and larger volumes of working capital, in order not to render already difficult conditions impossible, prolongations of repayments were authorized. Share capital increases also played a large role in credit provision, but the banks' role in providing a steadily increasing flow of working capital was inestimable. This is the picture emerging from the case studies of the PMKB.

The Green Book Register does not disclose the original request from the client; more often than not the reasons for the credit extension are withheld as well, and it also appears that some large clients in which PMKB had a special interest (usually a largish shareholding) also negotiated for and obtained so-called 'intern loans' from the Bank which are rarely recorded in the Register, but to which occasional references are made.

The selection of companies analysed in this paper is based on an endeavour to include as many industrial branches as possible, as well as companies which remained clients throughout the 1920s, in order to indicate the consistency of the policy which the Bank pursued towards them during the post-war years which included inflation, stabilization and a brief but relatively prosperous development period.

One indication that a special bank–client relation was being formed was the establishment of a so-called 'banker's agreement'. This agreement or undertaking in effect meant that in exchange for credit facilities, loans or overdrafts the client companies agreed to conduct all their financial transactions with PMKB for a stipulated period, usually for the anticipated duration of the credit extension. This would have ensured that all bank charges and commissions would accrue to the Bank (including those on share emissions), as well as the Bank being able to keep an eye on the companies' business activities to protect the Bank's investment.

The sample of companies includes the following industrial branches: mining, smelting; engineering; civil engineering; electrical industry; timber; textile; cloth weaving, ready garment manufacture; milling, food processing; chemical industry; artificial fertilizer; small arms; hunting cartridge manufacture.

The policy of the PMKB is well illustrated by the first two examples: Hardwood Producer Ltd and Hungarian Plywood Mfg Ltd.[22] Both companies had been clients of the Bank since before 1918, both enjoyed credit facilities which were extended on a short-term (three months) basis, which were renewed and increased repeatedly, and both conducted their banking business exclusively with PMKB. Company fusion took place in November 1921, presumably at the instigation of the Bank to reduce competition between them and to rationalize their trade practices.

According to the records Hardwood's initial overdraft limit was K650,000 in February 1919, which was increased to K2 million by 1920 and prolonged without repayment; whilst occasional commodity credits for bulk purchases were enjoyed, these latter appear to have been repaid.

Plywood was granted a K3 million overdraft facility in 1918 for three years, which by 1921 grew to a total of K26.5 million made up of four different loans. On fusion a combined K40 million overdraft was granted and in return the Bank was to appoint half of the directorate. By 1924 the credit limit had been increased to K1,500 million, but complete access to the company's books/records had been requested by the Bank to ensure overseeing the safety of the Bank's investment.[23] By October 1926 the credit limit went up to K7,350 million, not because the company was in any kind of financial difficulty, but because the post-stabilization credit squeeze slowed down business activity generally, and the Bank had to step in to continue providing credit during the lean period. The same overdraft facility was carried on (converted to Pengö 500,000 in December 1927) with a seasonal credit having been provided separately, and both of these were prolonged to 15 December 1929.[24]

The immediate post-war years' increases in the credit facility were in line with the slower pace of inflation, but as inflation gathered pace the overdraft limit grew from K40 million in 1922 to K1,500 million in 1924. During 1925/6, operating capital was scarce owing to the League of Nations Controller's insistence on concentrating on balancing the budget, and enforcing tight credit/monetary policies. This caused a slump in the economy, and further increases were approved in the overdraft provision from K1,500 million to K7,500 million in 1926. It is quite clear that monetary stabilization did not reduce the need for increasing capital injection by the Bank. Whether this was due to increased business activity (as might have been with the state-sponsored and fast developing textile industry) or difficulties experienced in coping with competition from domestic or inter-national sources can only be ascertained by following each company's archive material, which unfortunately are extant only for the larger concerns.

In the case of these two companies one can only make educated guesses, as Hungary lost the majority of its timber industry owing to territorial changes after the First World War, so the increasing credit demand after stabilization may well indicate having to expand pro-duction to satisfy domestic demand. The periodic adjustment of con-ditions attached to the credit provisions also reflect the Bank's attempt to keep up with inflation in order to protect its liquidity. For instance, the interest charged was determined by a cartel agreement among the large banks, initially based on the base rate of the Austro-Hungarian Bank, later on the Hungarian National Bank's (shown as Bk + 1.5% = 6.5% in 1920). This was supplemented by a quarterly 1 per cent commission on the outstanding amount. As monetary inflation quickened, the quarterly commission grew to 0.375 per cent in 1920, and to 1 per cent in 1921. When a longer-term (two-year) loan was negotiated in 1920[25] a fixed sum of K30 per cubic metre of wood sold had to be paid to the Bank over and above the existing interest/com-mission rates to recoup losses on the depreciating loan.

Indicative of how scarce working/investment capital was during the post-stabilization credit squeeze is the case of Hungarian Brown-Boveri Ltd.[26] When in March 1925 they prolonged their K500 million overdraft by a month, the cartel interest charged amounted to 14.5 per cent, plus 1 per cent turnover commission, plus 0.75 per cent bank commission. This being an engineering company of Swiss origin producing turbines, even the 1 per cent turnover commission must have been considerable revenue to the Bank, over and above the high 14.5 per cent interest rate, and equally a substantial cost to the manufacturer.

Surprisingly, the textile industry, which was a government-sponsored industrialization project in order to reduce Hungary's trade deficit by import substitution, was not given preferential treatment by the Bank. Hungarian Konfectio[27] had been charged in 1920 min. 5.5 per cent interest, plus 1.5 per cent turnover commission, plus quarterly 0.5 per cent bank commission on the outstanding amount. By 1923, over and above cartel interest a monthly 3 per cent bank commission was charged,[28] a so called 'credit insurance commission'. Whenever a foreign currency loan was requested, such as for a compulsory quota of hard currency to be contributed by industrial companies to help accumulate reserves for the newly set up Hungarian National Bank (MNB valuta loan), or having to find foreign currency for the compulsory purchase of MNB shares in 1924, the interest charged was 15–16 per cent p.a.[29]

Occasional references were made to substantial *intern credits* as in Posztogyar[30] K1,500 million in July 1926, which in this case was included in the Register because it had to be prolonged, but originally it was presumably kept out of sight because compared to the share capital of the company it was disproportionately large. It is not known how long this intern credit had been in operation, or for what purpose (investment or working capital) it was used.

The next example, Nitrogen (artificial fertilizer),[31] was financed jointly by the two large banks, MAH 60 per cent, PMKB 40 per cent, and as early as November 1918 when the French put the company into operation, the Bank's conditions to extend credit included a request for an exclusive 'banker's agreement' for fifteen years, and commission on sales, rather than interest charged. In case the French venture did not become profitable, the Bank stipulated the right to cancel the credit or to convert the loan amount to shares held by the banks. Again, the amount of the loan grew in line with inflation, from K4 million in 1918 to K3,000 million in 1925.[32]

Much the same story can be told for the two food-processing companies.[33] Both enjoyed increasing credit facilities, for an 'indefinite period', both continued beyond stabilization, and apart from the commodity credits the facility was extended to 1929.

Rimamurány-Salgótarján Iron Works Ltd was one of the largest joint interest venture concerns between a large coalmine (Salgó) and a smelting concern (Rima), created in 1921.[34] PMKB was the main banker (75 per cent) with Wiener Bank-Verein as partner (25 per cent). an agreement to this effect was drawn up for ten years to provide credit facility to the company. A note in 1922 refers to a change in the banker's agreement, which stipulated a 50–50 interest by the two banks and the credit limit raised to K700 million.[35] This agreement appointed the two banks' representatives to the Vice-Presidency in each company. It also linked the Rima and Salgó Boards: each company was to nominate two directors and exchange them to sit on the Executive Committee and the Supervisory Board.[36] In 1923 it is disclosed that over and above 'present intern credit' an additional K2,000 million was granted for two weeks. Even if we assume that the additional amount was repaid in time, the next reference[37] still indicates that a P1 million (equivalent to K10,000 million) loan was still outstanding and prolonged to as late as June 1928. This was granted in spite of a large $3 million restructuring loan from Liesmann & Co. New York in 1925.[38] One explanation of the need for continued bank support may have been Rima's large production capacity which remained a problem despite product diversification and increasing exports on the largely protected markets of Eastern Europe.[39]

Salgótarján Köszén Rt.'s (coalmine) record in the Register only indicated three months' acceptance credits and bills of exchange credits which were guaranteed by the Bank, and even these were prolonged repeatedly. Under the Bank's Document Register,[40] however, the intern credit arrangements are revealed. This 'intern credit' amounted to K2 million in 1914, when a new 'banker's agreement' was signed for five years, which was increased and prolonged to an amount of K1,000 million in 1923, and further extended to K3,450 million in December.[41] Furthermore, during the later 1920s when foreign capital was again available, a $2.05 million two-year loan had been negotiated by PMKB at 7.5 per cent, with three Swiss banks providing the bulk of the loan and $1.3 million in 1928. Part of this was made up by PMKB and Wiener Bank-Verein each contributing $350,000. This dollar loan was repaid on 21 April 1931.[42]

Szobi Quarry Ltd also has a full record in the PMKB Green Book Register. This company was particularly supported by the Bank as a potential profit spinner, as it was anticipated that it would take advantage of the reconstruction of rail and road system of Hungary and would also benefit from the development of road transport with the advent of the automobile as a new mode of transport. This company was set up during the war,[43] and records in November 1919 a share capital of K3 million, of which 50 per cent was owned by the Bank. This entitled the Bank to nominate half of the directorate, as well as in 1920 to extend a K1 million overdraft, initially for two months. This was prolonged and increased to K2 million in April 1921, and prolonged again to June. The amount was increased over the months to K3.5 million in January 1922 and in May an additional K6 million was granted for construction work for seven months.[44]

The conditions stipulated that if the loan was not repaid on time the Bank could insist on a share issue to recoup the loan. This appears to have happened[45] in March 1925 when it is noted that the Bank then held a 54 per cent majority of the shares (previously 46.66 per cent). To enable the company to sell on credit to public authorities and thus to utilize its increased capacity the Bank approved an overdraft of K2,000 million in 1924. It is indicative of the scarcity of capital at the height of the inflation that this credit was considered to be a viable proposition although in addition to the conditions of the credit a high cartel interest rate plus a commission of 3 per cent monthly had to be paid.[46]

Again it is notable that the post-stabilization deflationary measures imposed by the League of Nations' Controller forced the Bank to maintain its credit policy towards the company. This time in order to extend its production capacity a credit was provided[47] for an 'indefinite period' in 1927. The reason for this appears to be not the desire of the Bank to increase its shareholding or influence/dominance in the company, but because no other source of credit was available until the latter part of the 1920s, when foreign capital began to flow in, albeit only towards the larger companies and mostly on a short- to medium-term basis.

During the period 1925 to 1928 these additional credits cost the company over and above cartel interest and commission a so-called 'factura commission' of 5 per cent on public utility deliveries and 3 per cent on private sales based on turnover. This was reduced to 2 per cent in 1928,[48] indicating that shortage of venture capital must have been a very real bottleneck in the development of the manufacturing industry.

Vadásztöltény (hunting cartridge manufacturing) also operated on cartel interest and commission and a substantial percentage of factura commission. This was 10 per cent in 1922, 15 per cent in 1924, at the height of the inflation,[49] as the price for the credit facility. The harshest conditions applied were in 1925, during the deflation period, when the K500 million overdraft was increased to K3,000 million and cartel interest plus 7 per cent p.a. credit insurance commission, plus 10 per cent turnover commission was charged. The credit was continually prolonged[50] and the record shows the substantial amounts of factura commission collected: for instance, from July to December 1924 K1,919 million, for 1927 P98,593.[51] Even as late as 1927 the price of credit was high: the cartel interest plus monthly 0.125 per cent commission amounting to 10.7 per cent plus a 6 per cent turnover commission must have further reduced profitability.[52]

Similar PMKB financing support was experienced by United Incandescent Lamp and Electric Ltd. Apart from three-monthly draft credits[53] (often prolonged), the company also utilized substantial 'short-term' prolonged credit injections during the inflation period. During 1923 extension of facilities and increases were common, K1,000 million to K2,000 million,[54] but policy continued into the late 1920s for an 'indefinite period'.[55] A separate loan was provided for share purchases in 1925 when together with Niederösterreichische Escompte Gesellschaft PMKB extended a K2,300 million credit.[56] The same two banks organized a $600,000 loan on the current account for a year on a 50–50 basis in January 1927[57] at 8 per cent, which relatively low rate indicates that the source was foreign. Nevertheless, Pengö credit provisions continued despite this dollar loan; in 1928 it amounted to P1.5 million.[58]

The First Budapest Steam Mill Ltd is another example of pre-First World War interest being supported by PMKB. Post-war shortages necessitated the first recorded loan in 1920 which financed Yugoslavian corn imports for spirit distillation, for which K20 million was extended for a year (returning cartel interest and 5 per cent of the profit on the transaction). Apart from the normal PMKB 'intern credit' which in 1921 amounted to K200 million on current account and K500 million for drafts,[59] which had grown to K2,000 million by 1926, short-term foreign currency credits in Yugoslav crowns were maintained to facilitate export ranging between SHS K7.5 million in 1921 to SHS K17.5 million in 1923.[60] In addition Czech crown credits were also extended, Kč1 million in 1924 at 20 per cent interest prolonged six months later at 15 per cent, as well as in Romanian lei.[61] After stabilization of the currency this well-known milling concern attracted short-term foreign capital. PMKB procured a six-month credit of $600,000 at 10 per cent in November 1924. This was replaced by a £500,000 credit extended by Guinness Mahon & Co. of London in June 1925, with PMKB collecting an additional $4^1/2$ plus 2 per cent interest. This appears to have been extended as late as 1928,[62] with PMKB taking a 10 per cent share in the credit provision. Another major source of short-term credit was the Schweizerische Bankverein who together with PMKB on an 80–20 per cent basis extended a $1 million credit in May 1926. It was a kind of rolling credit with an anticipated monthly usage of $300,000, and each amount utilized was to have been repaid within nine months. In May 1928 this was reduced to $250,000 (PMKB taking a fifth share) and prolonged further.[63]

The consequence of stringent financial policy pursued by architects of Hungarian stabilization was not unanticipated. As Siepmann reported to the Foreign Office on the consequences of stabilization: 'Hungary is entering upon a difficult period . . . The difficulties are partly due to fiscal, but mainly to financial and hardly at all to fundamental economic causes. Outwardly these difficulties may be expected to take the form of high interest rates, a struggle between the reluctance or incapacity of buyers and the holders of commodity stocks, distress among the middle classes, unemployment (though not on any dangerous scale) and frequent failures among the smaller firms . . . and for special reasons not peculiar to Hungary, in iron and steel, leather and (more occasionally) textiles.' It was anticipated, however, that 'business fusions and amalgamations (especially among banks and finance houses) and the consequent economies due to reduction of overhead charges and better management' will alleviate problems. It was predicted optimistically that 'the whole process should be accomplished without heavy loss, except where the parasitical growth resulting from currency inflation have to be got rid of'.[64] It was not at all appreciated how far and how long the capital scarcity would affect the whole manufacturing industry.

The case studies here analysed provide evidence that even well-established and well-managed firms, who did not suffer from 'parasitical growth', had to pay a crippling price for the only source of credit available to them. It appears from the records that the Bank, far from trying to maintain or extend its finance monopoly in the economy – as Hungarian historiography still contends – was forced by historical obligations and economic circumstances and pressured to continue to maintain the liquidity of the client companies, at times going against sound banking principles.

The long series of initially short-term credit extensions (three to six months) as overdraft facilities, and their continuous prolongation, sometimes lasting for a decade or longer, are evidence of this practice, even if in the first place it was not seen by the Bank as a policy. The fact that during the inflation years of 1918–24 the 'short-term' overdraft credits were increased repeatedly to keep pace with monetary inflation as well as prolonged, also attests to this policy of having to bail client companies out, when no other source of finance was available.

Most surprisingly, this practice continued even after stabilization: since only the large and well-known companies attracted foreign investment, the smaller companies paid a high price for their domestic credit supply. Nothing indicates more the critical shortage of venture capital in Hungary than the high cost of domestic credit, i.e. 10.7 per cent plus 6 per cent factura commission in 1927, compared to the 'lucky' few like Salgó 'only' having to pay 7.5 per cent interest on its foreign loan with a 0.5 per cent commission to the procuring banks in 1928.[65]

Perhaps the most eloquent expression of the regression of long-term lending can be gleaned from the PMKB balance sheet from 1900 to 1930 (even to 1940) (table 10.3). Whereas during its pre-First World War development, concurrently with increasing accumulation of savings and share capital, the long-term lending had been a much larger volume than short-term placements, in 1939 long-term lending (K585.9 million) was 32.6 per cent above the level of short-term lending (K441.9 million).

It is further evident that during the war and inflation years long-term loans were being repaid in depreciating currency to the extent that in 1922 (before inflation totally distorted the statistics) the long-term lending of K639.2 million had been reduced to only 20.3 per cent (K3,143.1 million) of short-term lending. This trend against long-term lending did not improve greatly after the stabilization of the currency in 1924, when banks and companies were obliged by law to restore financial accounting (value of assets and liabilities) to a realistic value (the so-called 'gold' balance sheet of 1925) and express

Table 10.3. *The development of PMKB's capital lending and participation trends (in million crowns & Pengö)*

	Share + reserves	Savings + current a/c deposits	Short-term lending	Long-term lending	Securities & participation
Pre-First World War					
1900	K54.8 million	K138.1	K170.1	280.3	28.8
1905	71.0	189.2	210.1	381.5	40.9
1910	117.6	311.4	324.4	482.0	98.5
1913	162.3	399.9	441.9	585.9	129.4
Inflationary years					
1918/19	314.2	K2,794.0	1,411.3	606.8	1061.5
1920	314.2	3,370.3	1,942.1	605.6	605.3
1921	320.0	4,058.6	2,140.2	615.6	756.1
1922	517.5	5,935.4	3,143.1	639.2	1169.4
Post-stabilization years (in Pengö)					
1925	P50.0	P82.3	P71.0	nil	44.7
1926	50.2	128.7	116.3	15.2	39.7
1927	50.6	190.4	174.1	39.7	42.2
1928	51.5	216.5	202.0	58.2	45.1
1929	52.6	245.2	205.2	68.1	45.0
1930	53.5	251.3	223.3	79.2	46.0
1940	51.9	323.1	383.5	55.2	85.7

Source: Compiled from *A Pesti Magyar Kereskedelmi Bank Százéves Története 1841–1941* (The Centenary of the Hungarian Commercial Bank 1841–1941) (Budapest, 1941), Addendum pp. 6–7, 12–13.

them in the new Pengö currency as well as eliminating the distortion of inflationary valuations.

Between 1925 and 1930 PMKB recorded a steady accumulation on savings and current accounts, yet long-term lending which admittedly started from a nil position in 1925, never reached let alone overtook the level of short-term lending. In other words, it never returned to the pre-war trend. In 1930 the latter was 182 per cent more than long-term lending. By 1940 the proportion between the two types of lending deteriorated even further.

The case studies certainly indicated heavy reliance on the Bank for capital mostly extended piecemeal on short-term bases, and the Bank's altogether changed lending policy is graphically illustrated in table 10.3 in absolute figures, as well as in a statistically more informative form in the percentage of lending relative to PMKB's total capital in table 10.4.

Table 10.4. *Structure of assets of PMKB, 1900–30 (per cent)*

	1900	1910	1913	1925	1926	1927	1928	1929	1930
Cash	1	1	1	14	9	6	5	12	10
Bills & advances	34	34	36	50	57	61	60	54	55
Securities & participation	6	10	11	31	20	15	13	12	11
Long-term credits	56	51	48	—	8	14	17	18	19
Other	3	4	4	4	6	5	5	4	4

Source: Compiled from *A Pesti Magyar Kereskedelmi Bank Százéves Története 1841–1941* (The Centenary of the Hungarian Commercial Bank 1841–1941 (Budapest, 1941), Addendum, pp. 6–7, 12–13.

Examination of the PMKB's structure of assets (table 10.4) also confirms the trend indicated by the case studies. Bills and advances increase most markedly during the post-stabilization deflation period from the pre-war 35–36 per cent to 57–60 per cent of total assets in 1926 to 1928, while long-term lending dramatically drops from the pre-war 50 per cent to 19 per cent of assets in 1930.

The thesis that banks through shareholding and participation gained a dominant position as a result of their industrial financing is not confirmed by the investigation. The structure of assets indicates that pre-war securities and participation amounted to between 6 and 11 per cent, which was very similar to the late 1920s too. What is notable, however, is the dramatic increase in the 1925 'gold' balance sheet valuation figure (31 per cent of total assets) which might well indicate that during the inflation period the companies did indeed alienate some of their shares to the Bank in return for credit or share emission provisions/services. Nevertheless, it is also clear that the proportion of shares held did not indicate conscious accumulation in order to extend the Bank's dominance over industry. As far as the Bank's economic power was implied in the credit provision, it fluctuated with conditions of demand and supply and depended on what alternative sources of finance – profit plough back, foreign capital, other financial intermediaries – it was possible to tap. It does appear that the inflation period of 1918–24 did increase industry's dependence on the Bank. The 1925 percentage figure of securities held being so high indicates this. Furthermore, even after stabilization there was little scope for profit retention as margins were reduced by new taxes and the fiscal restraints also prompted companies to maintain their ties with their bankers for further credit provision. The larger companies were able to borrow from abroad, the terms of which were somewhat more favourable than on the domestic front, but since smaller companies had no such choice they had to suffer the higher rate for the credits provided. Certainly during the post-war reconstruction period the Bank extended surprisingly large short-term credits, particularly during the inflation and deflation period. A more 'prudent' credit policy, more in line with the companies' assets, on the other hand, would have undermined the otherwise sound smaller manufacturing companies. Since the Bank had sufficient insight into any expansion programmes to ensure their viability, and indeed often proposed concentrations/rationalizations which the companies found difficult to resist, the alternative, that is, a more restrictive credit policy, would have aggravated the macroeconomic consequences in terms of unemployment and production. Desire for 'dominance', however, is not indicated statistically because after 1925 when conditions returned to 'normal' the accumulated participation holdings were quickly reduced to the pre-war level, that is, 12 per cent of total assets in 1929.

As to whether the Bank pursued a 'missionary' role after the First World War, quantitative analysis is not conclusive about this thesis. Table 10.3 indicates that adding together short- and long-term lending, the result shows an upward trend in absolute terms before the First World War and afterwards as well. If, however, one analyses the structure of PMKB's assets (table 10.4), adding together Bills & advances and Long-term credits, the result – as a proportion of total assets – shows that pre-war lending of 90 per cent (in 1900) of total assets declined to 84 per cent by 1913 and 50 per cent in 1925, and the maximum reached before the depression only amounted to 77 per cent of total assets in 1928. It appears that during the post-war period when conditions did necessitate greater dependence on the Bank, the lending – as a percentage of total assets – did not increase, if anything it decreased.

The conclusion one can draw therefore is that during the reconstruction period in Hungary a more genuine interdependence developed between PMKB and industry. The companies, particularly the medium-sized ones, on the one hand, had no alternative but to use the Bank as intermediary for credit (foreign long-term loans were scarce even for large concerns). The Bank, on the other hand, was prepared to supply them with credit, albeit at a price, in order to safeguard its interests, be it in substantial or marginal shareholding in the companies. A more mundane reason might have been (even at the risk of stating the obvious) that companies were supported because prolonged financing interlinked the Bank's management with boards of directors and insight into business convinced them that the companies were viable propositions, so it made sense to continue lending especially as financial rewards accruing to the Bank were not negligible either.

One hypothesis of mine, albeit not tested empirically as yet, is that the break-up of the Austro-Hungarian Empire caused the Bank to lose a number of its branches to the successor states with consequent loss of banking business, which may have encouraged PMKB to involve itself in more intensive industrial financing activity at home to make up the shortfall in revenue, especially as it was perceived to be safe and secure as a result of directorate interlinkages. Furthermore, the Hungarian state also promoted domestic industrialization, with tax, freight concessions and rapid amortization on productive investment, which enhanced the commercial viability of the Bank's industrial financing policy. Nevertheless, as the volume of credit extension (long- and short-term) as a percentage of total assets did not reach the pre-war level, it is difficult to see a 'missionary' role played by the Bank during the post-war decade.

NOTES

* This paper was prepared for the International Workshop held at Uppsala University, Sweden, 10–12 September 1989. I am grateful to the British and Hungarian Academies for financial assistance towards the underlying research, and to Monash University for its support with travel grants. Also warmest gratitude should be expressed to the late Gy. Ránki, Director of the Institute of History at Budapest, who unfailingly assisted the research. Furthermore, the co-operation of the archivists at the Hungarian National Archives was most appreciated.

1 R. Hilferding, *Finance Capital: A Study of the Latest Phase of Capitalist Development* (London, 1981).

2 A. Gerschenkron, *Economic Backwardness in Historical Perspective* (New York, 1965). Both these theoretical assumptions are tested in the light of the present state of research by A. Teichova, *Rivals and Partners: Banking and Industry in Europe in the First Decade of the Twentieth Century*, Uppsala Papers in Economic History, no. 1 (1988).

3 J. Komlos, *The Habsburg Monarchy as a Customs Union* (Princeton, N.J., 1963), p. 114.

4 *Ibid.*; this is the thesis of the book. Also: P. Hanák, 'Hungary in the Austro-Hungarian monarchy: preponderancy or dependency?', *Austrian History Yearbook*, 3 (1967), 260–302.

5 *A Pesti Magyar Kereskedelmi Bank Százéves Története 1841–1941* (The Centenary History of the Commercial Bank of Pest) (Budapest, 1941), p. 62.

6 K. Jenei, *Pesti Magyar Kereskedelmi Bank és beolvadt vállalatai* (The Hungarian Commercial Bank of Pest and its affiliated companies) (Budapest, 1965) (Repertorium manuscript).

7 *Ibid.*, p. 18.

8 *A Pesti Magyar Kereskedelmi Bank*, p. 128.

9 *Ibid.*, p. 138.

10 *Ibid.*, p. 136. There is, unfortunately, no definition given as to what is meant by 'drawn into the Bank's sphere of interest'. Descriptions on how this process is achieved include facilitating share emissions, acquisitions of competitor company's shares with view to merger, extensions of overdraft facilities (main creditor), resulting in bank's shareholding in companies included in sphere of interest, with bank's representation on the Board of Directors of a given concern. György Köver in *Bank and Industry in Hungary before 1914* (Manuscript contribution to the Uppsala Workshop) also touches upon this problem, see p. 11.

11 *Ibid.*, p. 137.

12 Jenei, *Pesti Magyar*.

13 *A Pesti Magyar Kereskedelmi Bank*, pp. 164–5.

14 *Ibid.*, pp. 160–2.

15 *Ibid.*, p. 163.

16 *Ibid.*, p. 164.

17 *Ibid.*, p. 165.

18 E. März, *Austrian Banking and Financial Policy: Creditanstalt at a Turning Point* (London, 1984), p. 89.

19 *Ibid.*, p. 203.

20 Jenei, *Pesti Magyar*.

21 E. A. Boross, 'The effects of inflation on the Hungarian manufacturing industry' (PhD thesis, University of East Anglia, 1984).

22 Országos Levéltár (OL) (Hungarian National Archives) PMKB Z34 Green Books, 5224, 5680, 5710, 6181, 6275, 5122, 5292, 5535, 6430, 6431, 7689.

23 *Ibid.*, 9517.

24 *Ibid.*, 13593.

25 *Ibid.*, 5710.

26 *Ibid.*, 9821.

27 *Ibid.*, 5753.

28 *Ibid.*, 8622.

29 *Ibid.*, 9113, 9112.

30 *Ibid.*, 11053.

31 *Ibid.*, 5168.

32 *Ibid.*, 9904.

33 *Ibid.*, 5086, 5838, 8089, 8862, 10832, 11382, 12187, 13345, 13658, 6802, 7831, 8555, 10620, 11358, 12356, 13273.

34 *Ibid.*, 6434.

35 OL PMKB Z36 149cz N-Z 1922.

36 *Ibid.*

37 *Ibid.*, Z34/8646, 12968.

38 *Ibid.*, Z41/191g 1925; also in *A Pesti Magyar Kereskedelmi Bank*, p. 202.
39 Boross, 'The effects of inflation'.
40 OL PMKB Z41/83, 26 June 1914, 1550g/IX, 14 Sept. 1922.
41 *Ibid.*, Z34/8832.
42 *Ibid.*, 12915.
43 *Ibid.*, 5258.
44 *Ibid.*, 6309, 7101.
45 *Ibid.*, 9810
46 *Ibid.*, 9610.
47 *Ibid.*, 11657 in 1927.
48 *Ibid.*, 12816.
49 *Ibid.*, 6920, 8958.
50 *Ibid.*, 9836, 10668.
51 *Ibid.*, 9917, 12756.
52 *Ibid.*, 11714.
53 *Ibid.*, 8493, 8746.
54 *Ibid.*, 8685, 9096, 9330.
55 *Ibid.*, 12409, 12531.
56 *Ibid.*, 10048.
57 *Ibid.*, 11566.
58 *Ibid.*, 12409, 12531.
59 *Ibid.*, 5678, 7549.
60 *Ibid.*, 11356, 6829, 8023.
61 *Ibid.*, 9074, 9154, 7804, 8203.
62 *Ibid.*, 9575, 10047, 13257.
63 *Ibid.*, 10888.
64 Foreign Office (FO) 371/10772/C4189/260/26, Siepmann Report on the consequences of stabilization in Hungary, 15 March 1925.
65 OL PMKB X34/12915.

11 The rise and fall of German-inspired mixed banking in Italy, 1894–1936

DOUGLAS J. FORSYTH

The world economic depression of the early 1930s produced a major banking crisis in Italy, as in other continental European countries – including Germany and Austria – where commercial banking was dominated by mixed or universal banks. The two largest commercial banks in Italy, the Banca Commerciale Italiana (Comit) and the Credito Italiano (Credit), became insolvent in the course of 1930 and 1931, and a general banking panic was averted only by timely, and essentially secret government intervention. As a consequence of further losses posted by these banks during 1932, the worst year of the depression, government authorities undertook a more fundamental restructuring of the commercial banking system in 1933 and early 1934. Following these measures, the majority of the share capital of the Comit and the Credit, as well as the Banco di Roma – the third largest commercial bank in the country – passed into state hands. In Germany and Austria too control of most of the largest commercial banks passed into state hands as a result of liquidity crises and government rescue operations in the early 1930s. However, only in Italy did the financial crisis lead to major institutional reforms, including the termination of the commercial banks' former role as holding companies of industrial enterprises; the permanent nationalization of the largest commercial banks, and their reorganization as 'Banks of National Interest' (Banche di Interesse Nazionali); and the creation of a state holding company owning a substantial proportion of the country's manufacturing capacity (Istituto di Riconstruzione Industriale, Institute of Industrial Reconstruction, or IRI).

In Germany, the commercial banks had more modest portfolios of

179

industrial stock at the time of the crisis than was the case in Italy, and therefore the state did not assume control over a significant proportion of the country's manufacturing capacity. The seven major banks that failed in the crisis were reorganized and reprivatized again in the course of 1936 and 1937. Although the Nazi state created a new regulatory agency to oversee commercial banking (Aufsichtsamt für Kreditwesen), it made no attempt to alter radically the functioning of the universal banks or their relationships with industrial clients. In Austria the leading commercial banks had become industrial holding companies prior to the onset of the depression, as was the case in Italy. Here, the public rescue of the three largest commercial banks between 1931 and 1934 caused an important proportion of the country's industrial capacity to fall into state hands. Moreover, the weakness of the Austrian capital market prevented the government from reprivatizing the banks prior to the Anschluss with Germany in 1938. The Austrian authorities also restructured the commercial banking system, merging the three failed banks into a single organization (the Credit-Anstalt); however, in contrast to their Italian counterparts, they made no effort to transform fundamentally commercial banking practice or reorder the Credit-Anstalt's relationship with its industrial clientele.[1]

Only in Italy, therefore, did the financial crisis of the 1930s mark a major rupture in the history of financial institutions, and the relationship between banks and industry.[2] In effect, measures taken in 1933 (the creation of the IRI), in 1934 (the acquisition by the IRI of the equity portfolios of the commercial banks) and in 1936 (the banking reform law) terminated a forty-year era in Italian economic history in which mixed or universal banks had played a pre-eminent role in industrial finance, a period which began with the reorganization of the country's largest issue bank, the Bank of Italy, in 1893, and the foundation of the Banca Commerciale Italiana and the Credito Italiano in 1894 and 1895 respectively.

This paper addresses the question of why the outcome of the Italian banking crisis was so different from the banking crises elsewhere in Central Europe, despite broad similarities in the nature of universal banking throughout the region, and similarities in the proximate causes of the Austrian, German and Italian financial crises of the early 1930s. Two key aspects of the Italian situation will be addressed: (1) the weaknesses of the Italian industrial securities market; and

(2) tensions between central bank and Treasury authorities in Rome on the one hand, and the leadership of the big commercial banks, particularly the biggest commercial bank (the Comit), in Milan on the other.[3] It will be argued that the fundamental weaknesses of the Italian mixed banking system had already emerged prior to the First World War, but that the economic and financial consequences of the war, together with the fascist government's monetary and financial policies in the 1920s, exacerbated the problems confronting Italy's commercial bankers, leading in the early 1930s to the collapse and restructuring of the mixed banks, and sweeping changes in the ownership, organization and functioning of major banking and industrial concerns.

Mixed banking in Italy in the 'Giolittian era'

The German-inspired mixed or universal banks were the fulcrum of industrial finance in the so-called Giolittian era in the early years of the century. As Alexander Gerschenkron and others have demonstrated, the mixed banks, notably the Comit and the Credit, which were founded by German-led international banking syndicates in 1894 and 1895 respectively, played a leading role in promoting Italian economic growth. These two banks participated intensively in the so-called 'big spurt' 1898–1907, when average annual increases in industrial output reached 6.7 per cent, the highest sustained rate of growth in Italy prior to the 'economic miracle' of 1958–63. The mixed banks not only engaged in ordinary commercial operations, but also made long-term industrial investments. They actively participated in the formation of joint-stock companies by underwriting and purchasing securities. Bank directors commonly sat on the boards of companies with which the banks maintained close financial relations.[4]

But the rapid process of growth predicated on mixed banking bore with it significant costs. As Gianni Toniolo has recently noted, the involvement of deposit-taking banks in industrial promotion is inherently pro-cyclical and lends instability to the financial system.[5] The major commercial banks did not aspire to become holding companies by retaining majority interests in the industrial concerns whose securities they promoted. Rather, the key goals in the banks' industrial promotion activities were to earn profits through underwriting commissions, and by acquiring the normal, commercial

banking business of the firms they sponsored. Nevertheless, the practices of the commercial banks made them almost as vulnerable both to
fluctuations in the earning potential and in the equity value of the
manufacturing firms they maintained relations with, as if they owned
the firms outright. Banks made commercial loans against industrial
securities deposited as collateral, making their loan portfolios vulnerable to fluctuations in stock prices. Further, nominally commercial
loans were often used to finance fixed investments; in good times,
manufacturing firms would repay such credits by issuing stock or
bonds on the securities markets; in bad times, however, the banks'
commercial portfolios tended to become illiquid. The vulnerability of
the mixed banks to a decline in industrial activity ensured that a
recession in manufacturing would ripple rapidly through the banking
system and the economy as a whole. Relatively minor shocks on the
securities markets could produce crisis and stagnation for the entire
economy. Such was the case in 1907, when a third mixed bank
founded on the model of the Banca Commerciale and the Credito Italiano, the Società Bancaria Italiana (SBI), failed, provoking a general
collapse of industrial securities prices. The traditional preference of
Italy's middle classes for investments perceived as being more secure,
such as national and foreign government securities, and savings bank
deposits, was reinforced, while demand for industrial securities stagnated. As a consequence, Italian firms were no longer able to raise substantial sums of capital on the securities market. In the period
1907–13, the rate of growth of industrial output slowed to only 2.4 per
cent. On the eve of the First World War, Italy faced economic stagnation,
largely because of the virtual cessation of industrial investment.[6]

The role of the state in favouring investments in non-competitive
heavy industries tended to exacerbate the problem. The mixed banks
favoured industries that enjoyed tariff protection, subsidies and state
contracts. A significant proportion of the total share capital invested
in Italian joint-stock companies was tied up in iron and steel manufacturing, shipbuilding, armaments and companies exploiting subsi-
dized shipping lines. Such investments drained resources from the
consumer-oriented sectors of the economy, and the overall multiplier
effect of strategic investments was probably modest.

The structural vulnerabilities of Italy's financial system were aggravated by a long-standing, bitter conflict between Treasury and Bank of
Italy authorities in Rome and the leadership of the largest commercial

banks in Milan. The conflict had its origins in the financial crisis of 1893. At that time, the two largest commercial banks in the peninsula, the Credito Mobiliare and the Banca Generale, along with an important Roman issue bank, the Banca Romana, failed. It was in the wake of this crisis that the Banca Commerciale and the Credito Italiano were founded by German-led international banking syndicates. Meanwhile, Parliament enacted legislation consolidating three of the six issue banks which the Kingdom of Italy had inherited from the predecessor states to form the Bank of Italy. The Bank of Italy, which continued to share the privilege of issuing banknotes with two smaller southern banks, the Banco di Napoli and the Banco di Sicilia, was envisaged by the legislators as an instrument of stronger public regulation and intervention in the financial markets. However, the new issue bank was constrained to absorb the stricken Banca Romana, and emerged from the crisis with a portfolio of bad loans and overvalued real estates assets, which it was obliged to liquidate over the following two decades. The Bank of Italy was thus in no condition to pursue an active monetary policy in the early years of the 'big spurt', when the Banca Commerciale and the Credito Italiano were consolidating their positions in the Italian financial and industrial world. As the Bank of Italy became stronger after the turn of the century, it sought to play a more active role on the financial markets; however, the leading Milanese banks were unwilling to submit to its authority.

Sharp conflicts developed between the leadership of Italy's largest private banks and the premier issue bank in two key areas: the Milanese institutions resisted the Bank of Italy's efforts to regulate interest rates and the volume of bank credit; and they refused to participate loyally in syndicates headed by the Bank of Italy to rescue other banks in distress. The latter problem was particularly evident in 1907, when the Comit and Credit sabotaged the Bank of Italy's attempt to rescue the SBI.[7] The central difficulty of the Italian banking system was that it was particularly vulnerable to liquidity crises, given the involvement of deposit-taking banks in industrial promotion, while at the same time tensions between the commercial banks and the Bank of Italy made it difficult for the latter to effectively regulate the credit markets and exercise its lender-of-last-resort function in the event of a crisis.

There was also a political dimension to the tensions between the Bank of Italy and the major commercial banks. Unlike the leadership of central banks in other European countries, the officials of the Bank of Italy were not drawn primarily from the world of *haute finance*. Bonaldo Stringher, director of the Bank of Italy from 1900 to 1928 and governor until his death in 1930, and other top Bank officials began their careers as civil servants – Stringher had been Director General of the Treasury prior to assuming the directorship of the issue bank – and they were more sensitive to the goals and concerns of the Italian state's political and administrative leadership than they were to those of the financial community.[8]

The largest Milanese commercial banks often found themselves at odds with the Italian government over foreign policy. Before the war, they were frequently reluctant to participate in overseas investments urged by the government to reinforce Italy's colonial and imperial policy when such investments promised indifferent or uncertain economic returns. Although the foreign interest in the Banca Commerciale and the Credito Italiano declined to a modest proportion of share capital after the turn of the century, a substantial number of foreigners (of German, Austrian, Swiss and French nationality) still sat on the boards of both banks, where they could oppose investments in Balkan and Mediterranean projects suggested by the Italian Foreign Ministry. In addition to foreign board members, many of the executive directors of the two banks were foreign-born, making the two institutions vulnerable to charges of lack of patriotism. Such charges seemed to be confirmed by the determination with which the commercial bankers resisted the efforts of the Italian government and the Bank of Italy to regulate the credit markets, a determination reminiscent of the imperious behaviour of European bankers in Latin America or other semi-colonial environments at the beginning of the century. But while the major commercial banks resisted pressures to further the Consulta's aims in foreign policy, they were at the same time deeply involved in financing firms in the strategic sector that enjoyed the full range of tariff protection, subsidies and government contracts. The largest commercial banks thus found themselves in the contradictory position of being simultaneously financiers of rearmament at home, and opponents of adventurism abroad. In the process, the Milanese commercial bankers made important political enemies on the Left and on the Right: left-liberal reformers criticized the power of the banks, favouring more active government intervention in the economy; while conservatives accused the banks of undermining

Italy's great power aspirations due to their association with foreign financial interests, and lack of enthusiasm for the imperial programme of the Consulta.[9]

The tensions between the Milanese commercial banks and the government led the Bank of Italy and successive governments of both the Left and the Right to challenge the financial predominance of the Banca Commerciale and the Credito Italiano. Prior to 1907, Stringher sought to bring the two commercial banks to heel by favouring the growth of the Società Bancaria Italiana. Meanwhile, the Foreign Ministry co-operated with another commercial bank, the adventurist Banco di Roma, which established subsidiaries and financed enterprises in Libya, opening the way for the Italian invasion. However, neither the Società Bancaria nor the Banco di Roma were well managed: the SBI, as was noted, was badly hurt in the financial crisis of 1907, and only salvaged *in extremis* by the Bank of Italy, and the Roma was also on the verge of bankruptcy by 1914.[10] Another contradictory aspect of the tensions between Milan and Rome, therefore, was that the public authorities were driven to co-operate with the more speculative and even corrupt banks in their efforts to gain greater control over the financial markets, thereby further destabilizing the banking system.

Banking and industry during war and post-war stabilization, 1914–22

In Italy, as in other European countries, the deterioration in international relations and the ensuing outbreak of war in late July and early August 1914 produced a breakdown in international payments. Throughout the continent, governments suspended gold payments and imposed moratoria on commercial bills. But in contrast to most of the rest of Europe, the panic on the exchange and bill markets quickly produced a catastrophic decline in the market prices of domestic securities in Italy. The collapse of stock prices in turn threatened to undermine the basis of the entire Italian financial system. Industrial firms were heavily indebted to the banks and a significant part of these debts were held against collateral deposits of industrial stocks; therefore, any significant decline in the value of industrial securities threatened to undermine the country's largest commercial banks. Significantly, the price of bank shares fell more dramatically on the market than those of manufacturing firms. The collapse in stock and bond prices soon produced a run on bank deposits, which was directed particularly against the major commercial banks. The banks were consequently induced to turn to the issue banks with extraordinary rediscount requests.[11]

Initial attempts to meet the crisis by injecting liquidity into the markets proved fruitless. Therefore, on 4 August 1914 the government, in consultation with the Bank of Italy, took the extraordinary step of freezing bank accounts to halt the depositors' run. Significantly, among the other actual and future belligerents in the war, only Austria-Hungary imposed a similar freeze on bank deposit withdrawals.[12]

The moratoria on deposit withdrawals and commercial bills eliminated the immediate symptoms of the financial panic, but the threat to the liquidity of the financial system produced by the collapse of stock prices remained latent, despite the closure of the stock exchanges. Stocks and even government securities were traded informally in August at prices far below the last official exchange quotations and considerable scepticism prevailed as to whether the exchanges could be safely reopened again on 31 March 1915, as was envisaged by the moratorium legislation. In effect, the stock exchanges were not reopened until September 1917 (and they were closed again one month later, after the Caporetto military disaster), whereas in most of the other belligerent nations the stock markets were functioning normally again by mid-1915; a fact which further underscores the particular vulnerability of the Italian financial system to fluctuations in stock prices.

Even though the government decided to keep the stock exchanges closed during most of the conflict, it took two important measures in December 1914 to firm up stock prices. First, firms, including banks, were authorized to carry stocks in their portfolios at their market values on 30 June 1914 in their financial statements at the end of the year. Secondly, a new financial institution was created by a banking syndicate led by the Bank of Italy that was authorized to make advances to non-financial institutions against stock deposited as collateral at a margin of 50 per cent of its value on 31 July 1914 or 90 per cent of its nominal value.[13]

It is worth examining in some detail this new institution, the Consorzio per la Sovvenzioni su Valori Industriali (CSVI). It was the brainchild of Stringher, and represented an attempt to create a new institutional framework for dealing with the financial crises endemic to the Italian system of industrial finance predicated on mixed banking. Some of the features of the CSVI would resurface again with the creation of the IMI (Istituto Mobiliare Italiano) and the IRI in the early 1930s. The CSVI could charge interest rates equivalent to the official discount rate of the issue banks. It was authorized to rediscount its portfolio with the issue banks at 1.5 per cent less than the official discount rate. The CSVI began functioning in February 1915 with a capital of Lit. 22m, which had been subscribed by the three issue banks, two old public banks – the Monte dei Paschi of Siena, and the Banco di San Paolo of Turin – and the Savings Banks (Casse di Risparmio) of Lombardy, Turin, Genoa, Bologna, Florence and Palermo. At the time of Italian intervention in May 1915, the CSVI's capital was raised to Lit. 40m. It was authorized by statute to make advances for up to ten times its capital.[14]

The association of the savings banks and similar institutions such as the Monte di Paschi and the Banco di San Paolo in the new organization reflected Stringher's concern to extend the responsibility and risk associated with maintaining the stability of the financial system beyond the Bank of Italy to all major financial institutions. Stringher also aimed to create an institutional channel which would make available to industry the resources of the savings, and other public banks. In contrast to the commercial banks, the savings banks suffered from an embarrassment of liquid resources in relation to the types of investments they were authorized to make. Equally noteworthy was the initial exclusion of the commercial banks from the CSVI; Stringher evidently wished to create a new financial circuit that allowed him to establish a direct rapport with financially distressed manufacturing firms, bypassing the mixed banks.

But the CSVI neither remedied Italy's fragile financial structures nor protected the Bank of Italy from locking up its resources in the event of a collapse of stock prices and a major run on the commercial banks. With its modest share capital, the CSVI hardly divided the risk of meeting a financial crisis. The CSVI represented only a paper wall between illiquid firms and the issue banks, as the latter were expected to rediscount the CSVI's acceptances. In practical terms, the main function of the CSVI was to create a mechanism whereby the issue banks could legally make loans to industry in the event of a liquidity crisis without violating the issue banks' statutes, which forbade loans against anything other than first-class commercial paper or collateral deposits of state and state-guaranteed securities. These limitations would become clear during the post-war financial crisis, 1920–3, and once again during the Great Depression, 1930–4.

After the passing of the liquidity crisis in late summer 1914, the major commercial banks, and their industrial clients, were buoyed by the surge in demand for war materials, and they enjoyed a period of unprecedented liquidity and prosperity. Manufacturing firms paid off old debts to the banks, and huge war profits permitted new and some-times daring investments. For example, between 1915 and 1918 Ansaldo began building the pharonic iron and steel and electricity generating facility at Cogne, high in the mountains of the Val d'Aosta; Fiat built a steel-making plant and the mammoth Lingotto automobile factory in Turin, modelled after Henry Ford's facilities in Dearborn; Silvio Crispi rebuilt his cotton textile works in Upper Lombardy; and Franchi Gregorini, the Brescia-based steel and armaments concern, embarked on an ambitious programme of investments and expan-sion. Under the influence of 'productivist' ideologies, the govern-ment actively encouraged new industrial investments during the war, even though private firms competed with the military for scarce raw materials and labour. Construction of new plant was undertaken with public incentives such as tax write-offs, even when it was clear that new capacity would not come on the line until after the war was over, and that such investments would therefore detract from, rather than enhance, the immediate war effort. Of course, this policy was of a piece with the long-standing government strategy of promoting investments in defence-related industries, irrespective of comparative cost-advantage or markets.[15]

The commercial banks, in turn, were able to redress their troubled liquidity positions and improve their relative position within the bank-ing system at the expense of more conservative financial institutions, notably the savings banks. The banks were induced to recycle their profits and the liquid resources they accumulated through the influx of deposits in new industrial investments. This was particularly the case in 1919–20, after war-related state contracts dried up, and manufactur-ing firms once again looked for external financing, often to complete ambitious projects begun during the war.

The pell-mell industrial expansion of the war years caused the post-war recession to be more severe in Italy than in the other victorious powers, and the intimate relationship between Italian industry and banking transformed the economic recession into a devastating financial crisis. Industrial expansion had taken place without reference to post-war markets, and much of the new capacity built up during and just after the war became idle. Not surprisingly, the iron and steel, armaments and shipbuilding industries were hardest hit in the post-war recession. In the course of 1921–3, the two largest heavy industry conglomerates in Italy, Ilva and Ansaldo, and two of the four largest commercial banks, the Banca Italiana di Sconto and the Banco di Roma, essentially failed and had to be financially restructured with state support. In effect, the enormous public contribution to industrial expansion during the war – through armaments contracts, tax write-offs and the toleration of tax evasion – was continued after the war in the form of government-sponsored rescues of troubled banks and manufacturing firms, a process Franco Bonelli has termed 'the retroactive state financing of industry'.[16]

The long-running conflict between public officials in Rome and private bankers in Milan persisted during the war and post-war years, and aggravated the financial crisis of 1921–3. In the spring of 1914 a group of industrialists and bankers began efforts to create a third major commercial bank to contest the predominance of the Banca Commerciale and the Credito Italiano. The European war broke out before the new bank had opened its doors, and its foundation took place in the context of a nationalist campaign against the allegedly German-dominated Milanese banks during the period of Italian neutrality. This new enterprise, the Banca Italiana di Sconto (Bansconto), began operating on 31 December 1914, with a modest share capital of Lit. 15m. In July 1915 the institution was enlarged by merger with two smaller banks, including the greatly diminished Società Bancaria Italiana. The new bank made its headquarters in Rome, rather than Milan, and established close relations with Ansaldo, the only firm engaged in iron and steel production and shipbuilding that was outside the orbit of the Commerciale. The brothers Pio and Mario Perrone, directors of Ansaldo, became members of the board, and the most influential figures in the new bank. Armaments contracts allowed both Ansaldo and the Bansconto to expand rapidly during the war, and the new financial-industrial trust soon challenged the domination of the Milanese banks.[17]

From the beginning, the 'banca italianissima' enjoyed broad political support. The Ansaldo-Bansconto group maintained close relations with radical groups, through its financial support for *Il Popolo d'Italia*, Mussolini's interventionist newspaper, and *L'Idea Nazionale*, the newspaper of the radical-rightist Italian Nationalist Association. But its intimate relationship with Francesco Saverio Nitti was of even greater importance. Nitti, a corporate lawyer, professor and influential left-liberal deputy from Basilicata, had served as Minister of Agriculture, Industry and Commerce in Giolitti's fourth ministry, 1911–14. Hereafter, in 1914–15, he acted as legal consul to the group that established the new bank. Nitti later exercised a dominant influence on government financial policy as Minister of the Treasury from November 1917 to January 1919 and Prime Minister from June 1919 to June 1920. The southern Italian political leader believed that continuing the reformist policies of the pre-war era would require firmer government control over the banking system and the financial markets. In public, Nitti, and the financial press close to him, advocated 'bank co-operation', or the suppression of bank rivalries and the submission of the commercial banks to the leadership of the Bank of Italy and the Treasury. During Nitti's tenure at the Treasury in 1918 and again during his tenure as Prime Minister in 1920, the Bansconto made two unsuccessful hostile take-over bids on the Banca Commerciale. Although historians sympathetic to Nitti have confirmed the southern politician's public denials of complicity in the Bansconto's 'escalades' of the Commerciale, Anna Maria Falchero has recently argued, more convincingly in my view, that Nitti considered the Bansconto's actions as being in conformance with his programme of bank co-operation. Not surprisingly, Stringher and the Bank of Italy were at a minimum benevolently neutral during the first take-over attempt against the Commerciale in 1918. Meanwhile, another group of industrialists led by Giovanni Agnelli of Fiat attempted a similar 'escalade' of the Credito Italiano.[18]

The struggle for control of the Commerciale ended with the signing of an accord between the two rival groups dictated by Nitti. The accord envisaged an increase in the share capital of the Commerciale from Lit. 156m. to Lit. 208m., with the Ansaldo-Bansconto group being guaranteed a minority interest and a seat on the board of directors of the rival institution. The agreement did not give the Bansconto group control over the Commerciale, and thus did not satisfy the

Perrone brothers. Nitti and his followers insisted that the accord represented a compromise and that the Minister of the Treasury stood above the conflicting parties, a position that has been echoed in the recent literature. Falchero, in contrast, argues that the Perrone brothers lacked sufficient shares and sufficient liquid capital to dislodge the old controlling interests from the leadership of the Commerciale, and that under the circumstances the compromise arranged by Nitti was by no means disadvantageous to them. She points out that the Perrone brothers were at least successful in securing the participation of the Comit in an issue of Ansaldo stock in the summer of 1918, which raised its share capital from Lit. 100m to Lit. 500m, enabling the firm to continue its vast programme of investments and expansion.[19]

Several days later, Nitti persuaded – or forced – the directors of the four major commercial banks, the Comit, the Bansconto, the Credit and the Banco di Roma, to sign another accord. The text of this agreement was not made public, but it evidently committed the commercial bankers to co-operate with the Treasury, the Bank of Italy and each other on matters deemed by the government to represent the national interest.[20] Whatever the extent of Nitti's collaboration with the Perrone brothers in 1918, the bank accord represented an attempt to impose greater government control over the commercial banking sector, and was sufficient in itself to provoke the uncompromising hostility of the Milanese bankers. It was bound to remain a dead letter in a climate of strong mutual suspicion and animosity.

The second hostile take-over attempt against the Banca Commerciale was mounted in the spring of 1920, at a time when war-related state contracts were being wound up, and the Ansaldo-Bansconto group was beginning to experience serious liquidity problems. Having already immobilized the deposits of one of the country's largest commercial banks in a pharaonic programme of industrial expansion, the Perrone brothers concluded that only control of the resources of the Commerciale could save them from bankruptcy. When Giuseppe Toeplitz, the Polish-born executive director of the Comit, and his financial allies, the so-called Marsaglia group, successfully fended off this renewed take-over attempt, the collapse of the overextended Ansaldo-Bansconto empire became inevitable. The failure of the Bansconto in early January 1922 reproduced many aspects of the financial crisis of 1907: once again the Bank of Italy attempted to save a large bank from failure by forming a rescue syndicate comprising the other issue banks and the large commercial banks; and once again the lack of co-operation of the Credit and the Comit thwarted the efforts of the central bank.[21]

Banking and industry in the early years of the Fascist regime

As is clear from the discussion above, the Italian banking system entered the fascist era with none of the pre-war problems resolved. The collapse of the Bansconto reaffirmed the supremacy of the Comit and the Credit in Italian *haute finance*, and their independence from the centres of public monetary policy formation in Rome. But both banks emerged ravaged from wartime inflation, the post-war recession and the hostile take-over attempts. Not only the Ansaldo, but also manufacturing firms that moved within the orbit of the two Milanese banks experienced liquidity difficulties during the recession of 1921–2. In particular, the Ilva iron- and steel-making concern had to be restructured in the summer of 1921, at considerable financial sacrifice to the Milanese banks. Both banks emerged from the war with their financial positions eroded. In the Giolittian era, the major commercial banks had maintained capital plus reserves to deposit ratios of about 1:3; by the immediate post-war years this ratio had fallen to 1:10.6 for the Commerciale, and 1:11.3 for the Credito Italiano. Worse, the equity capital of both banks was essentially symbolic after 1920.[22] In order to defend themselves against hostile take-over attempts in the wake of the Perrone brothers' 'escalade' of the Commerciale, the two banks formed financial concerns that held the majority interest in their stock. The majority interests in these financial concerns were in turn owned by firms in which the two banks themselves held controlling interests. Therefore, through a circular pattern of ownership links, dubbed Chinese or Japanese boxes in Italian financial parlance, the two banks essentially owned themselves – with their depositors' money![23] The negative implications of this ownership structure for the stability of the banks is obvious.

The Bank of Italy, meanwhile, was once again constrained to lock up its own financial resources in the restructuring of the Bansconto-Ansaldo group. Domestic creditors of the failed bank, including depositors, received only a fraction of the sums owed them, but government authorities felt compelled to keep afloat Ansaldo and other insolvent industrial firms, including Alfa Romeo, that had relied on the Bansconto for credit. A year later, in late 1922 and early 1923, the incompetently managed Banco di Roma was also on the verge of financial collapse, and this time Mussolini's newly installed government felt obliged to undertake a full rescue. The Consorzio per la Sovvenzioni su Valori Industriali now came into its own, albeit not in the form in which Stringher had envisaged in 1914. The director of the Bank of Italy feared involving the savings banks and the other public institutions that had subscribed the capital of the CSVI in the ruin of the Bansconto and the Roma, and therefore an 'Autonomous Section' of the CSVI was created in March 1922 to lend money, first to Ansaldo and other stricken firms, and later to the Roma, against paper that the Bank of Italy could in turn rediscount. In its financial operations, the 'Autonomous Section' acted in effect as little more than a window of the issue bank. But it was also equipped with a managerial and technical staff, which reorganized the ailing manufacturing firms that had fallen under state control. For the first time, a public institution in Italy became owner of major manufacturing concerns. During this period, it was assumed that state control of industrial firms was temporary, and that they would be returned to the private sector as quickly as investors with sufficient financial and technical resources could be found. Ansaldo was shorn of some of its holdings outside the iron- and steel-making and shipbuilding sector, and outside of the Liguria region where its main facilities were located and reprivatized in the mid-1920s. The controlling interest in the reorganized firm passed into the hands of a new bank, the Credito Nazionale, which inherited the branch network of the old Banca Italiana di Sconto. Private investors could not be found for Alfa Romeo and other bits of the old Ansaldo complex, including the Cogne facility, and they remained in state hands until they passed under the ownership of the IRI in the early 1930s.[24]

The conflict between Rome and Milan was more acute than ever. Not only the leadership of the Bank of Italy, but also the new political regime regarded the Banca Commerciale with suspicion. Mussolini had been bankrolled by the Comit's archrival, the Ansaldo-Bansconto trust, during the war, and his newspaper had joined the jingoist campaign against the Milanese institution. According to some accounts, the fascist government considered launching an attack on the leadership of the country's largest commercial bank soon after it came to

194   Douglas J. Forsyth

power, and only refrained from doing so out of fear of the negative reactions such steps would provoke among domestic and foreign business groups.[25]

After the March on Rome, Italy experienced two years of economic recovery, coupled with relative price and foreign exchange stability, and moderate monetary expansion. By early 1925, however, Italy's international payments position was deteriorating, and the lira was coming under speculative attack. Domestic monetary expansion was fuelled by stock market speculation with bank credit. Mussolini's Minister of Finance, Alberto De Stefani, issued decrees restraining stock market activity in February and March, which led to a sharp decline in stock prices. The collapse of the stock market had the usual negative consequences on the liquidity positions of the commercial banks: they had lent to manufacturing firms against collateral deposits of stock, the value of which now plummeted; at the same time, their industrial clients were more dependent than ever on bank loans, as the collapse of the securities market foreclosed other means of raising capital.[26]

Meanwhile, in 1925 the government negotiated settlements of Italy's war debts to the United States and Britain. By the end of the year, Italy was ready to stabilize the exchange value of the lira as a prelude to returning to the gold standard. But in attempting to counter speculation against the lira in the course of 1926, the government and the Bank of Italy found themselves at loggerheads with the large commercial banks once again. While the authorities pursued restrictive monetary policies, the Milanese institutions expanded the total volume of bank credit to meet the needs of their illiquid industrial clients. The commercial banks could evade the restrictive policies of the Bank of Italy, and defeat the government's monetary policy, by selling off large blocks of Treasury bills. Italy, like France, had relied heavily on short-term bills to finance the war, and in 1926 over half of the total state debt was in the form of short-term notes.[27]

In response to this situation, the fascist government took a series of measures in 1926 to curb the independence of the commercial banks, and bolster the authority of the Bank of Italy. It ordered the forcible conversion of all outstanding Treasury bills into long-term consols which paid 5 per cent on 6 November 1926. In addition, a series of decrees between May and November 1926 strengthened the Bank of Italy and its control of the credit market. The issue privileges of the two southern Italian banks were revoked, and the Bank of Italy acquired a monopoly on the issue of banknotes. For the first time in Italy, commercial banking was subjected to special regulation going beyond the commercial code. Loans to single clients were not to exceed one-fifth of the bank's capital, without express permission of the Bank of Italy. Ratios of own to outside resources were set, and a fixed proportion of deposits exceeding these ratios had to be held either as deposits at the Bank of Italy, or in state or state-guaranteed securities. The opening of new banks or branches was subjected to the approval of the Ministry of Finance. Finally, a regulatory agency was established under the control of the Bank of Italy, which was empowered to inspect the commercial banks. Little is known about how the new legislation functioned. The Bank of Italy's regulatory powers were, in any event, still sharply limited. It was not empowered, for instance, to vary the quality or quantity of bank reserves.[28]

On 18 August 1926 Mussolini made his famous speech in Pesaro, in which he promised to defend the lira, 'to the last breath, to the last drop of blood'. The question of why the Duce insisted on pegging the lira at 90 to the British pound, instead of a rate closer to 120, as was recommended by his Finance Minister since 1925, Count Giuseppe Volpi di Misurata, and favoured by most of Italian business, has provoked a lively historical controversy. What must be stressed in the present context is that 'quota novanta' was strongly opposed by the Milanese financial community, and further weakened the position of the commercial banks. Mussolini and Volpi imposed a strong dose of deflation on the domestic economy to drive up the exchange value of the lira. The banks were forced to devote their liquid resources to keeping afloat those client firms which were so big, and so heavily indebted to the banks that their failure would produce a crisis of confidence in the solidity of the banks themselves: loan applications from less financially troubled firms increasingly were turned away. The stock market continued its inexorable decline. The banks bought up their own stock, and that of their client firms to prevent the stock market plunge from triggering a depositors' run. More and more, the large commercial banks took on the physiognomy of industrial holding companies.[29]

The settlement of the war debts and the stabilization of the lira opened the British, and particularly the American financial market to private Italian borrowing. The more profitable and financially solid firms, such as Fiat, Pirelli, and the electrical companies, including

Giuseppe Volpi's Società Adriatica di Elettricità (SADE), were able to emancipate themselves from the commercial banks by issuing obligations in the United States.[30] The clientele of the commercial banks was increasingly reduced to the least profitable firms, including those engaged in iron and steel manufacturing, shipbuilding and shipping. At the same time, the commercial banks seem to have redressed their own troubled liquidity positions by attracting hot money from abroad with high interest rates, much as did their German and Austrian counterparts during the same period.[31]

The banking crisis and the reform

Under these circumstances, it is hardly surprising that the world economic crisis precipitated a major banking crisis in Italy. In fact, the Italian banking crisis was already in an advanced state in May 1931, when the Austrian government announced that the Credit-Anstalt had suffered major losses, and that a state rescue operation was being undertaken to prevent its collapse. Beginning in 1929, public authorities in Italy intervened to save small and medium-sized banks on the verge of failure. Among these was the Banca Nazionale di Credito, which had taken over the branch network, and some of the industrial holdings of the failed Bansconto. In early 1930 the Banca Nazionale was merged with the Credito Italiano, with public support. It appears that the authorities favoured the Credit during this period, seeking to augment its size and detach it from its close traditional association with the Comit.[32] The new financial group resulting from the merger, with the encouragement of the Bank of Italy, sought to institutionally separate its commercial banking activities from its industrial promotion activities, by creating a financial holding company (first called the Banca Nazionale del Credito, later the Società Finanziaria Italiana or SFI). The Credit ceded its industrial portfolio to this new firm, while its directors, with the endorsement of the Bank of Italy, sought to restrict the bank's activity to commercial lending. Of course this did not affect the liquidity position of the group, as the firms in the SFI group continued to rely on the Credito Italiano to meet their financial needs; these needs grew in the course of 1930, as the general economic situation worsened.[33]

By the end of 1930 the Credit's directors were negotiating the terms of a government rescue with the authorities. A secret agreement was signed on 20 February 1931 between the Credit, the Bank of Italy and the Minister of Finance. The industrial interests of the Credit were divided into two holding companies, one of which, the Società Elettrofinanziaria, owned majority interests in the firms which the Credito directors and shareholders considered most solvent and most valuable. As is suggested by the name, electrical and telephone companies, including the Edison company, predominated. This group was to remain in the private sphere, although its annual reports were made subject to the approval of the Bank of Italy, and corporate interlocks with the Credit were to be severed. The other financial holding company, the SFI, contained the Credit group's least promising securities, including stock in iron and steel, and shipbuilding firms. The Bank of Italy made a non-interest-bearing loan to the SFI through an intermediate organization similar to the Autonomous Section of the CSVI for Lit. 330m, which it used to reimburse its debts to the Credit. The Credit's directors believed at the time that this loan would provide the bank with sufficient working capital to set it on its feet again. Although the Credit technically owned the SFI, the Bank of Italy accrued to itself the right to name half the members of the board, and approve the nomination of the president.[34]

While the Credit was attempting to divest itself of its non-remunerative industrial holdings in co-operation with the government in early 1931, the Banca Commerciale further increased its exposure to its client firms. With good reason, Giuseppe Toeplitz feared that the authorities would be less generous to his bank if it asked for state assistance. According to Ettore Conti, who was president of the Comit, but held little real authority, Toeplitz hoped the Comit might still 'double Cape Tempest', and survive the recession in full possession of its large portfolio of industrial securities. But the summer of 1931 brought deepening recession, the German banking crisis and the rapid withdrawal of hot money from Central European banks. The Comit, which by now had locked up most of its liquid assets in rediscounting operations with the Bank of Italy, went so far as to negotiate a foreign currency loan with the central bank by pledging its branch in London and its subsidiary in New York as security. Under pressure from his own staff, Toeplitz finally capitulated in September, when he flew to Rome to present Mussolini with a memorandum on the (disastrous) situation of the bank, and a proposal for government intervention.[35]

On 31 October, the Comit signed an agreement with the public authorities that was considerably less favourable than the one negotiated by the Credit eight months earlier. The Comit was forced to give more explicit guarantees that it would not hold more than a very modest amount of industrial securities in its portfolio in the future. All of its industrial securities holdings, in both solvent and insolvent firms, were transferred to a holding company, the Sofindit, to which the Bank of Italy appointed half of the board of directors, and reserved the right to approve the president. Through a complex series of financial operations, the Sonfindit reduced its debts to the Banca Commerciale, while the Bank of Italy's total exposure to the Comit group increased from Lit. 522m to Lit. 2,540m. This agreement too remained secret. Secrecy in Italy prevented the banking crisis from provoking a depositors' run, as occurred in Germany and Austria, leading Gianni Toniolo to conclude that in dealing with financial crises the existence of a dictatorship in Italy carried with it certain advantages.[36]

The agreements of 1931 did not provide a satisfactory basis for overcoming the financial crisis. The Bank of Italy's loans to the ex-Credit and Comit groups only met the immediate needs of the two banks and the industrial holding companies, and in 1932 – the worst year of the Great Depression – these groups posted further losses. Although the Sofindit and the SFI had been formally severed from the Comit and the Credit, they continued to rely on the two banks to meet their growing liquidity needs. The two commercial banks had agreed to limit drastically their role in industrial finance, but there was no new mechanism for providing investment capital to replace them.

The Istituto Mobiliare Italiano (IMI), which was created at the end of 1931, was evidently intended to fulfil this function. Like the CSVI, its share capital was subscribed by public institutions, including the post savings bank, and the provincial savings banks. The new organization was authorized to issue obligations guaranteed by the state for up to ten times its share capital of Lit. 550m. It was hoped that the state guarantee would attract investors reluctant to invest in private securities, and thereby finally create the broad market for industrial securities that Italy had never had. However, it quickly became apparent that the losses of the Sofindit and SFI would far exceed the financial resources of the new institution. Theodor Mayer, the IMI's first director, pursued an exceedingly cautious policy, declining to make risky loans or take full advantage of the institute's resources.[37] Meanwhile, the Bank of Italy's exposure to the commercial banks and the financial holding companies mounted to Lit. 7,382m at the end of 1932, or 54 per cent of the entire note circulation.[38] Not only the commercial banks, but also the Bank of Italy had become immobilized as a consequence of the financial crisis.

The decisive steps in resolving the crisis came in 1933–4, with the nationalization of all three major commercial banks – the Comit, the Credit and the Banco di Roma – and all of their former industrial holdings. Even the Elettrofinanziaria, which the government had left in private hands in 1931, was now nationalized. A new state agency, the Istituto di Ricostruzione Industriale (IRI), was created in 1933, and it acquired the entire block of industrial and banking securities previously held by the three banking groups in separate agreements signed in March 1934. Needless to say, bank directors associated with the old system, foremost among them Giuseppe Toeplitz, were forced to resign.

During its first years of activity the IRI pursued two goals: the liquidation of the Bank of Italy's resources locked up in loans to the commercial banks and their industrial groups; and the financial and technical reorganization of insolvent industrial firms. It was greatly aided in its programme by the recovery of economic activity and stock prices from early 1933. According to the agreements signed in March 1934, the IRI agreed to pay the three commercial banks approximately Lit. 10.7bn for their securities portfolios, 'in one or more payments', by the end of 1935 at 4 per cent annual interest. This sum was judged sufficient to provide the banks with fresh share capital, reserves and working capital, and allow them to extinguish their debts with the Bank of Italy. Through these agreements and other operations, the exposure of the Bank of Italy to the IRI group was reduced to just over Lit. 4.5bn by the end of 1936.[39]

Beginning in the final months of 1933, the IRI also undertook the reorganization of several important industrial enterprises, including the SIP, which owned most of north-central Italy's telephone exchanges; the shipping companies, most of which had fallen under public ownership; and Terni, a speciality steel, armaments and electrical concern.

The IRI received direct annual grants from the state, but its chief means of finance was the sale of state-guaranteed, tax-exempt obli-

gations. Although the IRI had some success in placing its securities
with the general investing public, large blocks of obligations were also
taken up by the savings banks and other public banks, finally realizing
Stringher's goal of involving these institutions in industrial finance.
Some pieces of the IRI's industrial empire were also reprivatized. It is
worth noting that the investment group associated with the old Credit
regained control of the Edison Company, and other stock formerly
held by the Elettrofinanziaria, a favourable treatment that was not
extended to business interests associated with the old Comit.[40]

The process of industrial and financial restructuring was completed
in 1936 with a bank reform law. Ownership of stock of the Bank of Italy
was limited to public institutions. It was no longer allowed to engage
in commercial lending, and was therefore confined solely to the role
of 'bank to banks'. The three commercial banks, in which the IRI held
the controlling interest, were declared 'Banks of National Interest'
(BIN). The banking legislation did not seek to distinguish between
commercial and industrial credit or restrict the type of lending activity
of the BIN, but it imposed strict supervision on banks' acquisition of
equity interests, in order to prevent the banks from turning into industrial holding companies again.[41]

The public sphere's supervisory and regulatory powers vis-à-vis the
banks was vastly expanded. Indeed, an English commentator writing
in 1938 observed that 'a powerful controlling organization had been
created, which, if used fully, would make the Italian banking system a
state organization in all but name'.[42] Control over the banking system
was nominally vested in a Committee of Ministers, presided over by the
head of government, but actual authority was exercised by a dependent organization, the Inspectorate of Credit and Savings, which was
chaired by the Governor of the Bank of Italy. The Committee (and the
Inspectorate acting in its name) was authorized to close banks and
branches, to fix active and passive interest rates, and to fix reserve
ratios. It could require advance approval for specified types of
financial operation, decide what proportion of profits should be set
aside as reserves and set limits on loans to individual clients.[43]

Conclusion: the peculiarities of the Italian response to the banking crisis

It is now time to return to the question raised at the beginning of this essay: why in Italy, did the banking crisis produce major institutional changes, including the creation of the largest state-owned manufacturing sector outside the Soviet Union, and the nationalization of almost the entire commercial banking sector? This question seems all the more compelling because recent research has tended to discount the possibility that either the Fascist Party or the corporativist apparatus that was being assembled in this very period had any significant influence on the IRI and the banking reform of 1936.[44] Indeed, the principal architects of both the IRI and the banking law, Alberto Beneduce and Donato Menichella, were government functionaries, not party members. Beneduce, in fact, had been a protégé of the liberal statesman F. S. Nitti before the March on Rome, and was distrusted in party circles.[45] Indeed, in many respects the reforms of the 1930s accomplished Nitti's old programme of bank co-operation.

Two key problems led to the demise of mixed banking in Italy: the weakness of the securities markets, and the extreme tensions between public authorities and private bankers. Both predated the rise of fascism. In the early 1930s, the Italian state took control of a large group of manufacturing firms, most of them in the strategic sector, because they were uncompetitive and chronically unprofitable, and because there were no private investors prepared to buy them. In the course of the 1920s, the major commercial banks had become industrial holding companies, owning the stock of manufacturing firms, and their own stock, with the money of the banks' depositors. These structural problems were grave enough in themselves, and they led in Italy – as did a similar state of affairs in Austria – to the nationalization of banking and industrial firms. However, the decision in Italy to permanently restructure the banking system and create a large state industrial holding company owed much to another factor: the desire of the public authorities to gain greater control over the credit system, and their long-standing conflict with the leadership of the commercial banks. This represented unfinished business of the Giolittian era.

NOTES

1 On the German banking crisis see K. E. Born, *Die deutsche Bankenkrise: Finanzen und Politik* (Munich, 1967); G. Hardach, 'Banking and industry in Germany in the interwar period 1919–1939', *Journal of European History*, 13, no. 2 (1984) (special issue on banks and industry between the wars), 203–4. On Austria see D. Stiefel, 'The reconstruction of the Credit-Anstalt', in A. Teichova and P. L. Cottrell (eds.),

202   Douglas J. Forsyth

International Business and Central Europe, 1918–1939 (Leicester and New York, 1983), pp. 415–30.

2 For a discussion of the uniqueness of the Italian response to the banking crisis of the 1930s see Gianni Toniolo's comments in Banco di Roma, *Banca e industria fra le due guerre. Atti del convegno conclusivo della ricerca promossa dal Banco di Roma in occasione del suo primo centenario* (Bologna, 1981), pp. 130–6.

3 The weakness of industrial securities markets in Italy has been widely discussed in the literature. Of particular interest is F. Vicarelli (ed.), *Capitale industriale e capitale finanziario. Il caso italiano* (Bologna, 1979). On the tensions between public authorities and commercial bankers see D. J. Forsyth, 'The politics of forced accumulation: monetary and financial policy in Italy, 1914–1922', PhD diss. (Princeton University, 1987).

4 A. Gerschenkron, 'Economic backwardness in historical perspective', and 'Notes on the rate of industrial growth in Italy', in *Economic Backwardness in Historical Perspective: A Book of Essays* (Cambridge, Mass., 1962), pp. 5–30, 72–89; J. S. Cohen, *Finance and Industrialization in Italy, 1894–1914* (New York, 1977).

5 Toniolo, in Banco di Roma, *Banche e industria fra le due guerre. Atti del convegno*, p. 132.

6 A. Confalonieri, *Banca e industria in Italia (1894–1906)*, 3 vols. (Milan, 1977–80); A. Confalonieri, *Banca e industria in Italia dalla crisi del 1907 all'agosto 1914*, 2 vols. (Milan, 1982); F. Bonelli, *La crisi del 1907. Una tappa dello sviluppo industriale in Italia* (Turin, 1971); F. Bonelli, 'Osservazioni e dati sul finanziamento dell'industria italiana all'inizio del secolo XX', *Annali della Fondazione Luigi Einaudi*, 2 (1968), 264–71; idem, 'The 1907 financial crisis in Italy: a peculiar case of the lender of last resort in action', in C. Kindleberger and J.-P. Laffargue (eds.), *Financial Crises: Theory, History and Policy* (New York, 1982), pp. 51–65.

7 Bonelli, *La crisi del 1907*; Confalonieri, *Banca e industria in Italia (1894–1906)*.

8 On Stringher see F. Bonelli, *Bonaldo Stringher, 1854–1930* (Udine, 1985).

9 My interpretation agrees substantially with that of Confalonieri, *Banca e industria 1907–agosto 1914*, esp. pp. 414–20, and contrasts with that of R. Webster, *Industrial Imperialism in Italy, 1908–1915* (Berkeley, Calif., 1975), pp. 310–22, and passim. See also B. Vigezzi, 'Otto Joel, il principe di Bülow e i problemi della neutralità', in *Da Giolitti a Salandra* (Florence, 1969), pp. 203–62.

10 On the Società Bancaria see Bonelli, *La crisi del 1907*. On the Banco di Roma see L. De Rosa, *Storia del Banco di Roma*, vols. I–II (Rome, 1983) (published privately, restricted distribution).

11 R. Bachi, *L'Italia economica nell'anno 1914* (Città di Castello, 1915), pp. 87–92; Archivio Storico della Banca d'Italia (hereafter ASBI), Consiglio superior, verbali, 24 August 1914.

12 E. März, *Austrian Banking and Financial Policy: Creditanstalt at a Turning Point, 1913–1923* (London, 1984), p. 131.

13 Bachi, *L'Italia economica nell'anno 1914*, pp. 240–4; Banca d'Italia, Servizio Segretario Particolare, Presidenza e giunta del consiglio superiore riunite in Comitato (hereafter Comitato), verbali, 20 December 1914.

14 R. Bachi, *L'Italia economica nell'anno 1915* (Città di Castello, 1916), p. 242; Banca d'Italia, Servizio segretario, Comitato, verbali, 31 May 1915.

15 On Ansaldo see R. Webster, 'La tecnologia italiana e i sistemi industriali verticali: il caso dell'Ansaldo', *Storia contemporanea*, 2 (1978), 205–39; on Fiat see V. Castronuovo, *Giovanni Agnelli. La Fiat dal 1899 al 1945* (Turin, 1971); on Crespi see R. Romano, 'Silvio Benigno Crespi', *Dizionario biografico italiano* (1984); on

Franchi Gregorini see A. A. Kelikian, *Town and Country under Fascism: The Transformation of Brescia, 1915–1926* (New York, 1986). See also A. Caracciolo, 'La crescità e la transformazione della grande industria durante la prima guerra mondiale', in G. Fuà (ed.), *Lo sviluppo economico in Italia*, 3rd edn, vol. III (Milan, 1978), pp. 195–248; L. Segreto, 'Armi e munizioni. Lo sforzo bellico tra speculazione e progresso tecnico', *Italia contemporanea*, 146/7 (1982), pp. 35–66; Forsyth, 'The politics of forced accumulation', esp. pp. 50–74.

16 F. Bonelli, 'Il capitalismo italiano. Linee generale d'interpretazione', in R. Romano and C. Vivanti (eds.), *Storia d'Italia. Annali I: Dal feudalismo al capitalismo* (Turin, 1978), pp. 1195–1255.

17 E. Galli della Loggia, 'Problemi di sviluppo industriale e nuovi equilibri politici alla vigila della prima guerra mondiale. La fondazione della Banca Italiana di Sconto', *Rivista storica italiana*, 82, no. 4 (1970), 824–86.

18 This interpretation essentially agrees with A. M. Falchero, 'Banchieri e politica. Nitti e il gruppo Ansaldo-Banca di Sconto', *Italia contemporanea*, 146/7 (1982), 62–92; and disagrees with F. Barbagallo, *Nitti* (Turin, 1984), and A. Monticone, *Nitti e la Grande Guerra (1914–1918)* (Milan, 1961). See also F. S. Nitti, *Rivelazioni* (Naples, 1948); V. Nitti, *L'opera di Nitti* (Turin, 1924).

19 Falchero, 'Banchieri e politica'.

20 *Ibid.*, p. 85.

21 Banca d'Italia, Servizio segretario, Comitato, verbali, 15 January 1922; A. M. Falchero, 'Il gruppo Ansaldo-Banca Italiana di Sconto e le vicende bancarie nel primo dopoguerra', in P. Hertner and G. Mori (eds.), *La transizione dall'economia di guerra al'economia di pace in Italia e in Germania dopo la prima guerra mondiale* (Bologna, 1983), pp. 543–71; P. Sraffa, 'The bank crisis in Italy', *Journal of Economic History*, 32, no. 126 (1922), 178–97.

22 Elaborated from data in U. Bava, *I quattro maggiori istituti italiani di credito* (Genova, 1926).

23 E. Conti, *Dal taccuino di un borghese*, 3rd edn (Bologna, 1986), pp. 301–2; G. Malagodi, 'Il "salvataggio" della Banca Commerciale nel ricordo di un testimone', in G. Toniolo (ed.), *Industria e banca nella grande crisi 1929–1934* (Milan, 1978), pp. 270–83, esp. pp. 275–6.

24 E. Cianci, *Nascità dello Stato imprenditore in Italia* (Milan, 1977), pp. 43–65.

25 Barbagallo, *Nitti*, pp. 459–61; U. Ojetti, *I Taccuini, 1914–1943* (Florence, 1954), p. 394.

26 G. Toniolo, *L'economia dell'Italia fascista* (Bari, 1980), *passim*; G. Toniolo, 'Crisi economica e smobilizzo pubblico delle banche miste (1930–1934)', in G. Toniolo (ed.), *Industria e banca nella grande crisi, 1929–1934* (Milan, 1978), pp. 284–352; J. S. Cohen, 'The 1927 revaluation of the lira: a study in political economy', *Economic History Review*, 2nd ser., 25, no. 4 (1972), 642–54. A summary of Toniolo's extensive and important publications on banking and industry in interwar Italy is available in English in P. Ciocca and G. Toniolo, 'Industry and finance in Italy, 1918–1940', *Journal of European Economic History*, 13, no. 2 (1984), 113–36.

27 Cohen, 'The 1927 revaluation of the lira', esp. pp. 648–9; Toniolo, *L'economia dell'Italia fascista*, esp. p. 108.

28 On the bank reform of 1926 see F. Belli, 'Le leggi bancarie del 1926 e del 1936–1938', in Banco di Roma, *Banca e industria fra le due guerre. Le riforme istituzionali e il pensiero giuridico* (Bologna, 1981), pp. 203–68; S. Cassese, 'La preparazione della riforma bancaria del 1936 in Italia', *Storia contemporanea*, 5, no. 1 (1974), 3–45; G. Carli, 'Alcuni aspetti dell'evoluzione funzionale dell'istituto di

emissione dalle sue origini ai nostri giorni', in *Studi in occasione del primo centenario della Corte dei Conti nell'unità d'Italia* (Milan, 1963), pp. 35–59.

29 On 'quota novanta' see Cohen, 'The 1927 revaluation of the lira'; R. Sarti, 'Mussolini and the Italian industrial leadership in the battle of the lira, 1925–1927', *Past and Present*, 47 (1970), 97–112; R. De Felice, 'Lineamenti politici di quota 90', *Nuovo Osservatore*, 50 (1966), 374–6. On the impact of the deflation on the banks see Toniolo, 'Crisi economica e smobilizzo pubblico', pp. 293–5.

30 On the borrowing of Italian firms in the United States see G. G. Migone, *Gli Stati Uniti e il fascismo. Alle origini dell'egemonia americana in Italia* (Milan, 1980); C. Sartori, 'Un aspetto del capitale finanziario durante la grande crisi: il caso del gruppo Volpi-SADE', in Toniolo (ed.), *Industria e banca nella grande crisi*, pp. 134–84.

31 This is the opinion of Toniolo: 'Crisi economica e smobilizzo pubblico', p. 294. See also the recollections of Giovanni Malagodi – who worked in Toeplitz's secretariat in the late 1920s and early 1930s – in 'Raffaele Mattioli (1895–1973)', in A. Mortara (ed.), *I protagonisti dell'intervento pubblico in Italia* (Milan, 1984), pp. 549–606, esp. p. 565. The historical archive of the Banca Commerciale has been recently reopened to scholars, and finally it may be possible to obtain more precise information about this, and other little-understood aspects of Italy's financial history.

32 Toniolo, 'Crisi economica e zmobilizzo pubblico', pp. 297–310.

33 *Ibid.*, pp. 298–301.

34 *Ibid.*, pp. 302–6.

35 *Ibid.*, pp. 306–7; E. Conti, *Dal taccuino di un borghese*, pp. 301, 307–8. The memorandum presented by Toeplitz to Mussolini, which was drawn up by Raffaele Mattioli (Toeplitz's secretary, and future executive director of the nationalized Comit), has been published in G. Malagodi, 'Raffaele Mattioli (1895–1973)', in Mortara (ed.), *I protagonisti dell'intervento pubblico in Italia*, pp. 602–6. See also G. Rodano, *Il credito all'economia. Raffaele Mattioli alla Banca Commerciale Italiana* (Milan and Naples, 1983), pp. 3–32.

36 Toniolo, 'Crisi economica e smobilizzo pubblico'. On the agreement with the Comit: pp. 307–19; on the 'advantages of dictatorship': pp. 284–5.

37 *Ibid.*, pp. 310–21; F. Cesarini, 'Alle origini del credito industriale: la gestione dell'IMI dalla costituzione ai provvedimenti per l'autarchia (1931–1938)', in Banco di Roma, *Banca e industria fra le due guerre. Le riforme istituzionali e il pensiero giuridico*, pp. 81–180.

38 Toniolo, 'Crisi economica e smobilizzo pubblico', p. 322.

39 *Ibid.*, pp. 332–48; M. Giotti, 'La gestione dell'IRI dalla costituzione alla vigilia della transformazione in ente permanente', in Banco di Roma, *Banca e industria fra le due guerre. Le riforme istituzionali e il pensiero giuridico*, pp. 181–202. The text of the agreement between the Bank of Italy, the Ministry of Finance and the Credit is published in Cianci, *Nascità dello Stato imprenditore*, pp. 353–61.

40 Toniolo, 'Crisi economica e smobilizzo pubblico', pp. 325–30; Giotti, 'La gestione dell'IRI'.

41 See Pasquale Saraceno's remarks in Banco di Roma, *Banca e industria fra le due guerre. Atti del convegno*, pp. 75–84, esp. pp. 81–2.

42 S. R. Cope, in A. M. Allen, S. R. Cope, L. J. H. Dark and H. J. Witheridge, *Commercial Banking Legislation and Control* (London, 1928), p. 275, quoted in S. Cassese, 'The long life of the financial institutions set up in the thirties', *Journal of European Economic History*, 13, no. 2 (1984), pp. 273–94.

43 Belli, 'Le leggi bancarie del 1926 e del 1936–1938'; Cassese, 'La preparazione della riforma bancaria del 1936 in Italia'.
44 *Ibid.*
45 On Beneduce see F. Bonelli, 'Alberto Beneduce (1877–1944)', in Mortara (ed.), *I protagonisti dell'intervento pubblico in Italia*, pp. 329–56; on Menichella see P. Saraceno, 'Donato Menichella e il rapporto Banca-Industria', *Rivista di storia economica*, 2nd ser., 1, no. 2 (1984), pp. 269–74.

12 Banking and economic development in interwar Greece

MARK MAZOWER

The interwar years were a period of economic and political transformation in Greece. A decade of almost continuous warfare separated the victories of the Balkan Wars from the final defeat at the hands of the Turks in Asia Minor in 1922. When peace came the country had virtually doubled in size and population and had to cope with an influx of over one million refugees on top of the post-war economic dislocation experienced by other belligerents. For the first time in Greece's history, industrialization was recognized to be a necessity – for social and political as well as economic reasons. Yet although industrial growth after 1922 was rapid, the manufacturing sector that evolved was inefficient and primitive. The explanation that follows differs substantially in emphasis from those dependency theories which attribute failures to industrialize successfully in the 'periphery' to external pressures such as unfavourable terms of trade movements or competition from the 'centre's' exports. The example of Greece suggests that such factors were rather unimportant in comparison with internal structural problems and domestic policy choices and attitudes. Symptomatic of such problems was the failure of the banking system to respond to the rapid post-war changes in the country's economy.

Paradoxically this was partly because banking itself was a well-established branch of the pre-war Greek economy. It had, according to one commentator, provided fertile soil for the special qualities of the Greek character: 'the accurate grasp of profitability, his entrepreneurial ability and shrewdness which made him an important element and feared competitor in exchange and trade, but delayed his

206

contribution to other branches of the economy, which required patience and application, such as agriculture and industry'.[1] Greek banking remained in the hands of Greeks, and foreign participation was of marginal importance. The system was dominated by its oldest institution, the National Bank of Greece, which was supplanted as the country's central bank in 1928 by the newly founded Bank of Greece. The National Bank was also the country's largest commercial bank: in 1929 it controlled over 40 per cent of the country's bank deposits, whilst another four medium-sized institutions owned another 37 per cent. Beneath them was a host of small, often rather short-lived banks which did not operate on a national scale. There was no tradition of specialized banking and the smaller banks simply duplicated the lending patterns of the National Bank, concentrating on short-term lending to commerce. The minuscule size of industry in pre-1914 Greece reduced its appeal to bankers and it was estimated that around the turn of the century the banks were involved with no more than a dozen industrial firms at the most. Foreign investors were chiefly interested in mining which was of some importance in the pre-war economy but would dwindle to comparative insignificance after 1922.[2]

However, the First World War altered the outlook for both industry and banking in Greece. Despite the absence of hard data, it appears that Greek industry expanded significantly during wartime and by 1921 manufacturing had achieved a prominence in the domestic economy unmatched by her neighbours.[3] The internal market was doubled as a result of the addition of the northern provinces, whilst the ending of transatlantic emigration, the influx of refugees and high rates of population growth all helped to create a cheap labour supply. Most importantly, attitudes changed: post-war governments accepted the need to encourage industrialization. In 1917 a committee was set up to study the question of tariff reform with protectionist as well as fiscal criteria in mind. Its findings resulted in the 1923 tariff revision which was finally implemented in 1926, providing most domestic industries with a higher degree of protection than they could actually make use of. Other legislation encouraged the formation of Chambers of Commerce and Industry, which spread throughout the country, providing a powerful voice for the business world in a society where interest group organization was still held back by paternalistic political structures.[4]

The banks benefited from the considerable capital accumulation which took place after 1914. Between 1915 and 1919 profits from the merchant marine amounted to around 800 million gold francs compared with a pre-war annual average of 25–30 million. The inflow of emigrant remittances was also unusually high, especially in the years 1919–21. Much of this capital found its way into the banks: in 1921 their deposits stood at twice the 1914 level in real terms; net profits of the six leading banks increased more than five times between 1919 and 1922. The only bank to emerge from the war in uncertain shape was the National Bank itself which had shouldered the burden of financing the Macedonian campaign and the expedition to Asia Minor, as well as defending the drachma after it began to depreciate in 1920. However, the depreciation of the currency, which had remained remarkably strong during before 1919, opened up another area of profitable activity for Greek banks – exchange speculation. By 1922 even the members of the consortium set up to defend the currency, including the National Bank, were said to be speculating against further falls! Thus while currency instability and inflation discouraged emigrant remittances, which dropped shortly after 1921, they provided new opportunities for the commercial banks. In the early post-war years numerous small and under-capitalized banks sprang up, provoking legislation in 1926 to curb their activities.[5] When the exchange rate steadied in 1927, before being officially linked with gold the following year, the commercial banks found their most profitable avenue blocked to them. There were few signs by this point that wartime gains had increased the Greek banking system's capacity for providing long-term capital to the domestic economy. On the contrary, despite the increasing importance of industry, bank lending seems to have been more liquid than before the war, as the uncertainties surrounding the exchange rate and the budget led to a relative increase in short-term deposits and therefore lending. One contemporary scholar contrasted the shift *towards* long-term lending in the advanced economies with the opposite trend in Eastern Europe and much of Latin America, where banking profits lay not in industry but in supporting export activity and exchange speculation. Yet post-war reconstruction required long-term investment, not just in industry but in agriculture and the resettlement of the refugees. The response of the commercial banks to these demands would reveal the limited value of the domestic capital market in financing economic growth.[6]

The task of resettling the hundreds of thousands of refugees was too great to be left to the private sector and in 1923 under the auspices of the League of Nations a Refugee Settlement Commission was set up, whose activities were financed by a loan floated the following year. The RSC settled refugees chiefly on lands vacated by the Muslims who had moved to Turkey under the provisions of the exchange of populations agreed between the two countries. However, although the refugee resettlement and the associated land reform, which turned Greece into a country of smallholders, were funded by foreign capital, the Greek banks were involved in various ways. The National Bank, which combined the duties of a central bank with commercial operations, adopted a deliberate policy of promoting the creation of agricultural co-operatives to facilitate lending to peasants. As a recent scholar has emphasized, the apparently impressive increase in the number of co-operatives during the 1920s must be understood in the light of the aims of this policy: indeed one may argue that the National Bank was aiming thereby to achieve complete control of the sphere of agricultural credit. Between 1920 and 1927 the proportion of its agricultural loans directed towards co-operatives rose from 31 to 71 per cent.[7] These developments alarmed other proponents of the co-operative ideal in Greece, who saw organizations that they had hoped would form the nucleus of autonomous local centres, encouraging unambitious improvements in farming methods, turned simply into credit subsidiaries of an unofficial part of the state apparatus, interested only in short-term gain.[8] Senior officials of the National Bank managed to resist calls from the Ministry of Agriculture for an independent Agricultural Bank, which was postponed until the intervention of the League of Nations after 1927. Given the Bank's priorities, in particular its reluctance to lend long-term, it is not surprising that it was mostly interested in export agriculture. Indeed in the 1920s the profits to be made through financial intermediation in the export boom encouraged many other banks to enter this market.

Two commodities alone – currants and tobacco – accounted for over two-thirds of total Greek export earnings. Of these the less important, and the crop with the gloomier long-term prospects, was the former. A complex system of guaranteed support prices and export taxes absorbed the annual surplus production. The administration of these arrangements which had once been in the hands of private concessionaires was controlled after 1925 by the Autonomous Currant Organization, which brought together representatives of the growers, merchants and the National Bank in a sort of corporatist initiative. It soon became clear, however, where power lay. When fierce international competition led exports to decline and strained the resources of the Organization, the National Bank insisted on reducing the voting power of the growers, lowering support prices and supervising the terms on which the surplus was sold to the domestic wine manufacturers, in whom the Bank also had a large interest.[9]

The critics of the National Bank's policy on co-operatives saw their fears borne out in the case of tobacco. The new co-operatives took advantage of the banks' desire to participate in the tobacco trade to burden themselves with debt; according to one area study the peasants viewed the co-operatives as a panacea for all ills and an easy source of credit for non-essentials. Tobacco growers, many of whom had only recently been settled on their land, borrowed money to pay for day workers so that they could expand cultivation. Here the National Bank was by no means the only source of such financing: numerous institutions and individuals hastened to establish a foothold in the market. The Ionian Bank alone, which employed more funds in the tobacco trade than any of its rivals, increased its lending in the port of Cavalla – the centre of the export business – from £105,000 to £560,000 between 1923 and 1929.[10]

The financial linkages between banks, merchants and growers were intricate and volatile: typically, the banks did not lend directly to the peasants, but to merchants – either importers or exporters – who were prepared to pay very high rates in view of the profits to be made from lending to the growers. Export merchants lent funds against the forthcoming crop; importers advanced supplies of coffee, flour, sugar and other items on credit. Often the village shopkeeper was a further intermediary between merchant and peasant. For several years this type of lending was vastly more attractive than involvement with industry: it was relatively liquid and profitable so long as the market held up. Not surprisingly, towards the end of the 1920s it had become a source of speculation: many refugees, newly installed in the towns of northern Greece, borrowed heavily to set themselves up as merchants. One young economist noted in 1928 that 'everyone, seeing the enrichment of the merchants, which in practice was merely superficial, wanted to turn himself into a man of business'.[11] But in 1929 the combination of a record tobacco crop with a more cautious buying policy by foreign customers drove prices down and brought the whole intricate credit system to the verge of collapse. The growers' inability to repay their debts triggered off financial embarrassment among the merchants and banks. By July 1931 over half the total funds employed in Cavalla were immobilized in old stocks.[12]

Where other crops were concerned, the solvency of the peasant smallholder had been in doubt for much longer: domestic wheat prices in particular had been falling in line with world trends for several years, increasing the financial difficulties of many small-holders. Their political weight was considerable – 60 per cent of Greek farmers grew cereals, 10 per cent tobacco – and the Liberal govern-ment responded in 1930 by granting a moratorium on peasant debts owed to private individuals, who were frequently the very merchants who were themselves in debt to the commercial banks. Political pressure was also brought to bear on the newly founded Agricultural Bank (which took over the National Bank's responsibility for agricul-tural credit) to keep advances to farmers at a high level. As the onset of the world depression weakened the commercial banks' links with the agricultural sector, the Greek state took a more active role in provid-ing financial support. The Agricultural Bank was certainly not in a position to provide the long-term capital which was required to restructure farming – to finance, for example, a shift in the south from currant-growing to citrus fruits; like that other institution constructed as part of the stabilization programme, the Bank of Greece, it began life on shaky financial foundations, unable to do more than perpetu-ate its precursors' short-term lending policies. Nevertheless, the state's readiness to recognize the need to supplement or even supplant the activities of private capital where agriculture was con-cerned stood out in contrast with its attitude towards the provision of industrial credit. To understand the reasons for this contrast we should begin by looking at the way Greek industry developed after the war.

The rapid increase in the country's population – especially its urban population – and the appearance for the first time in Greek history of an urban proletariat without ties to the land, made the development of industry a political as well as an economic imperative. This was recognized with some reluctance by the political elite who looked back with regret to the quiet, provincial life of pre-war Old Greece and generally refused to believe that Greece was a country with an 'industrial character'.[13] When one looks at the structure of her industrial sector one can find some justification for this view: despite tariff protection and very low labour costs Greek industry was backward and inefficient. The survey of manufacturing published in 1930 revealed that most concerns were small, family enterprises, employing fewer than five people, with a level of mechanization low even by Balkan standards.[14] Closer examination, however, shows that Greek industry was divided into two classes: one containing a large number of the small enterprises described above, and another comprising rather large concerns using more sophisticated technology. For example, in the case of olive oil processing, only 600 out of approximately 6,000 firms were mechanized and only eight were capable of chemical purification of the oil; in 1932, of the seventeen major incorporated olive oil companies, just two used 62.5 per cent of the total employed capital. Half of all cigarettes produced by some 150 manufacturers were from just three large concerns.[15] We are not exactly faced with a case of pure oligopoly: high transport costs meant that large companies could not easily dominate the small ones. Rather the national market was divided between major firms located close to their main source of demand – the urban centres of Athens and Piraeus – and tiny local firms supplying the country areas.

The industrialists who ran the large enterprises formed a close-knit group whose nucleus was the pre-war 'Zurich circle', so named after the city where several members had studied around the turn of the century. In the words of a younger colleague these men 'created great industries out of nothing' and emerged as leading spokesmen for the business world. They included Epaminondas Charilaos, the interwar president of the Athens Chamber of Commerce, his brother-in-law Nik. Kanellopoulos, and Andreas Chadzikyriakos, who was president of the Federation of Greek Industrialists and Minister for the National Economy during the Metaxas dictatorship. Among the companies they controlled were leading producers of chemicals, wines and spirits and cement. Another more isolated figure was a younger man, Bodosakis Athanasiades, an Asia Minor Greek who made a fortune provisioning the Ottoman army in the First World War before settling in Greece. Bodosakis's memoirs describe the close links between politicians – of all persuasions – industrialists and bankers, a world in which the leading bank in the country might be requested by a newly installed General to 'finance' a forthcoming plebiscite, or commanded to set up a domestic arms industry. They remind us that in the economic history of a country like Greece personal contacts – even if they will not feature prominently in this study – are as important as market forces.[16]

The large operations of the 'Zurich circle' required substantial financing and raised the question of establishing an industrial credit bank. Although precise figures are lacking, since Greek banks were under no obligation to provide a full breakdown of their investments, it is clear that banks shied away from lending to industry; nor was there a well-developed stock exchange. Although there were signs after 1918 that the commercial banks were aware of the more favourable environment in which industry was now operating, their lending still generally took the form of renewable short-term advances. In 1918 Charilaos and other businessmen founded the Bank of Industry but its activities never extended beyond financing its founders' own enterprises and in September 1932 it was declared bankrupt. A similar concern, the General Bank, which had been set up by the Popular Bank to act as its industrial credit branch, met the same fate. Other banks tried in the period of euphoria between 1918 and 1921 to found industrial companies: both the National Bank and its main commercial rival did this, with little success. Such failures made foreign capital an increasingly attractive answer to the problem of financing long-term investment. By the middle of the decade British and American investors were showing interest in the development of public utilities, road-building and land reclamation schemes. Direct foreign investment had been insignificant in pre-war Greek industry – outside the extractive sector – but this seemed about to change: in 1926 the National Bank joined forces with Hambros Bank to form the Hellenic Corporation Ltd (later renamed the Hellenic and General Trust), a holding company intended to provide long-term industrial credit. The following year the same banks set up the National Mortgage Bank.[17]

The formation of the Hellenic Corporation provided the first indications that the National Bank was beginning to develop what one scholar describes as a 'timid interest' in industry and to move beyond the financing of small family firms, often connected with refugee settlement. This interest was sharpened after 1928 by the loss of its note-issuing privilege to the new central bank, and then, the following year by the loss of its control of agricultural credit to the Agricultural Bank. The result of the return to gold and the accompanying monetary reorganization in 1928 was thus to turn the National Bank towards industry. Within the bank a section for industrial credit was created, which also seems to have acted for the Hellenic and General Trust. Between 1928 and 1933, as the other commercial banks began to reduce their level of investments, the National Bank pursued the opposite course, deliberately maintaining a high level of credit to industry.[18]

Through its stake in the Hellenic and General, the National Bank increased its participation in most of the country's leading industrial concerns. With this involvement came efforts to impose 'rationalization', though this – as elsewhere in Europe – meant different things to different people. To most politicians it implied supporting those branches of industry least dependent upon imported inputs and therefore most 'viable' in Greece; to a number of academics it meant lower costs and increased international competitiveness through amalgamation; to industrialists themselves it seems to have often meant putting a stop to the fall in profits that had been produced by 'excessive' domestic competition.[19] Pursuing this goal, the National Bank encouraged mergers and cartels in several branches of industry. But the Bank, operating as a commercial institution, understandably confined its concern to those areas where it was commercially involved, and shied away from the task of long-term restructuring. Its governor, John Drosopoulos, made clear in 1930 that in his view 'it was not the work of the banks to take an active share in the management of industrial enterprises and still less to immobilize their funds in such enterprises in a permanent manner'.[20] The consequences of such an outlook were twofold: on the one hand, a growing preference for investment in government bonds rather than industry; on the other, the provision of loans to a restricted group of 'safe' leading concerns to the exclusion of the majority of smaller firms. Thus, for example, Kanellopoulos's chemical fertilizer company received a loan of £600,000, while firms associated with Charilaos and Chadzikyriakos also received substantial assistance. Over half of the Hellenic and General's investments was channelled into a mere three firms. The foreign directors of the Trust soon became disillusioned with the limited investment opportunities offered in Greece and announced at the first general meeting that, contrary to the spirit of the original venture, the company would henceforth consider investing elsewhere.[21]

The other commercial banks were even less prepared for close involvement with industry. They were rarely represented on company boards. From Salonica, the second largest city in the country, a local bank manager reported that 'they only receive information when matters are really bad. Here there is also a tendency to look upon interference by the banks as a disgrace and as a sign of potential insolvency.'[22] Greek financiers and politicians, lacking any positive programme for improving industrial competitiveness and increasing exports of manufactures from their negligible level, confined themselves to wishing that the plethora of small firms which sprang up in the 1920s would be 'cleansed' by the oncoming depression. These hopes, however, were to be disappointed. To see why, we should turn to examine the changes in the banking system in Greece that accompanied the return to gold in 1928 and the effect these had on the transmission of the crisis.

Orthodox banking theory is based on the experience of developed economies. But change the institutional and political setting and the theory may cease to be applicable. Debating legislation in April 1931 designed to force the commercial banks to keep deposits with the new central bank, an opposition spokesman, taking issue with the Liberal government's appeal to the views recently expressed by Keynes in *A Treatise on Money*, asserted that Keynes 'clearly had the English and not the Greek money-market in his mind. Thus we may ask: is there really a parallel between the Greek and the British market? Here, gentlemen, there is such an enormous difference of conditions between the two markets that Keynes's theories may be borne out in England, and have no relevance to us.'[23] Indeed conditions were different, as one may judge from what happened in Greece when – as elsewhere on the periphery of the world economy between the wars – a central bank was established in accordance with the accepted principles of contemporary central banking: once it began operations in May 1928 it soon found many obstacles to smooth operation.

The first was political: the establishment of a potentially powerful new financial institution, basically as a precondition for the League of Nations' support in floating loans abroad, was bound to excite the hostility of existing banks and their supporters. Members of the opposition Populist Party had favoured turning the National Bank into a pure central bank and insisted that the newcomer was too weak to defend the national currency; such views gained weight, of course, as the unfolding balance of payments crisis depleted the new Bank's exchange reserves. Once in government, in 1933, Populist ministers repeatedly threatened to introduce legislation merging the Bank with the National Bank. And Venizelos too, the Liberal Prime Minister between 1928 and 1932, was critical of the new institution, which he regarded simply as the price that had to be paid for foreign financial assistance.[24]

Financially, the Geneva Protocol of 1927, which set out the terms on which the new institution was to be founded, left it in rather a vulnerable position. Though buoyed up with reserves which covered 80 per cent of the notes in circulation, it had been obliged to accept a large amount of illiquid state debt, which had been transferred from the National Bank, and which came to almost half its total assets. What was worse, the National Bank refused to hand over the deposits of a number of state institutions in violation of the Geneva agreement. It is not surprising that the new Governor of the Bank of Greece, Alexandros Diomedes, who moved there from the National Bank, expressed the view that the latter was, if anything, strengthened rather than weakened by this new arrival. In 1929 the National Bank opened a new branch in New York to reinforce its control over the flow of emigrant remittances, thereby excluding the central bank from a vital source of foreign exchange. In May 1931 at a meeting of the Financial Committee of the League of Nations – an important watch-dog over Central and East European banking between the wars – there was lengthy discussion of the 'enormous strength' and 'practical monopoly' exerted by the National Bank; Mlynarsky, the Czech delegate, warned that 'if the Bank of Greece is not strong enough to cope, the authority of the State should be called in to compel the National Bank not only to reduce its portfolio of drachma bills and foreign exchange, but also to re-discount bills with the Bank of Greece'.[25]

As these remarks suggest, the commercial banks – with the National Bank at their head – were ill disposed to accept the idea of central bank supervision. Only in 1931 did Parliament debate legislation designed to compel them to maintain deposits with the central bank, and when the bill was eventually passed its provisions were considerably less rigorous than the Bank of Greece's authorities had desired: it provided for a minimum liquidity ratio of 12 per cent which did *not* have to be kept at the central bank. This was an obvious constraint on the Bank's ability to control the volume of credit. Another problem was its lack of control over foreign exchange movements. This was significant since Greece relied on invisible earnings and capital inflows to balance its chronic visible trade deficit. The commercial banks were able to attract much of this exchange to their branches abroad before transferring it to Greece independently of the central bank. Even after 1928 they continued to accept deposits and make advances denominated in foreign currencies. All these factors made it difficult for the Bank of Greece to defend the drachma once its reserves began to run out. The president of the Bank for International Settlements wrote in the late summer of 1931 in response to Greek appeals for help: 'However sound the policy of the Bank of Greece may be, we would face great difficulty in approaching other central banks, in so far as the commercial banks in Greece appear to be following a different policy.' How – his letter continued – could foreign banks be expected to risk their own exchange holdings, when there were still foreign currency deposits within Greece unused by the Bank of Greece?[26]

One final difference between the positions of the Bank of Greece and, say, the Bank of England, was the former's inability to draw upon the two traditional methods of British credit control – open-market operations and changes in the official discount rate. The Bank's limited capacity to re-discount bills, combined with the fact that short-term government stock was unknown in Greece, made the former instrument unfeasible. Since the commercial banks were in a considerably healthier position than the Bank of Greece, they had sufficient funds to ignore changes in the discount rate, which was thus of limited value as an instrument of credit polity. Nor did it affect capital flows, which were more sensitive to considerations of security than they were to interest rate differentials. Considering all these factors, we may understand why the Deputy Governor of the Bank of Greece, Emmanouil Tsouderos, told the League of Nations Financial Committee on 7 September 1931 that 'in the present conditions, the rigid observation of the strictly orthodox principles governing the conduct of central banks may lead to results contrary to those which were desired'.[27]

It is not therefore surprising that the new central bank operated

from the start according to principles which members of the Financial
Committee would almost certainly have regarded as highly unortho-
dox. The Bank's response to the difficulties which faced it was a hesi-
tant and confused policy combining attempts at deflation with direct
competition for business with the commercial banks. Let us look more
closely at what this involved.

In the same year, 1928, in which the Bank of Greece began to function, the Liberal politician Eleftherios Venizelos, who dominated
Greek politics until his death in 1936, returned to power. Over the
next four years his government raised several large loans in Western
Europe to finance public works, aimed chiefly at land reclamation and
infrastructural improvements. The Liberal Finance Minister argued
rather defensively in March 1931 that 'if the national income were
adequate, or if the different productive sectors of the country operated in a more satisfactory manner, then the present policy of the
productive works would be excessive. In that case it would perhaps be
preferable to follow a more cautious policy of restraining expenditures and returning the state to its old limited role in accordance with
the tenets of the orthodox school ... But at present such a conservative
policy finds itself in plain contradiction to essential popular and social
interests.'[28] Greece's foreign debt grew rapidly and by the early 1930s
was a higher percentage of export earnings than in any other Balkan
country. Falling export prices caused the real debt service burden to
increase by 45 per cent between 1929 and 1931; with deficits on both
current and capital accounts on the Greek balance of payments, the
burden of adjustment was thrown on to the central bank.

With the exception of a period in 1930, net outflows of exchange
from the Bank of Greece's reserves continued from early 1929 right
through to the autumn of 1931. The ratio between its reserves and the
volume of notes in circulation – the so-called 'cover ratio' – fell from
75 per cent at the end of 1928 to 53 per cent at the end of September
1931; over the same period the slow contraction of the quantity of
notes in circulation alarmed the observers of the Greek scene on the
League's Financial Committee. A further loan had been raised for the
Greek government on the London market in the spring of 1931,
though most of the issue had been left with the underwriters and
Montagu Norman had warned that no further issues would be possible
for some time. In May the Committee concluded that though there
was 'no present cause for anxiety . . . the position is sufficiently dis-

quieting to make reform measures necessary'. Pressure on the Bank's reserves was partly attributed to deliberately hostile actions by the commercial banks. One delegate suggested engineering a further contraction through open-market operations since 'even a 10% reduction of the note circulation would make the other banks squeal!'[29]

In fact the Bank was attempting to exert its authority over the commercial banks in quite another fashion – by competing directly with them! To loud protests from the commercial sector it opened a network of branch offices throughout the country; its commercial advances rose from 168 million drachmas at the end of 1928 to 564 million the following year and 811 million in 1930. From the export port of Kalamata the local manager of the Ionian Bank reported how from the moment the staff of the Bank of Greece opened a branch in May 1930 'they gave us the impression which has proved correct, that they meant to compete with the other banks in most lines of business'. In Patras his colleague noted that the Bank and the National Bank were competing on an unprecedented scale, pushing down interest rates and enabling local businessmen to obtain 'excessive facilities at very low terms which cannot be justified by the actual position of the market'. The following year competition pushed provincial rates even lower and the Bank of Greece was – in violation of its own statutes – granting advances at 7 per cent when its own discount rate stood at 9 per cent![30]

Thus at the very time that the world crisis was causing trade to slow down and increasing pressures on the Bank's own reserves, it pursued a policy which was quite contrary to the orthodox deflationary remedy, thereby compounding the credit inflation which heavy competition among the commercial banks had created. There were at the end of the 1920s no less than ten banks operating in the tobacco port of Cavalla, and sixteen in Salonica, where one observer noted that 'it is evident we are going through a period of financial cleansing and reconstruction, the rhythm of which is simply delayed by the competition of the banks'. To experienced observers it was clear that a period of retrenchment lay ahead; the Cavalla manager of the Ionian Bank wrote in September 1929 that 'under the circumstances the year 1927/28 must be considered as marking the high level of profits and 1928/29 the high level of employed funds. For many years I do not anticipate such figures.'[31] However, if the Bank of Greece ignored

these warnings it was not just for reasons of its own; it was also suscep-
tible to heavy pressure from the Liberal government to sustain a mood
of confidence. Prime Minister Venizelos himself personally requested
both the Bank and the National Bank in June 1931 to intervene on the
Athens stock market in order to 'give a psychological boost to prices'.
The National Bank was also employed by the government for related
operations, such as buying up shares and bonds and – together with
the newly founded Agricultural Bank – maintaining a high level of
advances to peasant farmers.[32]

The Greek economy was thus spared the rigours of the sort of
deflationary regime which the League's Financial Committee recommended. It is unlikely that the Bank of Greece – even had it so wanted
– could have forced such a policy on the commercial banks, whose
position before the autumn of 1931 was generally secure. There were
few banking collapses, and these did not jeopardize the system as a
whole; what did occur was a transfer of funds by depositors from the
medium-sized banks to the National Bank, whose share of the major
banks' advances increased between 1928 and 1931 from 38 to 59 per
cent and of deposits from 53 to 65 per cent, making it even more difficult for the central bank to challenge its dominance of the commercial
sector.[33] But as the figures in table 12.1 suggest, the public did not lose
confidence in the system as a whole.

However, as we have already indicated, the authorities did *not* have
any confidence in deflation. Commercial bank deposits at the central
bank fell after early 1929. The official discount rate was cut in
November 1928 to 5 per cent where it remained until the autumn of
1931. Thus despite the occasional cries from the business world that
credit was too tight, it seems that if anything the opposite was true: as
one economist argued at the time, the Bank of Greece deliberately
followed an expansionary course from the time of its foundation. The
Bank's foreign adviser, H. C. Finlayson, informed Venizelos that 'the
Bank of Greece, unlike all the other central Banks in Europe, has been
content to play a purely passive role. It has not raised its discount rate
nor tried in any way to cut back its advances.'[34]

The relatively easy ride which the Greek banks enjoyed during the
international depression came to a halt with the onset of the European
financial crisis in the summer of 1931. The key blow was the British
decision to devalue sterling in September which left Greek politicians
and bankers disoriented and uncertain how to respond. Greece

Table 12.1. *The position of the commercial banks*

	Liquidity (%)	Deposits (mill. drs.)	Note circulation (mill. drs.)	Notes/Deposits (%)
1927	15.2	9,406	4,966	52.8
1928	14.5	13,020	5,870	45.1
1929	14.6	13,356	5,193	38.9
1930	18.5	15,660	4,803	30.7
1931	19.0	14,464	4,003	27.7
1932	17.4	13,736	4,714	34.3

Note: col. 1: capital + reserves/total liabilities.
Source: A. Kirkilitsis, *Ai trapezai en Elladi* (Athens, 1934), p. 19.

lacked the close financial ties which her northern neighbours had with Central Europe, but she was heavily dependent upon London for the continued financing of the public works.

At a meeting called by the Prime Minister the day after news of the sterling crisis reached Athens, it was agreed that Greece should remain on gold. The Liberal government had created a climate of complacency about the strength of the country's economy which – so spokesmen insisted – had so far managed to escape the worst effects of the international depression. Diomedes, the Governor of the Bank of Greece, insisted publicly on the night of 21 September that the crisis would be 'temporary' and that Greece would be less severely hit than elsewhere.[35] There were many reasons apart from these to advocate not following sterling: the politicians feared that devaluation would lead to renewed inflation and had also turned the stabilization into a sign of national virility; devaluation would also lead to an increase in the drachma cost of servicing the foreign debt, an unwelcome prospect with an election only a year away. Nor did the commercial banks dissent: in the event of devaluation they faced heavy losses on their foreign exchange liabilities. The only critic was the Bank of Greece's adviser, Professor Kyriakos Varvaressos, who telegraphed from London that he shared Sir Otto Niemeyer's view that the decision to remain on gold was 'hasty and ill-considered'.[36]

The news from London led to a run on the Bank, whose foreign reserves fell $3.6 million in one week; on 28 September exchange restrictions were rather belatedly introduced. Diomedes was forced to resign by Venizelos to be succeeded – after a politically charged struggle – by his former deputy, Tsouderos. A special committee was established to consider applications for foreign exchange, and Greek exporters were obliged to surrender their exchange earnings to the central bank in return for drachmas at the official rate. But in spite of these measures, the outlook for the Bank deteriorated: the outflow of exchange in the final quarter of 1931 was the heaviest since its foundation – more than double that which had occurred in the wake of the Wall Street crash. While exporters were unwilling to comply with the new regulations, import demand remained high as merchants built up stocks against an eventual depreciation. In December, Tsouderos requested Venizelos to bring in legislation compelling the commercial banks to surrender their holdings of exchange since 'we do not believe it is realistic to express the hope that by the efforts of the State and the Bank of Greece alone, we can balance our external accounts and at the same time avoid the gradual erosion both of our remaining disposable funds in gold abroad and of our exchange'.[37]

The commercial banks were facing fewer difficulties in the last months of 1931. One reason for this was the unimportance of lending to industry, or long-term lending generally. As elsewhere in southern Europe, the mildness with which the depression had affected Greece was widely attributed to the small degree of industrialization. The fact that several banks which did close down during the crisis had what by Greek standards were unusually close ties with industry only increased the traditional suspicion for such types of financing. Commercial portfolios were based on bonds and advances to commerce; in July 1931, for example, medium- and long-term advances of all kinds were only half the value of short-term advances.[38]

Drachma deposits with the commercial banks actually increased by 3 per cent in the last quarter of 1931, while there was only a slight contraction of credit. Despite the fact that many bank assets were effectively frozen, there was little evidence of public anxiety about the stability of the banking system itself. The explanation for this surely lies in the highly oligopolistic structure of the commercial sector, protected by the great weight and prestige of the National Bank.

But after the New Year the 'battle for the drachma' became fiercer and more desperate. This was the point at which import restrictions began to bite and – in Finlayson's words – 'brought commerce to a standstill'. As factories were forced to close for lack of raw materials, the business world showed signs of irritation with the politicians' view that the existing gold parity should be defended. Manufacturers criticized the banks for 'having originally been far too generous in granting credits, and now being over-cautious, exacerbating our difficulties'.[39] But the banks were themselves in an increasingly precarious position: the liquidity ratio of the 'big four' banks dropped from 16.8 per cent in December to 9.7 per cent in April, and from 17.8 to 12.5 per cent for the system as a whole. The withdrawal of deposits accelerated, whilst their cash base fell by one-third in the first quarter of 1932. At this point they turned to the institution they had previously fought against: the new central bank now came into its own as a lender of last resort. Between January and April the Bank's commercial advances rose from 300 million to 733 million drachmas – of which 500 million were direct advances to the commercial banks. According to Finlayson, 'the Bank of Greece . . . in its quality as lender of last resort, intervened at the proper time and adopted the wisest course'.[40]

However, the initial mismanagement of the response to the sterling crisis, followed by the protracted struggle to find a new governor, left it politically on the defensive. In November a leading economic adviser to the Populist Party, Dimitrios Maximos, published an attack on the Bank which – he argued – events had shown was incapable of functioning as an independent institution; he urged that it be merged with the National Bank since it could not survive without it. Members of the League of Nations' Financial Committee came to the defence of the Bank on this issue but offered little substantive help.[41]

In January Venizelos toured the capitals of Western Europe to seek financial assistance and the following month Niemeyer visited Athens on behalf of the Committee. The Bank's reserve situation was desperate since with invisible earnings having dried up, the Bank had to finance both the debt service and the trade deficit. In the first quarter of 1932 – the period when the Bank extended assistance to the commercial banks – the note circulation fell only 2.5 per cent despite a 19.5 per cent drop in the reserves. But the foreign help which alone could have kept Greece on the gold standard was not forthcoming. The League's Financial Committee issued a report at the end of March which recommended that Greece be included within the League's projected recovery plan. Although Venizelos wanted to hold out until the Lausanne Conference in June, when this plan was to be discussed, he was privately urged at Geneva in April to devalue the drachma without delay. Finlayson noted: 'it is indeed curious to reflect that the same persons who had advised Greece to stabilise its currency in 1928 should have been compelled to advise departure from gold in 1932, but I am certain they were right in each case; stabilisation was necessary in 1928 to surmount an inflation crisis, the opposite course is indicated today to meet a deflation crisis'.[42]

In Greece opinion had swung in the same direction. Many manufacturers had been supporting such a move for some time, arguing that it would allow a looser credit policy. They were now joined by the commercial banks. Remaining on gold, according to one, had led to 'withdrawals of bank deposits, an increase in the circulation of banknotes in its most unfavourable form, stagnation in the export trade, excessive profits for certain importers at the expense of the community as a whole etc.'. A memorandum from the general manager of the Bank of Athens to the Prime Minister aptly pointed out that 'it may fairly be said of our economy that the gold standard, which is designed to secure the payment of international debts, can only function upon the condition that they are not paid'. The only commercial bank to oppose the idea of leaving gold was, curiously, the National Bank, which had profited from watching the 'battle for the drachma' from the sidelines.[43]

This time, however, the National Bank was in the minority. Venizelos himself acknowledged with considerable reluctance that the drachma would have to depreciate, and this was announced at the end of April. The Bank of Greece was given greatly enlarged powers to supervise all gold and foreign exchange transactions and its hold over the commercial banks was extended further in July when the latter were obliged to hand over all their foreign exchange to the Bank as part of the so-called 'drachmification' law, whereby foreign exchange liabilities were taken over by the Bank and converted into drachma ones at a low rate of exchange. Largely as a consequence of this measure, the Bank's reserves rose from a low of 784 million drachmas at the end of May to 1,866 millions two months later. Trade and exchange controls were tightened and the drachma was allowed to float, falling almost 60 per cent against sterling before stabilizing at the beginning of 1933.

As one of their arguments against leaving gold the authorities at the National Bank warned that devaluation would lead to a run on the commercial banks. In fact what is striking about the experience of the Greek banks is their avoidance of the sort of crisis which occurred elsewhere in the Balkans. There was no Greek parallel to the failure of the Bank Marmorosch Blank in Romania or to the run on the banks in Yugoslavia after the summer of 1931. No Greek bank was as heavily committed to industry as the leading Romanian banks; nor, as we have seen, did the Greek central bank pursue the sort of severely contractionary policy adopted by the National Bank of Yugoslavia. There was a transfer of deposits from time- to sight-accounts, but the overall level of bank deposits rose after April 1932, and again it is clear that the strength of the National Bank of Greece reassured investors, although in the case of small banks in the provinces there *were* reports of depositors withdrawing funds 'to keep them in their own safes or to invest in property'.[44] The commercial banks pursued a rather restrained lending policy, not regaining their pre-crisis level until August 1934, by which time the domestic recovery was well under way. On the other hand, the Bank of Greece continued the active lending policy it had begun before the crisis. In Patras it was reported to be taking advantage of its new control of foreign exchange to extend its control over the financing of currant exporters. Central bank lending rose as a percentage of commercial bank lending from 4.3 per cent in January 1932 to 17.2 per cent at the end of the year and 25 per cent by the end of 1935.[45]

From the middle of 1932 capital which had been withdrawn from the banks was invested in real estate, starting a boom which continued for several years, especially in the Athens region. In addition many family businesses were traditionally self-financing and were thus not affected by the credit policy of the commercial banks. In October the US commercial attaché observed that the crisis was eased by the country's 'hidden reserves' as traders and businessmen drew on their own funds. 'Business in Athens', he noted, 'goes on with almost no appearance of a financial crisis.'[46]

These financial factors – the absence of a prolonged banking collapse, the limited reliance of industry on bank credit – help explain why Greece recovered so quickly after leaving gold. But of course the more important reasons are not negative ones; they include the record harvests of 1932–3 which boosted rural demand for manufactures, the impact of export restrictions and above all the devaluation itself. The drachma fell further than any other currency in Europe, providing domestic producers – as elsewhere in the Balkans – with the benefits of a 'real' devaluation. In 1936 the Royal Institute of

International Affairs reported in its survey of economic conditions in south-eastern Europe that 'in Greece there has been an almost spectacular recovery'.[47]

Greek industry prospered in the autarkic conditions of the 1930s. Growth rates in the first four years after 1932 were surpassed only by the USSR and Japan. Industrialists were able to pass on increases in costs to the consumer. Real wages fell whilst profitability rose sharply after the difficult years of 1929–31. However, impressive growth was not accompanied by modernization; the crisis did not, as had been hoped at the end of the 1920s, 'cleanse' the market of the large number of small, inefficient, family firms. On the contrary, these were rather well equipped to survive the financial crisis and enjoy the protected environment of the 1930s. As Ivan Berend has observed, what has to be explained is why high rates of growth were accompanied by a widening of the technology gap that separated the Balkan states from Western Europe.[48]

This gap could only have been closed if the state had provided incentives to industry to modernize, but in fact the policy of successive Greek governments was the reverse of this. Not only did they discourage industrial expansion, fearing that the firms created under a highly protectionist regime would be unable to compete on world markets once a liberal international economic order was re-established. They also hindered businessmen's attempts to reinvest profits in imports of machines to replace existing installations; that this was badly needed was demonstrated by a report on the textiles industry which found that in 1936 at least one-third of the existing machinery was in need of immediate replacement and that most of it was at least thirty to forty years old.[49] Thus profits were diverted to other uses – financing the real estate boom or spending on luxury goods. A rough calculation suggests that between 1932 and 1936 profits of leading industrial concerns came to around 2,000 million drachmas, yet in the same period the value of new investment in installations and buildings amounted to under 650 million drachmas.[50] However, this policy was not entirely unwelcome to established businessmen since it had the merit of preventing new competitors entering the market; the only real opposition to it came from 'experts' in the universities and the press whose views carried little political weight.

Greece's default on her foreign debt in 1932 meant that henceforth economic development would have to be financed from her own

Table 12.2. *Long-term lending and industrial growth*

	A	B	C	A/B	A/C
1930	5,343	17,890	6,671	29.9	80.1
1935	5,811	18,023	10,177	32.2	57.1
1939	4,716	21,670	14,113	21.8	33.4

A: long-term bank lending (excluding Bank of Greece, Agricultural Bank)
B: total bank lending (by same banks as A)
C: value of gross industrial output.
Sources: Oikonomia tis Ellados; Elliniki Oikonomia, various issues.

resources. It seemed plausible to argue that – as Kindleberger has generalized for the underdeveloped world – with a primitive money market a basically poor country like Greece would find this task beyond it. In 1937 the ex-Governor of the Bank of Greece, Alexandros Diomedes, warned that the country was reaching 'the limits of autarky' and that the only way to relieve her shortage of domestic capital was to seek a final settlement of the external debt and regain access to Western money markets.[51] Yet it is difficult to argue that further industrial growth required more capital than the banks could provide: between 1931 and 1939 the total value of new installations and buildings in industry amounted to less than one-quarter of the increase in bank lending. In other words, the problem was not lack of capital itself so much as the lending preferences of the banks.[52] The financial crisis reinforced the conservative instincts of the commercial banks and appeared to offer ample justification for their reluctance to lend long-term. There is no available data on the extent of commercial banks lending to industry. But there are statistics on overall long-term lending, which make it clear that this type of credit was of diminishing significance during the 1930s. The key example of this is provided by the National Bank itself, which, as we have seen, increased its domination of the commercial system. Whilst its short-term lending grew steadily throughout the 1930s, its long-term advances increased slightly after 1932 before declining again after 1936; by 1939 they represented 16.5 per cent of its total advances compared with 47.4 per cent in 1930. In the system as a whole, including the National Mortgage Bank, the figures in table 12.2 indicate that long-term lending remained static.

As before the crisis bank lending was funnelled into chosen industries with close ties with the National Bank, which continued to encourage the trend towards concentration. This had an increasingly obvious geographical dimension and as the recovery continued a contrast emerged between the flourishing condition of the Athens–Piraeus area and the economic stagnation in provincial towns. In Patras, a major port before 1932, business remained depressed well into the recovery, while the strikes and urban unrest in Salonica reflected the inhabitants' feeling that – as one Governor-General of Macedonia put it – they had no way of wresting power out of the hands of the 'Brahmins' in Athens. Leading firms shifted to the capital and others followed: between 1932 and 1936 membership of the Athens Chamber of Commerce and Industry increased at a rate unmatched until the 1960s. The Metaxas regime was sufficiently disturbed by this to commission a report on the problem by the Supreme Economic Council which estimated that roughly half the major industries in the country were centred around the capital. By the end of the decade the National Bank was disbursing three-quarters of its industrial credits through its Athens office.[53]

Critics of Greek banking argued that this was yet another symptom of a poorly functioning system of credit allocation: it was quite avoidable, since the developed state of branch banking in Greece (unlike elsewhere in the Balkans) made it possible to channel credit into the provinces. What needed to be overcome was the prevailing suspicion of industry.[54] It was this very suspicion that had led official policymakers at the beginning of the interwar period to leave the question of industrial investment to the market. It is revealing that the nearest institutional equivalent to the Agricultural Bank was a *private* venture, the Hellenic and General Trust. Industry benefited from certain financial policies – such as the expansionary monetary policy after 1928 and the depreciation of the drachma after April 1932 – but these could hardly be said to have been followed as part of an industrial policy. The need for 'rationalization' had been recognized, but again left to private initiative. As the example of the Hellenic and General Trust showed, the private sector was reluctant to enmesh itself in the task of reorganizing industry. Nor could 'rationalization' be entrusted to the 'cleansing' effects of the crisis: the post-1932 recovery showed that the outcome was the increasingly monopolistic exploitation of the domestic market by firms which had few incentives to modernize. Paradoxically the lack of the sort of difficulties which led in Italy to the formation of IRI made it less urgent for the Greek state to intervene in restructuring the credit system: both the banks and industry survived the crisis relatively well. This interpretation of the interwar decade suggests that in a newly industrializing country like Greece economic development was not doomed to distortion or failure as a result of external pressures, but neither could it be left to the market. Financing long-term goals was a risk domestic capitalists preferred to forgo, especially in such a turbulent era. In Greece the capital *was* available but it required state intervention to channel it in the right direction. This was not forthcoming and as a result the participation of the commercial banks in industry remained extremely limited, and impressive short-term growth rates masked an increasingly backward economic structure.

NOTES

1 A. Kirkilitsis, *Ai trapezai en Elladi* (Athens, 1934), foreword.
2 T. Galanis, *Trapezikai meletai* (Athens, 1946), p. 6; Kirkilitsis, *Trapezai*, p. 86; X. Zolotas, *I Ellas eis to stadion tis ekviomichaniseos* (Athens, 1926), pp. 26, 42.
3 M. Jackson and J. Lampe, *Balkan Economic History: 1550–1950* (Bloomington, Ind., 1982), pp. 338–40; M. Mazower, 'Towards autarky: the recovery from crisis in Greece, 1929–1936', unpublished D.Phil. thesis (Oxford University, 1987), pp. 24–5.
4 Department of Trade (E. C. D. Rawlins), *Report on the Industrial and Economic Situation in Greece for the Year to April 1922* (London, 1922), p. 10; Department of Trade (R. F. H. Duke), *Report on the Industrial and Economic Situation in Greece for the Years 1923 and 1924* (London, 1925), p. 6.
5 Zolotas, *Eis to stadion*, p. 33; E. Mears, *Greece Today: The Aftermath of the Refugee Impact* (Stanford, Calif., 1929), p. 207; D. G. Bristoyiannis, *La politique de la Banque Nationale de Grèce* (Paris, 1928), pp. 126–42; K. Kostis and T. Veremis, *I Ethniki Trapeza stin Mikri Asia (1919–1922)* (Athens, 1984), *passim.*
6 Kirkilitsis, *Trapezai*, pp. 42–3.
7 K. Kostis, *Agrotiki oikonomia kai georgiki trapeza* (Athens, 1987), p. 187.
8 A. Sideris, *I georgiki politiki tis Ellados kata tin lixasan ekatonaetian* (Athens, 1934), pp. 342–4; Ch. Evelpides, 'L'agriculture en Grèce', *Les Balkans*, 5, no. 1 (Jan.–Feb. 1934), 28–71.
9 Kostis, *Agrotiki oikonomia*, pp. 192–4.
10 F. Altsitsoglu, *Oi giakades kai o kampos tis Xanthis* (Athens, 1941), pp. 196–9; Ionian Bank Archives, St Antony's College, Oxford (hereafter IBA), Cavalla Yearly Report 1929/30, 'Review of the Results of the Last Ten Years'.
11 A. Angelopoulos, 'Ai anonymoi etaireiai en Elladi', *Archeion Oik. kai Koinonikon Epistimon*, 8 (1928), 31.
12 IBA/Cavalla, Half-Yearly Report 1930/31.
13 George Pesmazoglu, Minister for the National Economy, in *Viomichaniki Epitheorisis*, July 1934.
14 Ethniki Trapeza tis Ellados, *Oikonomiki Epetiris: 1933* (Athens, 1934), p. 54.

15 Ypourgeion tis Ethnikik Oikonomias, *Elliniki viomichania* (Athens, 1931), pp. 234–5; *Efimeris Chrimatistiriou*, 30 Sept. 1934; I. Serraios, *Peri tis eisagogis monopoliou kapnou en Elladi* (Athens, 1934), pp. 33–7.
16 ETVA, *Elliniki viomichania apo ton 190 sto 20o aiona* (Athens, 1985), pp. 14–15; Bodosakis Athanasiades, copy of unpublished typescript of untitled memoirs in author's possession, pp. 136–9.
17 Kirkilitsis, *Trapezai*, p. 87; M. Dritsas, 'La Banque nationale de Grèce et l'industrie', unpublished thesis (University of Paris 1, 1984), p. 57; *The Banker*, 25 (Feb. 1928), 289–91.
18 Dritsas, 'La Banque', pp. 45, 62–3; National Bank of Greece (hereafter NBG), *Report for the Year 1929 of the Governor of the National Bank of Greece* (Athens, 1930), p. 9; NBG, *Report for the Year 1930* (1931), pp. 11–13; *Report for the Year 1931* (1932), p. 14.
19 *Oikonomologos Athinon*, 22 Nov. 1930, 10 Jan. 1931; *Near East and India*, 10 April 1930; P. Dertilis, *La reconstruction financière de la Grèce et la Société des Nations* (Paris, 1929), pp. 217–18.
20 NBG, *Report for 1929*, pp. 24–5.
21 N. Anastasopoulos, *Istoria tis elliniki viomichanias*, vol. III (Athens, 1947), p. 1579.
22 IBA/Salonica, Yearly Report 1930/31.
23 S. Stefanopoulos in *Efimeris ton syzitiseon tis Voulis* (hereafter ESV), session 60, 1 April 1931, p. 1364.
24 E. Venizelos in *ibid.*, pp. 1382–5; K. Kostis, *Oi trapezes kai i krisi, 1929–1932* (Athens, 1986), pp. 107–11.
25 Archeion El. Venizelou, Benaki Museum Athens (hereafter AEV), 342, 'Notes of the discussions on our reports: Geneva', 11 May 1931; Kostis, *Trapezai kai krisi*, pp. 43–54.
26 *Ibid.*, pp. 62–98; Archeion Emm. Tsouderou, Bank of Greece, Athens (hereafter AET), 101/52, Diomedes to Tsouderos, 10 Sept. 1931; AET 65/12, McGarrah to Diomedes, 17 Sept. 1931.
27 AET, 'Keimena': League of Nations Finance Committee, 42nd session, procès-verbal, p. 6.
28 ESV, session 47, 12 March 1931, p. 949.
29 AEV 342, Tsouderos to Diomedes, 2 May 1931; Kostis, *Trapezes kai krisi*, p. 139; Bank of Greece, *Report of the Governor of the Bank of Greece for the Year 1931* (Athens, 1932), 37; AEV 342, 'Notes of the discussions of our reports: Geneva', 11 May 1931.
30 Kostis, *Trapezes kai krisi*, pp. 74–98, 140; IBA/Kalamata Yearly Report 1929/30; IBA/Patras, Yearly Report 1929/30, Yearly Report 1930/31; T. Galanis, 'I politiki tis Trapezis tis Ellados', *Ploutos*, 24 Jan. 1932; British Foreign Office, Public Record Office, Kew, FO 371/19517 R4809/646, Niemeyer to Britain, 23 July 1935.
31 IBA/Cavalla, Yearly Report 1928/29.
32 AEV 424, Venizelos to Koryzis, 30 June 1931; *ibid.*, Venizelos to Tsouderos, 30 June 1931; NBG, *Report for 1931*, p. 14; IBA/Cavalla Yearly Report 1930/31.
33 My calculations from Kostis, *Trapezes kai krisi*, pp. 64–5.
34 P. Christodoulopoulos, *Pistotiki politiki kai periodikai kriseis* (Athens, 1930); I. Venezis, *Emm. Tsouderos* (Athens, 1966), p. 68.
35 *Eleftheron Vima*, 24 April 1932; I. Venezis, *Chronikon tis Trapezis tis Ellados, 1928–1952* (Athens, 1955), pp. 100–1; IBA/General Manager's Report for 1932/33.
36 G. Pyrsos, *Symvoli eis tin istorian tis Trapezis tis Ellados*, vol. I (Athens, 1936), pp. 88–9.
37 AET 65/1, 'Situation and development of the cover', 4 Dec. 1931; AET 344, Niemeyer to Tsouderos, 16 Dec. 1931.

38 Trapeza tis Ellados, *Deltion*, Aug. 1931; AET 74/1, 'Table 3'.
39 AET 65/20, Finlayson to Venizelos, 10 Feb. 1932; *El. Vima*, 16 Jan. 1932.
40 AET 74/1, 'Situation of the commercial banks in Greece', 9 March 1933; AET 72/5, 'The policy of the Bank of Greece and the situation of the commercial banks', H. C. Finlayson, 31 May 1932.
41 *Proia*, 5 Dec. 1931; AEV 345; Niemeyer to Venizelos, 29 Feb. 1932.
42 *Ta peninta chronia tis Trapezis tis Ellados* (Athens, n.d.), appendix; AET 62/9, 'Unofficial notes of a meeting held in Geneva', 13 April 1932; AET 77/1, 'Greece's departure from the gold standard', 9 May 1932.
43 *Deltion Emporikou kai Viomichanikou Epimelitiriou ton Athinon*, June 1932; AET 60/1–3, memoranda from the commercial banks.
44 RIIA, *The Balkan States, 1. Economic* (London, 1936), pp. 57–60, 105–10; IBA/Patras, Yearly Report 1931/32.
45 IBA/Patras, Yearly Report 1931/32.
46 IBA/Sparta, Yearly Report 1931/32; IBA/Volos, Yearly Report 1933/34; IBA/Chios, Yearly Report 1931/32; Karl Lott Rankin Papers, Mudd Library, Princeton University, Box 2 (1930–3), 'Greek commercial debts', 28 Oct. 1932; Box 3 (1934–6), 'Annual economic report for Greece: 1933', 10 Jan. 1934.
47 RIIA, *Balkan States*, p. 65.
48 I. Berend, 'Balkan economic development', *Economic History Review* (May 1984), 268–73.
49 AOS, *Erevna kai gnomodotisis epi ton viomichanion tou vamvakos* (Athens, 1937), pp. 8–14.
50 Anastasopoulos, *Istoria*, p. 1580; NBG, *Oikonomiki Epetiris*, various.
51 C. Kindleberger, *The World in Depression: 1929–1939* (London, 1973), p. 190; AOS, *Elliniki oikonomia kata to etos 1936* (Athens, 1937), introduction.
52 Anastasopoulos, *Istoria*, p. 1580; *Oikonomiki Epetiris 1939*, vol. II, pp. 220–33.
53 AOS, *To zitima tis synkentroseos ton viomichanion en Elladi* (Athens, 1940); G. Burgel, *Croissance urbaine et développement capitaliste: le 'miracle' athénien* (Paris, 1981), pp. 142–64, 171, 218; FO 286/1052, 'Salonica Monthly report no. 4 for Nov. 1929'; FO 371/20392 R1436/1110, 'Conditions in the Patras district for Feb. 1936', 7 March 1936.
54 Galanis, *Trapezikai meletai*, p. 118.

13 Why Canadian banks did not collapse in the 1930s

IAN M. DRUMMOND

Canada's commercial banks did not collapse during the Great Depression, nor did they require to be taken over or reconstituted by governments.* This is a remarkable fact, in that the depression in Canada was as deep as in Central Europe or the United States. Furthermore, in comparison with her 'great neighbour to the south' Canada was far more dependent on its export trade, which was especially depressed. The grain trade, the market for pulp and paper, and the world demand for non-ferrous metals, as well as the overseas demand for cars and parts, all suffered severely. So did many domestically oriented manufacturing industries, in part because for almost a decade there was so little domestic capital formation.[1] Yet no bank failed.

In Germany, Italy and Central Europe, banks had difficulty because they were overcommitted to particular borrower firms which, in depression conditions, found themselves in difficulty, dragging their banks down with them. Some banks, furthermore, had incurred large short-term external obligations; when these were withdrawn, or when withdrawal was feared, another kind of trouble could and did engulf the borrower-banks. It is also suspected that in Germany, banks were further weakened by a flight of German capital. The same thing happened in the United States during 1931 and perhaps in spring 1933, but the roots of the American banking collapse are usually thought to have been different: a flight from bank deposits into currency and 'hard money', the limited lending power of the Federal Reserve System, the banks' inability to liquidate securities without serious loss, the unwillingness of the 'Fed' to support securities

232

through open market operations. When we ask why Canada's banks passed through the slump without visible scathe we inevitably think of these troubles in other lands.

How did Canada's banks survive the Great Depression? It has been suggested[2] that the main credit must go to Canada's branch banking system. By 1929 Canada contained only eleven incorporated commercial banks – 'chartered banks' in the Canadian terminology. A process of merger and geographical branching had long since converted seven of these banks into nation-wide branch systems, while two had branched regionally. The remaining two were specialized institutions – a metropolitan subsidiary of a United Kingdom parent, and a small local bank that was merged out of existence early in 1930. Thus in 1930 the surviving ten banks had 4,083 branches in Canada, three banks also had branched into the Caribbean, and several had branches and agencies in Newfoundland, Mexico, elsewhere in Latin America, Britain, France and the United States. Many but not all of these external branches were full-service retail operations. Table 13.1 summarizes the banks' financial position in the early years of the 1930s.

It is obvious enough that the branch system ought to have had the effect of spreading the lending risks, a task that unit banks would have found impossible, or costly. Such considerations would presumably be especially important in a national economy that was as small as the Canadian: in 1931, for instance, there were only 10.3 million people in the country, and in 1929 the GNP in current Canadian dollars was $6,139 million. Risk spreading, and the sense that the banks were large and solid institutions, would presumably help to forestall internal drains – 'runs on the banks'. It would also enable banks to absorb losses from bad loans, so long as these resulted from the misfortunes of individual firms or localized economic activities. This latter advantage, however, need not occur if the whole economy is depressed. That was the case of Canada's economy during the 1930s, and also of the other lands where Canadian banks were active. Branching, therefore, cannot be the whole story, and may not even be very much of it.

Nor can one give the credit to 'wise central banking', thus constructing a different sort of contrast with the United States.[3] If a country possesses no central bank, there can be no central bank policy for historians to praise or criticize. And Canada possessed no central bank until 1935, when the Bank of Canada, created by legislation in 1934,

Table 13.1. *Selected chartered bank assets and liabilities, 31 December (million Canadian dollars)*

	1929	1931	1932
Notes in circulation	175.4	141.0	127.1
Advances under the Finance Act	81.7	46.5	57.0
Due to banks abroad	107.0	47.1	19.7
Deposits payable in Canada	2163.7	1926.6	1843.7
Deposits payable elsewhere than in Canada	441.6	310.1	328.7
Capital paid up	142.9	144.5	144.5
Rest or reserve fund	158.1	162.0	162.0
Gold	73.3	65.8	53.3
Dominion notes (excl. deposits in Central Gold Reserves)	130.9	128.8	153.2
Mortgages on real estate sold by the banks	7.3	6.2	6.4
Deposits in Central Gold Reserves	56.1	25.7	19.9
of which gold 14.6 10.7 11.1 ⎫			
Dominion notes 41.5 15.0 8.8 ⎭			
Railway and other bonds, debentures, stocks	57.4	62.0	48.9
Dominion and provincial government securities	297.0	477.9	562.4
Due from banks abroad	101.7	109.6	108.6
Call and short loans in Canada	262.3	134.7	103.2
Call and short loans abroad	245.2	83.1	91.5
'Other current loans and discounts in Canada'	1402.8	1082.1	964.0
'Other current loans and discounts' abroad	250.6	188.4	151.7
Loans to the Government of Canada	0.0	0.0	0.0
Total assets	3521.1	2997.7	2582.1

Source: Bank Returns as printed in Canada Gazette.

began to operate. Once it had commenced operations the Bank did certainly appear to be well-managed.[4] In particular, it contrived a considerable monetary expansion during the late 1930s. But by then the worse of the depression was over, and no one would have thought that the Canadian banks were in any particular danger.

Canadian historians have not often wanted to give much credit to 'wise government policy' under some heading or other. As we shall see, the framework of Canada's banking and currency law may well have been of considerable importance, even though the relevant arrangements had been made years or decades before, and with no idea of 'bank-rescue' in a serious slump. We shall also see that certain government actions in 1930–1 may well have been important. Nevertheless, in part the survival of Canada's banks can be seen as a triumph of serendipity.

As we shall see, in one important respect Canada's banks were very exposed in 1929–31. Yet in certain other respects they may have been less exposed than the banks of Central Europe and the USA. Certainly their non-agricultural loans were less concentrated, and a good deal more liquid, than in Central Europe, although in the thirties some Canadian bank loans were certainly 'locked in' or 'locked up'. As for loans on securities, already by 1928 the Canadian banks were nervous about the prospects in the stock markets of North America, and they took collective steps to raise their required margins on stock loans, thus limiting their exposure. Exploiting an oddity in Canada's currency law, they also drew gold from the national reserve and used the gold to accumulate external earning assets. This action was important because the currency law immobilized the gold so long as the government held it, while the banks' external assets were both liquid and spendable. The banks had also accumulated 'secondary reserves' in the form of securities, both Canadian and American, which could be sold in case of need. By doing so they had, of course, exposed themselves in the same way as the US banks – they might have to liquidate securities on a falling market. But for Canada's banks this risk would remain only a potential one. Although securities were indeed sold from time to time, the Canadian banks never had to liquidate under pressure from depositors who were demanding coin or currency.

In 1929 Canada's chartered banks had Canadian assets of $2,873 million. These declined to $2,463 million in 1932, and then revived gradually, reaching $3,315 million in 1939.[5] The banks' note and deposit liabilities moved in step with their assets, falling from $2,585 million to $2,206 million, and then rising to $3,037 million. Thus the supply of bank money fell by 17 per cent, while the currency circulation fell less, and the money supply, broadly defined, by 13 per cent. Money GNP fell by 38 per cent, real GNP by 14 per cent and the GNP deflator by 16 per cent.[6] These facts are reported partly to clarify the divergence between Canadian experience and American, and partly to indicate why few Canadian historians or economists would argue that 'monetary forces caused the Great Depression',[7] at least so far as Canada is concerned.

Besides the chartered banks, Canada possessed a few surviving unincorporated 'private banks', but by 1929 these were so insignificant that we can safely ignore them here. In addition there were two incorporated savings banks in the Province of Quebec. Their assets, $78 million in 1929, hardly changed in the early and mid-1930s. The nation also contained a variety of bank-like institutions that Canadian economists nowadays call 'near-banks', because, in addition to their various specialized activities, since the nineteenth century they have operated chequable savings accounts, although they are not subject to federal banking law nor may they call themselves 'banks'. Like the banks, the near-banks experienced no general crisis. They were able to adjust gradually to the changed situation, slowly reducing their liabilities and their mortgage holdings, gradually absorbing write-offs and write-downs, placing their funds in other ways – especially in government securities.[8] It is true that a good many near-banks were wound up, wound down or merged. But they vanished without much drama.

We can divide the near-banks into two components. The first consists of credit unions, the post office savings system and provincial government savings offices. The earmark of this component is that almost all liabilities consist of deposits. In the early 1930s the assets of this component hardly changed. There were $75 million in 1929, $70 million in 1932 and $90 million in 1939. Since few of their deposit liabilities were subject to cheque, since only the credit unions had lent to the public, and since post office and provincial savings deposits enjoyed the protection of government guarantee, we can ignore them here.

Potentially more relevant to our story are the remaining two sorts of near-bank – the mortgage loan companies and the trust companies. Their Canadian assets *rose* from $501 million in 1929 to $519 million in 1932; thereafter the mortgage company assets fell while the trust company assets rose a little, so that by 1939 the joint total was $488 million. But only about 15 to 17 per cent of the mortgage company liabilities consisted of deposits,[9] while for trust companies the percentage rose gradually from 17 per cent in 1930 to 27 per cent in 1935 and 31 per cent in 1945, of which it appears that about half may have been subject to cheque.[10] Obviously, even though the trust and mortgage companies were not small in relation to the chartered banks, with respect to the movements of assets and of bank money the story would be much the same even if we included them in our definition of the banking system: their assets did not change much, and too few of their liabilities were deposits, whether payable on demand or not.

Shareholders' equity in trust companies was much the same size as deposit liabilities, while for mortgage companies it was substantially higher. In addition, both trust and mortgage companies had borrowing arrangements with chartered banks. Thus although they held very small cash reserves, neither kind of institution stood in great fear of an internal cash drain, and by 1929 most of the trust and mortgage business was being done by large firms which were diversified regionally or nationally, much like the chartered banks.

Because so much of the near-banks' borrowing had been medium-term, carefully matched to the terms of their mortgage assets, and because they had diversified their assets to some extent, these institutions were surprisingly well protected. Furthermore, so far as farm mortgages were concerned, much of any loss would fall on the specialized government lending institutions, both Dominion and provincial. The first five such institutions had appeared in 1917. More followed. By 1934, the provincial loan schemes were owed $93 million, and the Dominion's Farm Credit Corporation, another $10 million. In these circumstances it is hardly surprising that during the 1920s the specialized mortgage companies had not grown, or that they had somewhat diversified their assets, so that by 1930 mortgages made up 74 per cent of these. The trust companies had not diversified in this way, but they had never been so specialized in mortgage-lending: during the years 1920–30, mortgages made up just under half of assets. Thus the near-banks were much more secure than might have been feared.

The near-banks and private banks could not issue paper currency of their own, but the chartered banks could and did circulate their own banknotes, and until 1935 there was also a circulation of Dominion government paper currency – the so-called Dominion notes, which had existed for some sixty years. There had been pre-existing issues of provincial notes, and in 1935 Bank of Canada notes replaced both the Dominion notes and, more gradually, the chartered-bank notes. It is very important to understand how the Dominion note issue was determined before 1935, and how these arrangements interacted with the behaviour of the chartered banks.

The basic scheme for the Dominion note issue had always been modelled on the English Bank Charter Act of 1844. There was a 'fiduciary issue' of stated amount, for which, however, a 25 per cent gold reserve was required. Beyond this, every Dominion note was supposed to be gold-backed at 100 per cent, gold being priced at

$20.67 per ounce. Dominion notes were legal tender, but were meant to be convertible into gold on demand at certain Dominion government offices. To this end, and in conformity with the basic law, the Dominion Department of Finance held gold reserves. However, gold convertibility had been suspended in August 1914, and had only briefly been restored: except in 1926–8, and briefly and intermittently in 1929–31, the Dominion authorities simply refused to supply gold. In autumn 1931 gold convertibility was formally suspended, and has never been reintroduced.

In addition, ever since August 1914 there had been a parallel arrangement for the issue of Dominion notes. Any chartered bank could apply to a Cabinet committee known as the Treasury Board for an advance. Many kinds of security could be pledged – any Canadian, other British, or US government security, Canadian municipal securities, promissory notes and bills of exchange secured on grain, or drawn for 'agricultural, industrial, or commercial purposes'. It follows that the Canadian banks could rely upon a very far-reaching governmental support, even though there was no central bank: should the banks need a 'lender of last resort', virtually all bank assets, except for call loans, would qualify for pledging. The resultant new issues of Dominion notes, indistinguishable from other Dominion notes, required no gold backing. And although a bank occasionally was told that it could not borrow quite as many notes as it had applied for, very few requests were ever refused. Thus the banks had at their disposal – and at their command – an ideal lender of last resort. Indeed, by the end of the Great War the banks had formed the habit of establishing their lines of credit just in case of need, depositing approved securities with the Dominion Department of Finance. The advances were called 'advances under the Finance Act', or 'Finance Act advances'.

The banks' own note-issues were originally meant to be rigidly limited to the amounts of their paid-in capitals. In circulation the banknotes coexisted with Dominion notes. There were no reserve requirements either for the banks' notes or for their deposit liabilities. Soon after 1900 banks began to complain about the inelasticity of their note issues, especially during the autumn crop-moving season. Accordingly, after some experimentation, in 1913 it was provided that any bank could issue more of its own notes simply by depositing gold or Dominion notes in what was called the 'central gold reserves'. Since in 1913 the Dominion notes were gold-convertible and strictly limited in amount, this arrangement then looked reasonable enough. But with the introduction of 'Finance Act advances' in 1914 it was much less so. Now the banks could cause new Dominion notes to be created, could borrow them, could deposit them in the central gold reserves and could expand their own circulations accordingly. Of course, they could also do other things with the newly created Dominion notes. These could be added to reserves, put into circulation, used for inter-bank clearing – even, in 1926–8, presented to the Dominion authorities for conversion into gold.

The 'Finance Act advances' had originally been meant to protect the banks against the risk of an internal drain following the outbreak of war. After 1918 they were continued because both government and banks had come to find them convenient. During the war the Dominion government had come to rely upon the banks for short-term advances. The banks were much more willing to provide such advances, whether to Ottawa or to the British government, if they knew that the resultant treasury bills were highly liquid. But there was no short-term money market in Canada. Hence the banks could and did pledge these Treasury bills to the Dominion, using them as dollar-for-dollar collateral. From the banks' viewpoint the advantages were obvious enough: the system provided unlimited domestic liquidity on demand, without central bank interference and cost, and without the need to create or use a money market. If we apply any rational criteria for the design of a system of monetary management to Canadian arrangements of course these appear to be lunatic. Indeed, when Ottawa returned to gold, Canadian economists said as much. Yet in 1923, when the banking legislation was overhauled, the arrangements were continued without significant change. Nor were they modified when Canada returned to gold convertibility in July 1926.

Eccentric though these arrangements may appear, they totally protected the banks against internal drains, without exposing them to the risks that a central bank might pursue a foolish policy, as in the United States and in so many other lands. And even if a central bank had existed, and had been wisely guided by the parents of Professor Friedman and Mrs Schwartz, Canadian conditions were not propitious for active open market operations. Although there was a large domestic long-term debt, the secondary market was thin; any large transactions would have been impossible. Meanwhile, since Canada was (and is) a small open economy, both the external price level and some interest rates were externally determined, so that the main impact of an expansionary monetary policy would have been on the floating exchange rate; within the country, the banks' borrowing and lending rates were remarkably resistant to change, as Ottawa found when, in 1932–3, it tried to negotiate an all-round reduction.

In principle, the mere existence of the Finance Act system ought to have made the banks much less nervous with respect to asset-management. It ought also to have discouraged runs on the banks, or even to have prevented them. If so, it would have had the same effect on the near-banks. Even though they could not borrow from the Department of Finance, the near-banks could and sometimes did borrow from the chartered banks, which in turn had access to the Department.

In practice, the arrangements may not have had a large positive impact on public sentiment. It was for the banks, and for the government, that the system mattered, and it was at least as valuable when the banks were not borrowing as when they were. As for the public, few knew of the system, and even fewer understood it. The bankers mentioned it as little as possible. They tended to think that if the public knew a bank had been borrowing from the government, the citizenry would lose confidence in that bank. Also, among bankers there was a good deal of fear that if the public knew the government could and did produce Dominion notes ad lib there would be a demand for 'cheap credit' – a pressure for a massive expansion of the note issue which no government would be able to resist. Every month the government published a detailed *Bank Return* that reported, in considerable detail, the relevant information bank by bank. But few citizens can have had the knowledge to make use of such recondite information (indeed, very few historians or economists have ever done so). And even fewer can have read the relevant statutes, nor would many citizens have understood their importance.

If 'Finance Act advances' and the Dominion note arrangements were convenient to the banks, they were also convenient to the Dominion government. Ever since 1914, under one measure or another, the government had possessed the power to abjure gold convertibility and to place an embargo on gold exports. And when Dominion notes were not convertible into gold at a fixed price neither were banknotes: the banks could satisfy the law by paying out Dominion notes in exchange for their own notes or for deposits. Furthermore, even without issuing a formal prohibition, it was easy for the government to massage the banks, precisely because these banks were so few, and so well organized through their Canadian Bankers' Association, a body that enjoyed special statutory standing. Thus the government could and on occasion did ask the banks to discourage capital export, gold conversions, or both. Administrative flexibility, 'moral suasion' and legal latitude could and did spare Canada the convulsions that often occurred in other lands when 'free gold' had been exhausted while emergency measures might require legislation.

Meanwhile, because the currency regime was so 'flexible' the government could safely rely on the banks for short-term credit and the banks could safely provide it. This fact may help to explain the remarkable growth in the banks' holdings of government securities after 1929. Admittedly, the banks may to some extent have been buying more government stock because the demand for private sector advances was declining. But the point is that the nation's currency arrangements made it safe for them to do so. The *Bank Return* rarely showed any 'loans to the Government of Canada'. Even the Bank of Montreal, the government's financial agent, made such loans infrequently and for very short terms. Admittedly, too, in normal times the banks held few government securities. In December 1929, Dominion and provincial securities were only 8 per cent of chartered bank assets. But ever since the middle of the First World War, the Dominion government had relied on the collectivity of the banks for short-term loans on the security of treasury bills. The normal arrangement was simple. The Department of Finance would make contact with the Canadian Bankers' Association and explain how much help it needed; the Association would apportion the bills among the banks, roughly in proportion to paid-up capital. Once the bills had been issued, a bank could pledge or deposit them at the Finance Department.

In 1930–3 these arrangements were of special importance. Between 1928 and 1932, in spite of some tax increases, Dominion revenues fell by more than 50 per cent. Total Dominion expenditure, propelled by relief outlays and by rescue operations for several of the provincial exchequers, meanwhile rose by 19 per cent. During 1926–9 the Dominion budgets had produced comfortable surpluses; in 1932–3, the Dominion deficit was 37 per cent of Dominion expenditures. Thus the financial position was desperate. The domestic new-issue market could and did absorb large quantities of Dominion issues. It had been doing so since 1915; it would do so throughout the thirties. But its absorptive and digestive power was thought to be limited, especially under the conditions of 1931–4. Until 1935 Canada had no central bank. The New York market, where the Dominion authorities had borrowed modestly and usually on a medium-term basis since 1915, had collapsed in disarray by 1931. London was sympathetic but could not be forthcoming. Hence the importance of the Canadian banks – and of the Finance Act.

The Dominion government could hardly have 'spent Canada back to prosperity'. It was simply too small relative to the whole economy. In 1929, Dominion spending on goods and services was only 3 per cent of GNP, and total spending including transfers was 6 per cent. The government was not staffed or organized to attempt a really large spending programme, nor in federal Canada did it have the powers to do so. Indeed, no amount of government spending could have helped the prostrate export industries, except in so far as it might have forced down the price of the Canadian dollar. Even so, it would clearly have been counter-productive, not only for the 'real economy' but for the stability of the financial system, if the Dominion had been unable to mount the relief and rescue operations that it did, or to continue some of its spending on goods and services.

It appears that until 1932 neither politicians nor officials understood any of the above. Although it performed some currency functions, the Department of Finance was small and ill-staffed. In November 1929 the civil servant who had headed that Department since 1920 died. He had spent his working life inside the Department; he once admitted that he knew nothing of economics. In 1929 his assistant was about to be convicted of the theft of bonds and money from the Department. Below these folk there were many clerks, but there was little expertise. And only in November 1932 did the government select a new permanent head for the Finance Department. The new appointee, Professor W. C. Clark, was an academic specialist in money and finance who had also worked with an American financial house.[11] From Clark's office there came, for the first time, serious policy towards monetary topics. Clark was in accord with the wishes of the Prime Minister, who wanted to establish a central bank and who eventually, following a Commission of Inquiry and over the bankers' opposition, did so. But even Clark, like every Ottawa official of the time, had few talented subordinates. Although he managed to employ some able associates, they were few, and everyone, including Clark, was overwhelmed with administrative detail. Perhaps that was one reason why Clark wanted a central bank for Canada.

Soon after Clark was installed in office, the Dominion government tried to use the Finance Act mechanism to expand the monetary base. This was the first and last purposive use of the arrangements. The government persuaded the banks to borrow $40 million under the Act. As Bryce writes, 'This action . . . had only a small monetary effect.'[12] There was no real reason to expect that it would or could have done much. After all, the behaviour of the banks was not constrained by the size of the domestic reserve base – gold plus Dominion notes. Given the mechanisms we have described, they could have whatever domestic reserves they thought they needed.

Nor would the external position threaten the Canadian banks. They had not emulated the Austro-German pattern of the 1920s – attracting and accepting foreign short-term money so as to expand their domestic assets. Thus they faced little or no risk of an external drain in times of trouble. It is true that six of the banks did report some 'deposits elsewhere than in Canada'. In December 1929 these totalled $442 million, or 13 per cent of all bank liabilities. But at least two-thirds of this total appears to reflect the foreign retail-banking operations of the Royal Bank, the Bank of Nova Scotia and the Canadian Bank of Commerce, which in various ways conducted branch-banking in California and the Caribbean; almost all the rest reflects the external business of the Bank of Montreal. These banks, furthermore, held $495 million in external assets – call and short loans, plus other current loans and discounts after provision for 'bad and doubtful debts'. External assets thus exceeded external liabilities, even if one takes no account of the banks' $73 million in gold. This gold served no domestic monetary purpose: in Canada gold coin hardly circulated, while the banks could and did redeem their own banknotes in Dominion notes, which they could freely obtain via 'Finance Act advances'. In principle and in practice, therefore, the banks' gold was indeed available for international use in case of need. But the need was unlikely to arise, and so far as one can tell it did not. Although some gold was exported in the early thirties, there were no disruptive external drains such as those that afflicted Britain, Central Europe and the United States in 1931. Admittedly, after Britain left gold there was an alarming speculative flight from the Canadian dollar. But that dollar was already a floating currency which no one tried to 'defend', except with words. If the Dominion authorities had really been attached to the gold standard, things might have been much more alarming.

In principle the nation's overall external position might have imposed a strain on the banks. But it never did so. Once more, this was more a matter of good luck than good management. In 1929–30 Canada ran a current-account deficit. In both years there was a substantial capital inflow on account of portfolio investment, and a modest but useful net inflow on account of direct investment. Thus in 1929 the banks' external assets fell by only $88 million, and in 1930 they were unchanged: even so, at the end of 1930 the external assets were still larger than they had been in late 1927 or 1928. In 1931–2 there were continued but much smaller current-account deficits, and direct investment changed from inflow to outflow, but there was still a substantial net inflow on account of portfolio investment. Thus the banks' external assets fell by only $28 million in 1931, and $38 million in 1932. In 1933 the current account was effectively balanced, while direct and portfolio investment gave rise to an outflow, so that the banks' external assets fell by $24 million. From the end of 1929 to the end of 1933, the banks had disposed of 22 per cent of their external assets excluding gold, or of 19 per cent if gold is included. For the rest of the decade Canada continued to export long-term capital: both direct and portfolio investment were negative. But the current account was regularly in surplus in 1934 and thereafter. And the banks' external assets were rebuilt, though not to the levels of 1928–9.[13]

To understand the banks' good fortune, one would have to examine all the forces that worked to determine the current and capital items in Canada's balance of international payments. But it is obvious enough that, with respect to the rest of the world, Canada's banks began the depression from a position of some strength, even though in earlier years they had been stronger still. During 1929, their external call loans – a form of external secondary reserve that they had built up during 1928 – fell from 9.5 per cent of total assets to 7 per cent, while security holdings – another form of secondary reserve both external and internal – fell from 15.5 per cent of total assets to 12.7 per cent. Meanwhile, during 1929 their domestic loans and discounts expanded. Thus during 1929 they became significantly less liquid in two respects – their saleable secondary reserve assets diminished relative to total assets, and some of their growing domestic assets would shortly prove, under depression conditions, to be less liquid than had been expected. Even so, the banks still held external liquid assets (including gold) equal to 16 per cent of their total assets and 22 per cent of their deposit liabilities at home and abroad. Very few of their deposit liabilities were likely to be converted into other moneys in response to the kinds of fears that did so much damage in Central Europe, or for that matter in the USA.

But what if Canadian depositors were to lose their confidence in bank solvency? No amount of domestic liquidity could have protected them, especially if their ordinary 'loans and advances' were to become frozen. The result would have been a really large internal drain, and although Finance Act advances could prevent any bank from stopping payment, if used in such circumstances they might indeed produce an accelerating collapse of confidence. That is what the banks suspected and feared. But it seems that the public never did harbour suspicions about the banks. Given the structure of the economy and the depth of its depression, that is surprising. How might we explain the fact?

The banks of Canada were certainly different from those of the United States and Central Europe. Unlike the American banks and those of the Antipodes, Canada's banks did not lend on mortgage, although they were allowed to accept mortgages as secondary security. It was this legal arrangement which had produced the niche within which Canada's mortgage-loan and trust companies had flowered. Unlike the banks of Central Europe, Canada's banks had not become 'universal banks', nor did they overtly supply long-term funds to transport or industry. This meant that their 'secondary reserves' in the form of securities were comparatively small; it also meant that they had largely avoided the dangers that would have derived, in depression conditions, from long-term commitments to particular industrial firms. In late 1929, the banks held only $57.3 million in 'railway and other bonds, debentures, and stocks'. This was less than 2 per cent of total assets. The banks also tried to avoid the granting of overdrafts. Admittedly it does not follow that all of the 'call and short loans in Canada' or all of the 'other current loans and discounts in Canada' were genuinely liquid, or that all would be paid when due. But in important respects the banks began the depression in a position that probably compares well with the position of banks in many other lands.

We should also notice two structural characteristics of Canada's economy which probably helped to protect the banks. By 1929 the publicly owned sector was already quite large; furthermore, in mining and manufacturing many firms were foreign-owned. Government ownership is relevant because 'Crown corporations', as Canadians call such public enterprises, met their obligations throughout the slump: behind them stood the several exchequers, and behind these, directly or indirectly, the Dominion note issue and the Finance Act. Foreign ownership is relevant because the obligations of the foreign-owned firms could be, and doubtless often were, supported by the financial strength of their parents. In the past quarter-century, Canadians have often been critical of foreign enterprises, and nervous about the roles such firms play in the national economy. But if we are interested in the stability of the banking system, perhaps in the 1930s that role was not altogether an unhelpful one.

The pulp and paper industry was owned in part abroad, and in part at home. Having expanded rapidly in the 1920s, and having borrowed heavily, it found itself in severe difficulties when its export markets collapsed. Governments took some part in arranging for the industry's financial reconstruction. Although most of the industry debt was long-term and widely held, no doubt some was owing to Canadian banks, which therefore must have benefited to some unknown extent from the reconstruction of the industry. However, it does not appear that this element can have been very important to the banks.

It was the grain trade which posed problems for the banks, most of whom were involved in its financing, though not all to the same extent. Private grain merchants, who still handled about half of the trade, annually borrowed from the banks to buy grain, for cash, from farmers. With the slide in the world price of wheat, some of the private dealers would soon be in difficulties. But the one who had bought cheaply would escape, and so would their bankers in so far as the dealers were well capitalized, or had hedged, as many had done. The real problem would be the co-operative western 'Wheat Pools'.

There was one Pool in each of the three western prairie provinces. None of the pools had much liquid capital. None hedged. Every year each Pool accepted the wheat crops of its members, on whose behalf it would sell the wheat through a three-Pool central selling agency. On delivery, each member received an advance payment, final settlement to be made on the basis of the eventual selling price, less costs. The advances came from the banks. Just as if they were lending on common stock, when they lent money to the Pools, the banks insisted that the market price should always be at least 15 per cent higher than the advance per bushel. If the market price were to fall, the banks would issue a 'margin call'. The Pools would then have to 'cover the margin' on their existing loans, and lower the advance on any new bank-financed deliveries.

For the 1929–30 crop year the initial payment was originally fixed at $1.00 per bushel. As the world price fell, the initial payment had to be reduced: from 25 June 1930 it was $0.85. The Pools accepted 121 million bushels of wheat – slightly more than half of the prairie crop; on most of those deliveries, the initial payment was $1.00.[14] However, by the end of January 1930 wheat was trading at $1.20^3/4. The 'margin' above the one-dollar initial payment on a cash basis was 15 per cent, and on a May futures basis, 18 cents.[15] Obviously it was about to vanish, and the prospects were grim: the Pools did not have enough liquid capital to handle a 'margin call'. They would have to sell wheat, thus further depressing the price.

The Pool authorities approached the governments of the three wheat-growing prairie provinces, who quickly substituted their guarantees, so that the 'margin' need no longer be maintained.[16] These guarantees covered only the 1929–30 crop year, and neither banks nor Pools expected them to be renewed for 1930–1. Nor were they. In autumn 1930 the banks required the Pools to reduce their initial payments, which began at 70 cents per bushel, but which were shortly reduced to 60 cents, then to 55 cents, and then, on 11 November, to 50 cents. Even so, by 15 November the banks were threatening to end their financing, and to require the Pools to sell more grain, unless the Canadian government would provide a guarantee of $10 million. Prime Minister Bennett was at first willing only to make advances to the provincial governments, so that they could make advances to the banks. But within days he provided a limited and temporary guarantee, not for $10 million but for $5 million. A trusted friend of the Prime Minister was appointed to run the Pools' central selling agency. On 22 December, the Prime Minister announced that he had provided for 'orderly marketing' of the 1930 crop, and by the end of the year it was apparent that 'the federal government would provide the guarantees required to forestall a forced liquidation of the pools' unsold wheat'.[17]

How exposed were the banks? The problem had two components – the actual losses on the 1929–30 advances, and the potential for trouble if wheat prices were to fall further. The first element we know. To cover the 1929–30 Pool advances, the provinces had to find $22.8 million, all of which was eventually repaid by the Pools or forgiven to them. The second element cannot be known, partly because for the 1930–1 crop year, the federal government guaranteed the banks against 'any loss they may ultimately sustain' through Pool advances,[18] and partly because we do not know what would have happened to the price of wheat if the Pools had been forced to liquidate their large holdings and to refuse their members' deliveries. All we can safely say is that *for the entire prairie debt structure* the results would have been dire.

At 31 July 1930 Canada's wheat 'carry-over' was 126,582,000 bushels – nearly half of 1929–30 exports, and well over half of exports in 1930–1.[19] More than half of this wheat was under Pool management. Wheat, which had sold for $1.24 per bushel in the 1929–30 crop year, would realize only $0.54 in 1931–2. Without the active stockpiling policy that the new Pool manager continued for several years after autumn 1930, that price would have been a great deal lower. In capital and reserves the banks were worth no more than $290 million. A more serious collapse in wheat prices could have severely damaged Canada's banking system, and would probably have destroyed confidence in it.

There were precedents for such a rescue. During the First World War, a new transcontinental railway had got into financial trouble. It was discovered that a major Canadian bank had a claim on that railway, a claim much larger than the bank's capital. If the railway were to fail so would the bank. Ottawa nationalized the railway, assuming its debt.

In autumn 1931, other steps seem to have been taken. Professor Michael Bliss has described a series of measures that created or maintained artificially high values for a variety of securities. He argues that these measures were concerted among the Dominion government, the banks and the rest of the financial community, to prevent a 'domino effect that could follow a devaluation of securities to unregulated market prices'.[20] The effect would not have *directly* damaged the banks, because they held so few of the relevant securities. But it would have decimated the worth of their securities loans, a much larger figure. Many brokers would have failed; at least one large life insurance company would have been insolvent. One can imagine the effect on depositor confidence. Meanwhile, since the government depended on the banks for negotiated short-term financing, it had every reason to help and to calm the financiers.

We have noted that the chartered banks did not lend on mortgage. But the near-banks certainly did. Indeed, they specialized in that form of lending. Also, farmers could and did borrow from banks under a variety of headings, some but not all under government guarantee, and they also borrowed from implement companies and from retailers, all of whom, in turn, borrowed from banks. It has been estimated[21] that as late as 1937 prairie farmers owed $171 million, of which $63 million was owed directly to banks and financial institutions. In addition, there was plenty of mortgage paper in urban Canada: the nation was a land of home-owners. This debt pyramid rested fundamentally on wheat. Even as it was, substantial amounts of mortgage debt had to be written off, and much more was 'nursed', in the hope of better times. There was, after all, little point in foreclosure, and this drastic action was frequently impossible: all the provinces had enacted debtors' protection acts and moratoria of various kinds,[22] and so had the Dominion Parliament, although such actions may well have exceeded its constitutional powers. The result may well have been convenient to the banks. While they maintained 'secret reserves' which they could use to write off genuinely bad debts without affecting their published balance sheets, there was presumably a limit to the amounts that could be buried. But with moratoria in force, what counts as a bad debt?

I have argued that to explain the survival power of Canadian banks and near-banks one must draw on many elements – the branch system, the inherited asset structures, the absence of destabilizing external disturbances and commitments, the arrangements surrounding the issue of paper currency, and the fact that the government did not attempt to stay on the gold standard. Beyond this, and perhaps of equal or greater importance, were Prime Minister Bennett's 'rescue of the Pools', and his arrangements for fictive valuations in 1931. These measures may have been of especial importance in so far as the banks' own position had deteriorated during 1929, and because the depression would make their non-agricultural portfolios less liquid and more insecure. We cannot be sure what would have happened if the Prime Minister had not acted as he did. But the banks and near-banks had every reason to be grateful.

250   Ian M. Drummond

NOTES

* This paper has been revised and much improved on the basis of comments from Dr N. C. Quigley of Victoria University of Wellington, New Zealand. I have also benefited from a discussion with Professor Michael Bliss, Department of History, University of Toronto.
1 Data on these and all other macroeconomic topics come from Statistics Canada, *National Income and Expenditure Accounts*.
2 M. Friedman and A. J. Schwartz, *A Monetary History of the United States* (Princeton, N.J., 1963), pp. 352–3: 'In Canada, deposits remained as attractive as they had ever been.' The question is, 'Why was that the case?'
3 *Ibid.*
4 Cf. E. P. Neufeld, *Bank of Canada Operations and Policy* (Toronto, 1959).
5 Data on Canadian banks appear in various places, but can be most conveniently consulted in M. C. Urquhart and K. A. H. Buckley (eds.), *Historical Statistics of Canada* (Toronto, 1965). More detail can be found in the monthly *Bank Returns* that were published for many decades in the *Canada Gazette*.
6 *National Income and Expenditure Accounts*.
7 The phrase is Peter Temin's. See his *Did Monetary Forces Cause the Great Depression?* (Cambridge, Mass., 1972).
8 E. P. Neufeld, *The Financial System of Canada* (Toronto, 1972), pp. 423–8 and tables 7:4, 9:8.
9 *Ibid.*, table 7:4 (pp. 206–7).
10 *Ibid.*, table 9:5 (p. 309).
11 R. B. Bryce, *Maturing in Hard Times: Canada's Department of Finance through the Great Depression* (Kingston and Montreal, 1986), pp. 34, 66–81.
12 *Ibid.*, pp. 53–4.
13 Calculations based on *Historical Statistics* series F71, 93–6, 98.
14 Figures from D. A. MacGibbon, *The Canadian Grain Trade 1931–1951* (Toronto, 1952), pp. 4, 34.
15 *Idem, The Canadian Grain Trade* (Toronto, 1932), pp. 350–1.
16 On the débâcle of the Pools the best secondary source, and the only archivally based one, is C. F. Wilson, *A Century of Canadian Grain: Government Policy to 1951* (Saskatoon, 1978). The following account relies on Wilson, ch. 14, pp. 264–307.
17 *Ibid.*, p. 293.
18 Letter, Prime Minister R. B. Bennett to Beaudry Leman, President of the Canadian Bankers' Association, 20 January 1931, reproduced in Wilson, *Century of Canadian Grain*, pp. 293–4.
19 MacGibbon, *Grain Trade 1931–1951*, p. 6, table I.
20 Michael Bliss, *Northern Enterprise: Five Centuries of Canadian Business* (Toronto, 1987), pp. 416–19, especially p. 417.
21 MacGibbon, *Grain Trade 1931–1951*, p. 10, citing W. J. Waines, *Prairie Population Possibilities* (Study prepared for the Royal Commission on Dominion-Provincial Relations) (Ottawa, 1940).
22 See W. T. Easterbrook, *Farm Credit in Canada* (Toronto, 1938) for details on moratoria and on the government loan bodies.

14 Japanese banks and national economic policy, 1920–1936

W. MILES FLETCHER III

The interwar era in Japan witnessed major developments in the banking sector that continue to shape it today.* A brief overview of the development of the banking industry will help to place these changes in a historical context. Despite a high degree of commercial activity that arose in the Tokugawa era (1600–1867), Japan had no Western-style commercial banks until the 1870s. After the Meiji Restoration of 1867, the nation embarked on a programme of reforms based on Western models. The innovations included a national system of compulsory education and Asia's first constitution. As part of this campaign, the government unified the currency and encouraged the formation of private banks to help spur industrial development. In 1897 the nation adopted the gold standard and by 1913 it could boast the existence of 1,600 'ordinary' (commercial) banks.[1]

The progress of the banking industry became evident in its swift organization into powerful interest groups. By the turn of the century Osaka, Tokyo and three other cities each had bank assemblies dedicated to studying pertinent issues and to representing the views of local financial institutions. In 1891 the Tokyo assembly formed the first clearing-house to handle financial transactions and to 'plan the progress and reform of the general banking industry'.[2] The vital role that banks played in helping secure financing for the huge costs of the Russo-Japanese war of 1904–5 enhanced the banks' prestige. As if to acknowledge this, the Finance Minister in 1908 started a custom of announcing each year's budget at a meeting of the National Federation of Clearing-Houses. Three years later a banker, Yamamoto

Tatsuo, became Finance Minister – the first business executive to enter a Cabinet.[3]

Meanwhile, the government had created special banks to serve specific purposes. Modelled on the Banque Nationale de Belgique, the Bank of Japan started operations in 1882. Raising funds by issuing notes, the bank discounted commercial bills and became the fiscal agent of the government. By the end of the century the Industrial Bank was organized to make long-term loans to industries, and the Hypothec Bank extended credit in the agricultural sector. Other banks provided capital for the nation's emerging empire. The Bank of Taiwan focused on economic development in that island colony, and the Bank of Chosen provided capital for enterprises in Korea. All of these banks took the form of semi-private institutions under government supervision. Even the Bank of Japan, which seemed most closely tied to the government, obtained one-half of its funds from the private sector; the other four banks received all of their funds from private sources. The government, however, had powerful means of influence. It had the right to appoint or approve top officers in each bank and to scrutinize their policies. These institutions accounted for one-fifth to one-third of the paid-up capital and reserves of banks in the early twentieth century.[4]

The interwar decades had a major impact in several ways. First, bankers' views towards fiscal and currency policies changed dramatically – from yearning for small and balanced national budgets and the orthodoxy of the gold standard to accepting its abandonment and adjusting to huge governmental deficits. Secondly, the government became much more involved in banks' operations; the controls associated with the mobilization for full-scale war with China after 1937 capped a long-term intensification of interaction between government officials and private banks. Meanwhile, within the financial sector consolidation progressed apace. This article aims to clarify the evolution of national policies that nurtured these trends and thus forged an important legacy for the banking industry in succeeding decades.

A return to the gold standard

Deciding whether or not to return to a gold standard became the major financial issue for Japan during the 1920s. At stake were the nation's pride in identifying with the major industrial powers of the West as well as prospects for future prosperity. Japan had abandoned the gold standard in 1917, mostly because many European nations had done so during the First World War and the United States had stopped exporting gold. The American decision to resume gold shipments in 1919 thrust the issue into prominence once again.

Economic conditions complicated the debate. The World War had brought an unprecedented boom to Japan. Total economic production in nominal terms expanded 3.6 times between 1914 and 1919, while in real terms the gross national product increased by 50 per cent in the same approximate period of time.[5] Not only did the European nations want Japanese products, but Asian markets were left open to Japanese penetration as European exports dwindled. For the first time since the nation's industrial development began, Japanese exports registered a surplus over imports for five consecutive years. Given a respite from Western competition, the chemical and metal manufacturing sectors began to develop. Then in 1920 a post-war recession hit in full force as civilian European industries started to recover and began to supply their own markets and recapture foreign ones. Japan's industrial production plummeted, and the trade surplus dissipated.

Some banking leaders viewed these new economic woes as proving the need for a return to economic orthodoxy as represented by a gold standard. Inoue Junnosuke, the head of the Bank of Japan and one of the most prominent business leaders in the nation, argued stridently for a convertible currency based on gold, because the resulting deflation would slash the prices of goods and thus revive Japan's foreign trade. Unless the Japanese could export goods to purchase raw materials, industry could not develop. Inoue pointed out that if one set the index for Japanese prices in 1913 at 100, they had now inflated to 200, while American and British prices lagged far behind. Japan also suffered from comparatively high interest rates, as the use of overseas gold reserves, which had accumulated during the World War, to pay for extra imports lessened the supply of capital at home. A healthy trade surplus would thus lower interest rates and spur investment.[6]

Inoue also believed that the gold standard would bring economic stability through letting 'natural' market forces unfold. He criticized the 'makeshift policies' of the government towards the economy and the manipulation of the exchange rate through the use of overseas reserves. These yielded unpredictable results that complicated planning for international trade. Japan most needed a stable exchange rate determined by the balance of trade.[7]

Inoue's advocacy of an end to the embargo on gold attracted attention to the issue because of his eminence in the business community. Japanese executives also had to take notice of a League of Nations conference in Genoa in 1922 that proclaimed the goal of European nations to restore free trade in gold. Some executives, such as the textile industrialist Mutō Sanji, agreed with Inoue: only a gold standard could revive the economy by deflating prices and permitting the economy to regulate itself.[8]

Others harboured doubts. Even within the banking sector sceptics arose, especially in regard to the timing of switching to a convertible currency. Yashiro Norihiko of the huge zaibatsu bank, Sumitomo, wondered whether enacting a gold standard in the fragile condition of the economy would invite a sharp downswing rather than the expected benefits of the gold standard – generally lower prices and hence increased exports. Along these lines Miyajima Seijirō, the president of a major textile firm, worried that a strong yen could lower the prices of imports that might threaten nascent industries now protected by tariffs. Kushida Manzō, an executive from another large zaibatsu bank – Mitsubishi – insisted that the exchange rate would have to attain its old parity of 50 dollars per 100 yen before the embargo on gold could end. Some business leaders pointed out that when Japan had maintained a gold standard before 1917, the nation had regularly sustained an annual deficit in foreign trade.[9]

To explore whether a consensus existed, Finance Minister Ichiki Otohiko invited business leaders to his home in the autumn of 1922. The discussion uncovered a broad vein of caution, especially among the bankers. Instead of risking disruption by returning to free trade in gold, Oyama Kenzō of Osaka's Sanjū-yon Bank and Ikeda Kenzō of the Daihyakyu Bank preferred to suppress prices through restrictions on government spending and measures to discourage private consumption. Kodama Kenji from the semi-official Yokohama Specie Bank that handled foreign currency transactions favoured a delay in implementing any change.[10] In keeping with the doubts expressed at the meeting, Ichiki announced afterwards that he would not pursue a gold standard in the unsettled financial situation.

Over the next several years, opinion on the gold standard remained split. The great earthquake that destroyed Tokyo in September 1923 added to executives' jitters about the economy. To encourage recovery in the capital city, the Bank of Japan had to extend large amounts of credit through loans to banks and discounting of commercial paper for companies. The government guaranteed the bank's possible losses up to a limit of 100 million yen.[11] During the next year a major conference of officials and executives took up the issue. Ikeda Seihin, the managing director of the large Mitsui Bank, argued for immediate enactment of a gold standard at this special meeting of officials and executives. Kushida Manzō from Mitsubishi now relented and gave his support too. Other banking executives, however, remained adamantly opposed. These included Yukawa Kankichi from the Sumitomo Bank, Yūki Toyotarō from the Yasuda Bank, and Sasaki Yūnosuke of the Daiichi Bank. They believed that the exchange rate had to stabilize at a high level before the embargo could end. A low rate would enable foreigners to snap up Japan's gold reserves at bargain basement prices, and the nation would soon lose its stores of the precious metal. The group's report concluded that the nation should prepare for free trade in gold by reducing government and private consumption, reforming the organization of industry, suppressing imports and developing exports. The government should institute the gold standard only when it would not 'have unusual influence on the general business community'.[12]

The division of opinion on the gold standard inhibited any new actions by the government. The debate revealed, however, no substantial dissent within the banking community from the long-term goal of reinstating a convertible currency as a means of returning to economic normalcy. Reduction of government spending and general deflation still appeared to offer the only paths to prosperity. Disputes centred on issues of tactics and timing, as some executives worried about the damage a sudden change might bring. Ironically, continued economic difficulties worked not to inhibit change but to increase the pressure for it.

After the 1920 recession, a sense of economic malaise pervaded the rest of the decade. The growth of the real gross national product slowed considerably. The stagnation of the agricultural sector, embracing about one-half of the population, dampened demand. Although the industrial growth rate as a whole maintained a good pace, especially in comparison with European nations and the United States, executives had cause for concern. Sharp cuts in military expenses affected newly developed heavy industry. Slumping prices and profit rates in some manufacturing sectors ushered in a period of modest civilian investment; much of the nation's economic growth became dependent upon expenditures by regional governments on public works. The foreign trade ledger stayed in chronic deficit.[13] Finally, the financial panic of 1927 shook confidence in the economy. In April the failure of the Suzuki Trading Company that had borrowed heavily from the Japanese Bank of Taiwan sparked a run on domestic deposits. Only the Bank of Japan's massive transfusion of 2 billion yen to banks and the hasty imposition of a moratorium on financial transactions brought the situation under control.

Subsequently the clamour for a gold standard revived. Inoue Junnosuke continued his advocacy of the cause, as he harped on the need to trim government spending and the trade deficit. A financial retrenchment would cause a recession, but 'today's situation is a recession whose end is completely unseen. It is a recession from which there are no predictions for recovery.' Left alone, the current troubles would worsen. A temporary setback induced by the gold standard at least offered the hope of prosperity in the long run.[14] Yamamuro Sōbun of the Mitsubishi Bank looked forward to the stable exchange rates that would result. Predictable prices of imports would aid planning for companies conducting foreign trade and investing their funds abroad.[15]

Within the banking community, two former opponents of the measure now rendered qualified support. Yūki Toyotarō from the Yasuda Bank decreed that ending the embargo could put the economy back on a 'normal path'. Especially if the nation's trade achieved a favourable balance, few problems would arise. Reversing his long-standing opinion that an exhausted business community could not survive a jolt of deflation, Sumitomo's Yashiro finally decided that the time for free trade in gold had arrived. Norway and France had recently aligned their currencies with those of Germany, Italy and England; only Japan among major industrial powers lagged behind in adopting the gold standard. The trade situation was improving, and the exchange rate was nearing parity. Japan might as well try the gold standard soon.[16] Reflecting the new mood, the major banking associations – the Tokyo and Osaka Clearing-Houses – both passed resolutions calling for a convertible currency. Ikeda Seihin, as the head of both the Mitsui Bank and the Tokyo Clearing-House, predicted a 'new start' for the economy because of the lower production costs that would accompany deflation and the 'readjustment' of the business community through mergers and cartels.[17]

Other sectors of the economy had a variety of reactions. Large trading firms backed a gold standard, and the Kōbe and Tokyo Chambers of Commerce issued declarations of support. Some manufacturers anticipated benefits from lower prices for raw materials, but others feared that the strong yen would damage their exports and that deflation at home would slash their margin of profit. Perhaps because of an internal division of opinion two major business groups – the Japan Economic Federation and the Japan Spinners Association – did not make official statements on the issue.[18]

Finally, the Cabinet of General Tanaka Giichi convened an Economic Council in the autumn of 1928. This gathering of prominent executives from various sectors reached agreement in December. As summarized by the President of the Japan Economic Federation, Gō Seinosuke, the group recommended that the government should reinstate the gold standard by the middle of the next year while taking special measures to protect industries through tariffs and to promote exports. These would include a new export insurance system and the extension of more credit to small firms.[19] When Inoue became Finance Minister in July 1929, hopes rose for the rapid enactment of free trade in gold. Several months later, he decided the time had come: the nation had registered a trade surplus for four months and the exchange rate at $48.00 per hundred yen was approaching the old parity. Dismissing the stock market collapse on Wall Street as a temporary fluke, Inoue announced that Japan would return to the gold standard on the first day of the new year.

Normalcy, as the bankers defined it, had been restored. The nation could now find its way out of the economic doldrums. Bank executives could take pride in having played a major role in keeping the issue of free trade in gold alive and in lobbying for it. Still, they had taken nearly a full decade to achieve a unified stand among themselves. Moreover, the ultimate consensus that evolved in the Economic Council had to recognize and respond to the fears of sceptics from other industries. The government acted only after a broad-based consensus had formed.

The bank merger movement

The economic troubles of the 1920s made officials and executives become preoccupied with the basic health and strength of the banking system. This trend became most evident in officials' increasingly determined efforts to effect mergers among banks.

The issue of encouraging the consolidation of banks had emerged early in Japan's industrial development. A mere two decades after Western-style banks had begun to form, the Tokyo Bank Assembly petitioned the government to set minimum capital requirements for banks. Members feared that the instability of the smallest institutions would harm the credibility of the whole financial system. The Ministry of Finance responded by drafting a 'Bank Merger Law' in 1896 that streamlined procedures for such actions. Despite this legislation, the number of banks rose rapidly from 1,054 in 1896 to 1,890 in 1901. Worries about this proliferation led the Ministry of Finance to issue regulations requiring new banks to have a minimum capitalization of 500,000 yen; in 1911 this amount was doubled for banks in large cities.[20]

After the World War the situation continued to disturb officials. Inoue, as head of the Bank of Japan, believed that only if banks merged could they provide the large amounts of capital needed to 'reorganize' industries that had expanded during the war and make them more efficient. Finance Minister Takahashi Korekiyo argued that companies in all sectors had to expand in order to deal with competition in foreign trade. Observing how a number of small banks had failed in the post-war recession, Takahashi also perceived the vulnerability of small enterprises.[21]

In July 1924 the Finance Ministry issued a special internal 'instruction' to encourage mergers. The Ministry did not try to impose them on banks but sought to guide regional executives towards that goal. Local officials of the Ministry were to form committees of bankers and other businessmen in each region in order to discuss the advantages of consolidation for local banks outside of the major cities. In the first half of the decade, 308 banks did combine operations.[22]

Still, this was not enough. In June 1926 a Preparation Committee for the Investigation of the Financial System began operating within the Ministry of Finance. For advice on matters directly relating to commercial banks' activities, this committee consulted with a special ad hoc committee of five executives from the Bank of Japan and four large private banks – Mitsui, Mitsubishi, Sumitomo and Daiichi. In August they recommended further promotion of mergers among regional banks and, in order to 'smooth the flow of money among regions', between city and regional banks too. The government also had to take steps to ensure the durability of merged banks and newly created ones. Ministry officials, however, had some qualms about encouraging the dominance of the large banks. The Preparation Committee's report in October endorsed the merger policy to prevent unnecessary competition but omitted any reference to combinations of city and regional banks.[23]

In September a new Committee to Investigate the Financial System began deliberations. A sub-committee formed to scrutinize the operation of ordinary banks. This group, chaired by Inoue, consisted of prominent bank executives, such as Ikeda Seihin (Mitsui), Kushida Manzō (Mitsubishi), Yashiro Norihiko (Sumitomo), Yūki Toyotarō (Yasuda) and Sasaki Yūnosuke (Daiichi). The relationship between city and regional banks proved the most controversial issue. Officials retained their reservations about the possible effects of mergers between the two types of banks. Speaking to the committee, Matsumoto Osamu predicted that this policy would terrify local bankers into thinking that they could not survive without a link to a zaibatsu bank. A rush of hastily planned mergers would result. Den Akira feared that capital would concentrate in Tokyo and Osaka. Japan was simply not ready for the British or Canadian system of 'branchism', in which a few large banks built branches all over the nation. To maintain a plethora of small banks, on the other hand, would only invite the failure of many of them. Hence, Japan had to pursue its own solution of fostering the gradual consolidation of regional banks. Then ' ... the time to become like England will arrive.' Yūki Toyotarō of Yasuda and Sasaki Yūnosuke of Daiichi countered by insisting that city banks' absorption of some regional ones would not restrict the flow of capital to the countryside. One scholar has suggested that committee members stressed this point not because the zaibatsu wanted to monopolize regional banking but because they wanted to avoid accepting any new government limits on their activities.[24]

This group's final report in November recommended a strengthening of the merger policy through stricter minimum levels of capital to be applied to existing banks as well as new ones. The report also

suggested that the Ministry of Finance had to exercise more supervision to ensure an improvement in the management of the new banks
produced by mergers. Finally, the committee was willing to allow combinations of large city-based banks – such as the ones represented on
the committee – with regional banks. The Investigation Committee
accepted the report of the special sub-committee.[25]

This report became the basis for a new Bank Law that was submitted
to the Diet and passed in 1927. As explained by one official, the legislation intended to improve the management of regional banks and
help them compete in turbulent and treacherous economic conditions. According to the new standards set for banks' capital, more
than one-half of the current 1,417 banks would be unable to continue.[26]

In the words of one Japanese writer, the 1927 Bank Law had an
'epochal effect on rearranging the financial world'. Aside from having
to possess higher amounts of capital in order to operate, banks had to
subject their management to tighter scrutiny from the government.
For example, a bank could no longer engage in other businesses. A
director of a bank had to receive permission from the Ministry of
Finance in order to work for another company. Ten per cent of profits
had to be held as a reserve fund. Government audits became much
more detailed, and the penalties for providing false information
increased.[27]

The new law engendered little opposition. Small banks and businesses were most likely to protest; many of the former stood to lose
their autonomy, while the latter could see familiar sources of capital
vanish. One would expect that resistance, if it existed, would surface
among the Chambers of Commerce, because these groups included
as members so many small and medium-sized enterprises. Still, the
Japan Chamber of Commerce supported the law. A statement in June
1927 backed the merger policy as essential to enhance the role of
regional banks by cultivating a few strong ones. 'In order to make
regional banks still play a role as regional financial organs, [the
government] should in the future make regional banks merge as
much as possible and prevent the evil of fruitless competition.'[28] In
1928 Inoue Junnosuke wrote that the new law made him 'very happy'.
He hoped that co-operation among financial institutions would
replace excessive competition for deposits and reckless lending practices that used unsecured notes and company bonds as collateral.[29]
Acknowledging the fears of small businesses, Ishii Kengo of the

Daiichi Bank argued that the financial 'traditions of banks that were being merged had to be preserved' and that emphasizing mergers between regional banks would 'deepen their hometown character'.[30]

Whether the law was epochal or not, the Finance Ministry commenced an intensive campaign to merge regional banks. New guidelines urged officials to aim at creating one or two major banks in each region – ideally in each of the forty-five prefectures – of the nation. Local ministry officials were to take an active role in fostering mergers by meeting with banking executives and mediating the deals if necessary. In October 1927 the Ministry applied pressure by carrying out an audit of 490 small banks. The investigation allegedly aimed not at forcing mergers but 'to make executives realize the need for them . . . '. As bait, the government could hold out the prospect of special financing from the Bank of Japan to cover a bank's bad loans. Moreover, the new regulations forbade a bank from meeting the new capital requirements by raising more funds by itself.[31]

In 1927 and 1928, 312 banks participated in mergers. True to the intent of the original plan, most of the consolidations occurred among regional banks. The financial panic of 1927 did cause a dramatic shift of deposits away from small institutions to the large city banks. The top five, for example, saw their share of national deposits soar from 24 per cent in 1926 to 40 per cent in 1931. The large banks, though, evinced little interest in expanding their networks of branches. In one case, when the Higo Bank on the southern island of Kyūshū – itself the product of a recent merger of three local banks – ran into difficulties, the Yasuda Bank agreed to provide managerial help, underwrite the bank's notes and to transfer five branches to it. The Higo Bank became a subsidiary of Yasuda, but this turned out to be a rare case. Content with serving large companies, the city banks hesitated to venture into the unfamiliar and more volatile business of providing funds to small enterprises.[32]

By early 1930 the Tokyo Chamber of Commerce could note approvingly both the rationale and results of the merger policies. They had followed 'a world trend that had contributed to industrial development', especially in England and Germany. Since the nineteenth century, for example, over 90 per cent of Britain's banks had vanished, and only twenty-two banks remained. In this situation, Japan had had to take similar measures to prepare for 'world economic war'. As a result, banks had increased their reserves of capital and had earned a growing trust from the public.[33]

The world-wide depression and the gold standard

Contrary to Inoue's belief that the stock market crash in the United States deserved little notice, it marked the start of a severe depression in that nation. The impact soon spread to other nations, including Japan. The most direct effect came from the collapse of the American demand for raw silk, Japan's most important export. The steep drop in the price of silk reduced the income and purchasing power of Japanese farmers, many of whom depended upon sericulture as a secondary occupation. As domestic demand fell, so did industrial production and employment. The world-wide nature of the economic depression created another problem: ubiquitous deflation caused prices everywhere to drop. Although the prices of Japanese goods and services declined, the nation's products did not become more competitive, because comparable goods in other markets became cheaper too. In terms of value, the nation's industrial production and foreign trade withered.

The banking sector suffered too, as even large zaibatsu concerns ran into difficulties. For the industry as a whole, profit rates plummeted by the second half of 1931. After 1929, deposits at the Yasuda Bank fell by one-half. Profits tumbled, as both interest rates and the amount of loans decreased. In December 1931 a report of the bank stated that 'the economic world faced an important crisis'. Similarly, the Mitsui Bank emphasized the terrible economic situation in a report in 1930, and chief executive Ikeda Seihin took to expressing the impact on the bank by referring to this period as 'an era of difficulties'. In March 1932 Mitsui acknowledged a loss for the first time; Mitsubishi and Sumitomo followed suit.[34]

Still, support for the gold standard remained strong within the banking community. Imai Takuo of Sumitomo warned that deserting the standard at the old parity would harm the 'trust' of the nation abroad. Stressing the need for stable exchange rates, Noguchi Kōki of Daiichi inveighed against 'changing directions in the middle of a stormy voyage across the sea'. Sumitomo's Yashiro thought that raising productivity would prove more effective than fiddling with monetary policy. Mori Kōzō of Yasuda expressed the most doubt by saying that he would reconsider the need for a convertible currency if the situation worsened.[35]

When England abandoned the gold standard in September 1931, pressure for Japan to do likewise mounted. For two years the opposition Seiyūkai party had been battering the incumbent Minseitō Cabinet for the deteriorating state of the economy. Inoue Junnosuke's stringent spending policies and his insistence on maintaining the gold standard made him the main target for blame. Now critics could point to the British example. Some executives argued that Britain was trying to gain an advantage in trade through devaluing its currency and that Japan should do the same.[36] A broader discontent was evident in the vehement criticism that Mitsui received for purchasing a large amount of dollars towards the end of September. Although Mitsui protested that it was simply trying to cover its losses from investments in England, the media suspected that the bank was really conniving to profit from the imminent end of the gold standard and devaluation of the yen.[37]

Public statements by financial executives presented a strident defence of free trade in gold. On 5 November the Fifth Day Society (Itsukakai) – an informal gathering of leaders of the finance industry – issued a declaration urging the government to persevere despite the 'unease' caused by recent events. The next day Inoue discussed the government's economic policies with a group of major business leaders, including bankers Ikeda, Yashiro and Kushida Manzō. They reaffirmed their faith in the gold standard as the 'basis of the economy'.[38]

Political events, however, conspired against Inoue's stubborn adherence to his policy. His party, the Minseitō, gradually weakened. Not only could the rival Seiyūkai attribute the nation's economic woes to the Cabinet, but the party also proved incapable of asserting its will as it attempted to curb the Imperial Army's attack on Chinese forces in Manchuria in the autumn of 1931. Finally, when a Minister resigned in December in a futile ploy to force a merger with the Seiyūkai the Cabinet collapsed. Within a day after assuming power, Seiyūkai Premier Inukai Tsuyoshi announced an end to free trade in gold. Two months later Inukai's party won a resounding victory at the polls. Although most banking executives may have continued to believe in the beneficial long-term effects of the gold standard, this faith had to bow to economic and political realities.

Overcoming the depression and dealing with the military

Amid these economic difficulties, the bank merger programme began to encounter some resistance. Between 1929 and 1932 over fifty banks per year merged. Convinced that the programme had gone far enough, sixty-five members of the National Regional Bank Federation petitioned for relief in 1931. They wanted an extension of the five-year grace period granted by the Bank Law to allow small banks to raise enough capital to meet the new standards. The Tokyo Chamber of Commerce argued for a cautious attitude towards mergers for the sake of securing a smooth flow of capital for local businesses. The Ministry of Finance countered that only a handful of banks would benefit from a longer grace period and that a change would be unfair to those banks that had already co-operated through implementing mergers. A bill granting an extension of ten years passed the Lower House of the Diet but stalled in the House of Peers. The movement for consolidation, however, did ease. Between 1933 and 1936 an average of less than sixteen banks merged each year because of both growing resistance and a strengthening economy.[39]

Japan engineered a relatively swift recovery from the depression in several ways. The abandonment of the gold standard brought a sharp devaluation of the yen; this spurred a surge in exports to the extent of inviting new trade barriers in most major markets of the world. Meanwhile, the government greatly expanded its budget to fund both the war in Manchuria and new programmes, such as increased subsidies for shipbuilding. The budget for 1932 exceeded that for 1931 by almost 50 per cent. Much of the increase was financed by national bonds issued by the Bank of Japan; it, in turn, sold these to private banks. Between 1931 and 1936 the economy grew at a real rate of 4 per cent per year.[40]

Not surprisingly, the banks shared in this prosperity. For example, at Yasuda deposits and loans increased substantially, and the bank invested heavily in the new national bonds. The Mitsubishi Bank also reported rising deposits and loans, as well as large purchases of national bonds. In general, prospects for the economy seemed to brighten.[41]

Although the deficit-spending policies of the government reversed the consensus behind fiscal retrenchment and the gold standard in 1929, the banks could not argue against the evident success in stimulating the economy. The banks co-operated not only by purchasing national bonds but also by aiding the low interest policy of the Bank of Japan. To ease the burden of interest on the government, the Bank of Japan in 1932 and 1933 embarked on a campaign to cut interest rates. The discount rate fell to an unprecedented level of 3.65 per cent, and the rate on bonds went from 4.5 per cent to 4 per cent, the lowest level since 1910. The Bank of Japan requested large banks to help by reducing interest rates on their deposits and loans nation-wide. The large banks were to force rates down in each region by dropping rates at their branches. The banks responded positively and effectively.[42]

By 1935, however, both the Ministry of Finance and the banking community began to worry about fiscal policy. Takahashi Korekiyo, the mastermind behind the deficit budgets, voiced concern in July about the escalation of 'evil inflation'. Warning that the consumption of bonds would spawn burgeoning interest payments, he advised that the budget needed trimming and the government had to 'plan the smooth operation of bond policy'. Accordingly, he proposed slower growth in the next year's spending and a decrease in bonds.[43] Leaders of the banking community endorsed this switch in policy. Yasuda's Mori Kōzō, president of the Tokyo Clearing-House, said that 'the guaranteeing of such a policy of gradually reducing deficit bonds will have a good influence on maintaining their market value and make the future of their absorption bright . . . If public finances are not balanced, the absorption of bonds cannot continue forever.' Later he commented that the decline in bonds was something that 'we must greatly welcome'. Because the total value of national bonds was becoming excessive, future governments would have to hold to 'the iron principle of healthy finances'.[44]

The sudden and abortive army coup of 26 February 1936 dashed hopes for these new fiscal policies. The troops from the first division in Tokyo who seized parts of the capital failed in their goal of instituting a martial law regime under the direct rule of the Emperor. They succeeded, however, in assassinating Finance Minister Takahashi. Moreover, after the revolt the Cabinet fell and was replaced by one much more amenable to the wishes of the military. Baba Eiichi, president of the Hypothec Bank, replaced Takahashi. He shocked the financial world by announcing sharp changes in major policies. He outlined a budget that mandated a substantial increase in spending, new taxes and no reduction of national bonds. Addressing the

Federation of Clearing-Houses in June, Mori Kōzō expressed the concerns of bankers. The financial world, he said, felt 'unease' over the proposed reform policies of the Cabinet. Executives feared large rises in taxes and the onset of financial speculation because of interest rates that had dropped to unprecedented low levels. He also emphasized the need to progress through 'international co-operation' to develop the nation's trade. Baba sought to reassure his former colleagues by noting that the proposed tax rises aimed ultimately to decrease dependence on bonds. He had faith in the economy's ability to absorb more of them, and the government would take steps to control any speculation that resulted from low interest rates.[45]

In May 1936 Baba also unnerved bankers by announcing the goal of reducing the number of regional banks to one for each prefecture. His rationale emphasized the benefits for large numbers of citizens. In an era of very low interest rates, consolidation of regional banks would make them stronger and more competitive with the city banks. As a result, deposits would become more secure. Having fewer banks would also ease the task of government regulation.[46] This plan provoked strong opposition from bankers and others. Mori noted the widespread concerns about 'extreme controls'. Although national regulation was necessary, 'practical content about extent and methods' demanded 'careful study'. After surveying its members, the Japan Chamber of Commerce issued a statement against Baba's policy, because it would harm the financing of small enterprises and would ignore the special characteristics of each region. The Tokyo Chamber lamented the concentration of capital in a few banks.[47]

By the start of 1937 public criticism of Baba's fiscal policies reached the point that Army Minister Terauchi Hisaichi judged that the budget was doomed. His resignation caused the Cabinet to fall. When Yasuda's Yūki Toyotarō assumed the portfolio of finance, he sought to sooth the jitters of the banking community. He proclaimed that he had no intention of enforcing Baba's merger policy and, to Mori's delight, reduced the budget and the new taxes. Mori, however, discerned some remaining problems – speculation in the stock market and a decrease in the amount of bonds that the Bank of Japan had been able to sell in the past year. The Cabinet had to return to the policy of paring deficit spending. He reflected on the possible dangers that lay ahead: 'Plans not suited for a nation's power would damage credit, induce speculative investment, bring confusion into the financial world and overturn the basis for the national economy.'[48]

Within two months, however, the strategic and political situation would change immeasurably. A clash between Chinese and Japanese forces in North China brought full-scale war. Military expenditures over the next four years soared 300 per cent and the government's debt by 280 per cent. As the fighting dragged on into 1938, the government imposed tighter controls over the economy in order to mobilize for war. For example, the Temporary Funds Adjustment Act required banks to seek approval from the Ministry of Finance for long-term loans over a set amount. During the following year the Diet passed a National Mobilization Law that granted the government authority over every aspect of the economy. In these circumstances the emphasis on consolidating banks intensified for the purpose of facilitating wartime controls. The explicit goal became one bank for each prefecture. The number of banks declined from 424 in 1936 to 186 by the end of 1941. By the end of the Pacific War in 1945 that number had fallen to 61.[49] Only 5 per cent of the banks that had existed in 1926 remained!

Conclusion

The interwar period saw the development of an increasingly close and complex interaction between the banking community and the government. Taking an active concern with fiscal and monetary matters, bankers worked to influence related national policies. That reaching a consensus on the gold standard required the entire decade of the 1920s indicated that the financial community hardly constituted a unified bloc. Banks, however, played an important role in focusing public attention on the issue and in eventually persuading the government to cut spending and to enact a convertible currency in 1930. When the Cabinet switched to deficit spending in 1932, the large banks co-operated in helping the Ministry of Finance carry out the new policy. In regard to the campaign to consolidate the banking sector, executives from the zaibatsu banks advised government officials in the 1920s, won some concessions on policy guidelines and supported the programme. As it continued, however, into the 1930s, it encountered resistance, first from small banks and then from large ones that feared the rise of extended bureaucratic controls under Finance Minister

Baba Eiichi. In each instance, the government's policy moderated for a while.

If the banking community could at times affect national policies, that influence also had clear limits. The government did not implement free trade in gold without consent from all major business sectors. In 1931 international economic events and the actions of the Imperial Japanese Army forced abandonment of the gold standard, which executives had continued to defend in public. The brief army rebellion in 1936 and the China War that began in July 1937 swept away all hopes for bringing fiscal policy under control. Moreover, the 'extreme controls' that the bankers feared so much – including pursuit of the goal of one bank for each prefecture – came into effect.

These developments had a significant impact on the post-1945 Japanese economy. The close interaction between the Ministry of Finance, the Bank of Japan and the private banking sector continued after 1945 in informal and formal ways. The former included the authority granted in 1947 to the Ministry of Finance to control banks' interest rates and the well-known 'window guidance' through which the Bank of Japan could determine the maximum amount that each city bank could lend during each quarter of each year.[50] The banking sector also retained its high level of consolidation. Despite the aim of the Allied occupation (1945–51) to 'democratize' the banking industry by breaking it up, it proved resilient. Few new banks appeared. Three decades later, the commercial banking sector comprised thirteen large city banks and sixty-three regional ones. As one scholar has suggested, this circumstance may well have aided the availability of capital for Japan's rapid economic recovery from the devastation of the Pacific War and the nation's subsequent impressive record of economic growth.[51]

NOTES

* I would like to thank the University of North Carolina Press for permission to use material from my book, *The Japanese Business Community and National Trade Policy, 1920–1942* (1989).

1 R. W. Goldsmith, *The Financial Development of Japan, 1868–1977* (New Haven, Conn., 1983), p. 47.

2 Tokyo Shōkō Kaigisho, *Keizai dantai sôran* (Tokyo, 1941), pp. 171–3 and 151–2, and Hara Akira, 'Zaikai', in Nakamura Takafusa and Itō Takashi (eds.), *Kindai Nihon kenkyū nyūmon* (Tokyo, 1977), pp. 180–1.

3 Nihon Kōgyō Kurabu Gojū Nen Shi Hensan Iinkai, *Nihon kōgyō kurabu gojū nen shi* (Tokyo, 1972), pp. 20–1.

4 See W. W. Lockwood, *The Economic Development of Japan* (Princeton, N.J., 1967), pp. 249–50 and 514–16, and Goldsmith, *The Financial Development of Japan*, pp. 46–7 and 51.

5 Itō Masanao, 'Zaisei kin'yū', in 1920 Nendai Kenkyūkai (ed.), *1920 nendai no Nihon shihonshugi* (Tokyo, 1983), p. 87, and Goldsmith, *Financial Development*, p. 72.

6 Inoue Junnosuke, 'Nao seiri kinshuku jidai', 25 November 1922, in Takahashi Kamekichi (ed.), *Zaisei keizai nijū-go nen shi* (Tokyo, 1932), vol. VI, pp. 258–60, and Inoue, 'Chūkan keiki o imashimu' (January 1922), in Inoue, *Kokusaku keizai o kataru* (Tokyo, 1930), pp. 27–32. I treat the debate over the gold standard in more detail in W. M. Fletcher III, *The Japanese Business Community and National Trade Policy, 1920–1942* (Chapel Hill, N.C., 1989), ch. 2.

7 Inoue, 'Chūkan keiki' and 'Onshitsu ura no zaikai', in Inoue, *Kokusaku keizai*, pp. 31–2 and 44–65.

8 'Kin yushutsu kaikan sanpi', *Osaka jiji shinpō*, 17–31 August 1922, in Nihon Ginkō Chōsakyoku (ed.), *Nihon kin'yū shi shiryō, shōwa hen* (Tokyo, 1969), vol. XXIII, p. 650, and Mutō, *Jitsugyō seiji* (Tokyo, 1926), pp. 181–3.

9 'Kin yushutsu kaikin sanpi', pp. 650–5. Zaibatsu were huge combines that comprised many different kinds of companies. The largest were Mitsui, Mitsubishi, Sumitomo and Yasuda.

10 'Ichiki ōkurashō shusai kin kaikin mondai kondankai', *Chūgai shōgyō shinpō*, 8–9 September 1922, in Nihon Ginkō Chōsakyoku, *Shiryō*, vol. XXIII, pp. 567–8, and Aoki Kazuo, 'Kin kaikin to Inoue ōkurashō no omoishutsu', in Nihon Ginkō Chōsakyoku (ed.), *Nihon kin'yū shi shiryō, shōwa hen* (Tokyo, 1968), vol. XXII, p. 1.

11 H. Patrick, 'The economic muddle of the 1920s', in J. B. Morley (ed.), *Dilemmas of Growth in Prewar Japan* (Princeton. N.J., 1971), p. 246.

12 'Dai yonmen kin'yū bukai giroku', 7 May 1924; 'Kin'yūbu tokubetsu iinkai (kawase) dai ikkai kaigi yōroku', 14 May 1924; 'Kin'yūbu tokubetsu iinkai (kawase) dai nikai kaigi yōroku', 15 May 1924; Teikoku keizai kaigi kin'yūbu tokubetsu iinchō, 'Gaikoku kawase kaizen hōsaku oyobi kingin yushutsu kaikin . . . ', 15 May 1924, in Teikoku keizai kaigi, Kin'yū bukai kaigi roku, available in the Kokuritsu Kōbunsho Kan (National Archives) in Tokyo, Japan.

13 Goldsmith, *Financial Development*, pp. 73–4; Takeda Haruhito, 'Kyōkō', in 1920 Nendai Kenkyūkai (ed.), *1920 nendai*, pp. 349 and 352–5; Nakamura, *Senzenki Nihon keizai seichō no bunseki* (Tokyo, 1971), pp. 128–56; and Hikida Yasuyuki, 'Sangyō kōzō', in 1920 Nendai Kenkyūkai (ed.), *1920 nendai*, pp. 52–68.

14 Inoue Junnosuke, *Kokumin keizai no tachinaoshi to kin kaikin* (Tokyo, 1929), pp. 1–40, esp. pp. 33–40.

15 Yamamuro Sōbun, 'Kin no kaikin ga hitsuyō', *Daiyamondo*, 15 August 1928, in Nihon Ginkō Chōsakyoku, *Shiryō*, vol. XXIII, p. 41.

16 'Kin kaikin to honnen no zaikai', *Tōyō keizai shinpō*, 1–15 January 1927, and Yashiro Norihiko, 'Kyōkō de sokushin sareta kin kaikin', *Ekonomisuto*, 1 May 1928, in Nihon Ginkō Chōsakyoku (ed.), *Shiryō*, vol. XXIII, pp. 668–9 and 38–9.

17 Tokyo Ginkō Kyōkai, *Tokyo tegata kōkanjo kyūjū nen no ayumi* (Tokyo, 1977), p. 64, and Miwa Ryōichi, 'Kin kaikin seisaku kettei katei ni okeru rigai ishiki', *Aoyama keizai ronshū*, 26 November 1974, 181–6.

18 Kōbe Shōkō Kaigisho Hyaku Nen Shi Henshū Bukai, *Kobe shōkō kaigisho hyaku nen shi* (Kōbe, 1982), pp. 234–6, and Miwa, 'Rigai ishiki', pp. 189–98. For a survey of opinions of executives in various industries, see Nihon Kōgyō Kurabu Chōsaka, *Kin yushutsu mondai ni kansuru Nihon kōgyō kurabu kaiin no iken*, November 1928, in

Keizai shingikai, Shijun dai nigo tokubetsu iinkai kankei shorui, available in the Kokuritsu Kōbunsho Kan in Tokyo, Japan.

19 'Keizai shingikai, Dai sanmen sōkai giji roku', 21 December 1928.

20 Gotō Shin'ichi, *Shōwaki ginkō gōdō shi: ikken ikkōshugi no seiritsu* (Tokyo, 1982), pp. 2–12, and Kabushiki Kaisha Yasuda Ginkō Rokujū Shūnen Kinen Jigyō Iinkai (ed.), *Yasuda ginkō rokujū nen shi* (Tokyo, 1940), p. 344.

21 Katō Yoshihiko, *Honpō ginkō shi ron* (Tokyo, 1957), pp. 293–6, and Gotō, *Shōwaki ginkō gōdō*, pp. 13–15.

22 Gotō, *Shōwaki ginkō gōdō*, pp. 11 and 17–19, and Katō, *Ginkō shi*, p. 298.

23 Katō, *Ginkō shi*, p. 307; Gotō, *Shōwaki ginkō gōdō*, pp. 20–1; and Yaoita Masao, *Shōwa kin'yū seisaku shi* (Tokyo, 1943), p. 56. The members were Horikoshi Tetsuzō (Bank of Japan), Shimoda Morizō (Mitsui), Yamamuro Sōbun (Mitsubishi), Ohira Kensaku (Sumitomo) and Akashi Teruo (Daiichi).

24 Gotō, *Shōwaki ginkō gōdō*, pp. 21–3; Katō, *Ginkō shi*, pp. 303–6; and Makimura Shirō, 'Chihō ginkō kan no kankei', in Asakura Takakichi (ed.), *Ryō taisen kan ni okeru kin'yū kōzō* (Tokyo, 1980), pp. 362–3.

25 Katō, *Ginkō shi*, pp. 303–4, and Gotō *Shōwaki ginkō gōdō*, pp. 23–5.

26 Gotō, *Shōwa ginkō gōdō*, pp. 23–5, and Katō, *Ginkō shi*, p. 304.

27 Yaoita, *Shōwa kin'yū*, pp. 57–63. W. M. Tsutsui, *Banking Policy in Japan: American Efforts at Reform during the Occupation* (London, 1988), pp. 10–11, points out gaps that remained in the regulation of bank management.

28 Zenkoku Shōgyō Kaigisho Rengōkai, 'Ginkō gōhei ni kansuru kengi an', 16 June 1927, in Nihon Ginkō Chōsakyoku (ed.), *Nihon kin'yū shi shiryō, shōwa hen* (Tokyo, 1969), vol. XXV, p. 558.

29 Inoue Junnosuke, 'Kin'yūkai no dōyō o kaerimite zaikai no zento o omou', 20 May 1928, in Nihon Ginkō Chōsakyoku (ed.), *Nihon kin'yū shi shiryō, shōwa hen* (Tokyo, 1965), vol. XXVI, pp. 99–100.

30 Ishii Kengo, 'Ginkō kyōkō to sho shōkō kin'yū', *Ekonomisuto*, 5, 1 July 1927, in Nihon Ginkō Chōsakyoku (ed.), *Shiryō*, vol. XXVI, pp. 632–3.

31 Gotō, *Shōwaki ginkō gōdō*, pp. 36–41, and Katō, *Ginkō shi*, p. 310.

32 Katō, *Ginkō shi*, pp. 310 and 312–13; Gotō, *Shōwaki ginkō gōdō*, p. 78; and Kabushiki Kaisha Yasuda Ginkō Rokujū Shūnen Kinen Jigyō Iinkai (ed.), *Yasuda ginkō*, pp. 347–9.

33 Tokyo Shōkō Kaigisho, 'Wagakuni ginkō no gōdō mondai', January 1930, in Nihon Ginkō Chōsakyoku (ed.), *Shiryō*, vol. XXVI, pp. 456–8 and 478–80.

34 Kabushiki Kaisha Yasuda Ginkō Rokujū Shūnen Kinen Jigyō Iinkai (ed.), *Yasuda ginkō*, pp. 367–9 and 375–6; Mitsui Ginkō Hachijū Nen Shi Hensan Iinkai, *Mitsui ginkō hachijū nen shi* (Tokyo 1957), pp. 249–51 and 255–6; and Takeda, 'Kyōkō', p. 353.

35 ' "Kyūheika kaikin jizuku" ka, "kaikin denaoshi" ka', *keizai jōhō*, 1 October 1930, in Nihon Ginkō Chōsakyoku (ed.), *Shiryō*, vol. XXIII, pp. 764 and 767, and 'Zaikai nan dakai saku', *Tōyō keizai shinpō*, 24 May 1930, in Nihon Ginkō Chōsakyoku (ed.), *Shiryō*, vol. XXIII, pp. 742–3. I analyse this renewed debate over the gold standard in *Japanese Business Community*, pp. 65–71.

36 Mutō Sanji, 'Kin yushutsu saikinshi o dankō se yo', *Chūgai zaikai*, 15 October 1931, and Tsuda Shingo, 'Mengyō wa kin saikinshi ga hitsuyō', *Daiyamondo*, 21 October 1931, in Nihon Ginkō Chōsakyoku (ed.), *Shiryō*, vol. XXIII, pp. 199 and 202–3.

37 Nakamura Takafusa, *Shōwa kyōkō to keizai seisaku* (Tokyo, 1978), pp. 160–1, and Yanagisawa Takeshi (ed.), *Ikeda Seihin, zaikai kaiko* (Tokyo, 1949), pp. 159–62.

38 'Kin hon'i yōgō no tame dōryoku ni iken itchi', 5 November 1931, and 'Zaikai

yūryokusha kin hon'i sei yōgō moshiawase', 6 November 1931, in Takahashi (ed.), *Zaisei keizai*, vol. VI, pp. 1072–3.

39 Gotō, *Shōwaki ginkō gōdō*, pp. 41–4, 51 and 78.

40 Kabushiki Kaisha Yasuda Ginkō Rokujū Shūnen Kinen Jigyō Iinkai (ed.), *Yasuda ginkō*, pp. 376 and 379, and Goldsmith, *The Financial Development*, p. 108.

41 Kabushiki Kaisha Yasuda Ginkō Rokujū Shūnen Kinen Jigyō Iinkai (ed.), *Yasuda ginkō*, pp. 387–8; 'Kabushiki kaisha Mitsubishi ginkō gaikyō', January [1935]–December [1935] and January [1936]–December [1936], in Mitsubishi Shashi Kankokai (ed.), *Mitsubishi shashi* (Tokyo, 1981), vol. XXXVII, pp. 1059–62 and 1188–90; and Kiyomizu Ken'ichirō, 'Nentō shokan' and Kikumoto Naojirō, 'Nentō shokan', in *Ginkō tsūshinroku*, no. 600, 20 January 1936, pp. 2–3 and 17.

42 Kabushiki Kaisha Yasuda Ginkō Rokujū Shunen Kinen Jigyō Iinkai (ed.), *Yasuda ginkō*, pp. 377–8, and Goldsmith, *The Financial Development*, p. 114.

43 Yaoita, *Shōwa kin'yū*, pp. 259–63.

44 Mori Kōzō, 'Tegata kōkan o chūshin to shite no zaikai tenbō', *Ginkō tsūshinroku*, no. 600, 20 January 1936, p. 21, and 'Tegata kōkanjo shinnen bansankai enzetsu', *Ginkō tsūshinroku*, no. 601, 20 February 1936, p. 12.

45 Mori Kōzō, 'Tegata kōkanjo rengō konshinkai sekijō aisatsu', and Baba Eiichi, 'Dōjō ōkuradaijin no enzetsu', *Ginkō tsūshinroku*, no. 605, 20 June 1936, pp. 1–3 and 5–8. The Bank of Japan's discount rate fell to 3.29 per cent. See Goldsmith, *The Financial Development*, p. 114.

46 Gotō, *Shōwaki ginkō*, pp. 52–64.

47 *Ibid.*, pp. 61–2, and Mori, 'Tegata kōkanjo', 20 June 1936, pp. 1–3.

48 Gotō, *Shōwaki ginkō gōdō*, p. 65; Yaoita, *Shōwa kin'yū*, pp. 331–3; and Mori Kōzō, 'Tegata kōkanjo rengō konshinkai sekijō aisatsu', *Ginkō tsūshinroku*, no. 616, May 1937, pp. 1–3.

49 Goldsmith, *Financial Development*, p. 111, and Gotō, *Shōwaki ginkō gōdō*, pp. 66–9 and 78.

50 Tsutsui, *Banking Policy*, pp. 124–6; Haitani Kanji, *The Japanese Economic System: an Institutional Overview* (Lexington, Mass., 1976), pp. 168–9; and Koichi Hamada and Akiyoshi Horiuchi, 'The political economy of the financial market', in Kozo Yamamura and Yasukichi Yasuba (eds.), *The Political Economy of Japan. Vol. I. The Domestic Transformation* (Stanford, Calif., 1987), pp. 236–8 and 245.

51 Haitani, *Japanese Economic System*, pp. 149–50, and Tsutsui, *Banking Policy*, pp. 125 and 127.

Index

AB Kreditkassen, 89–91, 96
AB Nya Banken, 86
AB Privatbanken, 86
Agnelli, G., 190
Agricultural Bank, 209, 211, 214, 220, 228
Alfa Romeo, 192–3
Algemeene Bankvereeniging, 111–12
Allgemeine Österreichische Boden-Credit-
    Anstalt, 9, 141
Alpine Montan-Gesellschaft, 20, 21
Amsterdamsche Bank, 107
Ansaldo, 188–93
Athanasiades, B., 212
Austria
    Anschluss, 180
    bank cartel, 151
    banking crisis (1931), 1, 8, 17
    banking system, 135
    commercial banks (Vienna), 137–8
    Commission of Inquiry (1930), 131–2
    currency stabilization, 128
    deflation, 23
    devaluation, 130
    economic collapse, 150
    economic crisis (1925–33), 126–30, 133,
        151
    Electrical Power Companies, 21
    hyperinflation, 20
    industrial joint-stock companies, 122–53
        passim
    Industrie Inspektorat, 139
    inflation, 20, 23
    Krupp (Berndorf), 21
    mixed banks, 179
    Österreichische Alpine-Montan-
        Gesellschaft, see Alpine Montan-
        Gesellschaft

    Social Democrats, 23
    stabilization crisis, 128
    Steyr works, 21
    see also Österreichische Credit-Anstalt für
        Handel und Gewerbe
Austria-Hungary, see Habsburg Monarchy
Austrian National Bank, see Österreichische
    Nationalbank
Austro-Hungarian Bank, 166
Austro-Hungarian Compromise of 1867, see
    Hungary, Ausgleich

Baba, E., 256–66
Bairoch, P., 34
Baldwin, S., 35
Banca Commerciale Italiana, 179–85, 190–3,
    196–9
Banca Italiana di Sconto, 189–93
Banca Nazionale del Credito, 192, 196
    see also Società Italiana
Banco di Roma, 179, 185, 193, 199
bank(s), banking
    cartel, 63
    central, 3, 5, 11, 36–7, 39, 184, 192, 209,
        216–18, 220, 225, 233, 238–9
    chartered, 235–7
    commercial, 4–5, 28–9, 32–4, 81–4, 86–92,
        95–100, 137, 159–60, 179, 181–9, 192–5,
        199, 201, 207–8, 215–17, 219–25, 229,
        232, 251
    concentration, 52, 70, 84–5, 95, 97, 105–7,
        228, 258–68 passim
    deposit, 80–1, 109, 112, 114
    joint-stock, 84, 87–8
    legislation, 30–4, 80–5, 89, 94, 98–100, 116,
        195, 200, 215–16, 222, 233–4, 239, 258,
        260

local, 8, 109
mergers, *see* concentration
mixed, 2, 7, 9, 11, 24, 29–30, 32–3, 80, 83,
  104–6, 110, 112, 117–18, 134, 141, 153,
  158, 179–20-5 *passim*
municipal, 59, 70, 74, 109
nationalization, 200–1
provincial, 68, 70, 198
savings, 29, 59, 61, 68–70, 187, 198
socialization, 33, 50
universal, *see* mixed
zaibatsu, 254, 259, 262, 267
Bank-Associatie, 108
Bank for International Settlements, 39, 217
Bank of Athens, 224
Bank of Canada, 233–4, 237
Bank of Chosen, 252
Bank of England, 3, 36–7, 39–44, 217
Bank of France, *see* Banque de France
Bank of Greece, 5–6, 211, 216–25, 227
Bank of Italy, 5, 16, 180, 182–7, 191, 193-200
Bank of Japan, 252–3, 255–6, 258, 261, 264,
  266, 268
Bank of Montreal, 241, 243
Bank of Norway, 29, 96
Bank of Nova Scotia, 243
Bank of Sweden, 29
Bank of Taiwan, 252
Banque Belge du Travail, 111
Banque de Belgique, 105
Banque de Bruxelles, 30, 105, 112
Banque de France, 4, 9, 39, 41
Banque des Pays de L'Europe Centrale, 24
Banque Nationale de Belgique, 252
banking crises, 1–2, 7–8, 29, 85–7, 108,
  179–80
  see also countries
Bansconto, *see* Banca Italiana di Sconto
Baring Brothers, 42
Belgium
  Banking Commission, 113
  banking concentration, 106
  banking crisis, 2, 8, 117
  banking system, 105, 110, 117
  Catholic Party, 113, 115
  commercial banks, 32–3
  gold bloc, 112
  Liberal Party, 113
  mixed banking, 9, 30, 32–3, 104–6, 109,
    111–12, 114, 117–18
  Socialist Party, 113, 115
  state, bank and industry, 104–12 *passim*
Beneduil, A., 201
Bennett, R. B., 249
Bernhard, G., 56, 62, 67
Brussels Financial Conference, 72

CA, *see* Österreichische Credit-Anstalt für
  Handel und Gewerbe
Canada
  banking system, 233
  Canadian Bankers' Association, 241
  central gold reserves, 238
  chartered banks, 235–8
  'Crown corporations', 246
  'Finance Act advances', 238–40, 243
  gold convertibility, 238–40
  gold standard, 1, 13, 244
  Great Depression, 14, 232–3, 235, 244–5
  legislation (banks), 233–4, 239
  legislation (currency), 234
  mortgage loan companies, 236–7
  near-banks, 236–7, 240, 249
  trust companies, 236–7
Canadian Bank of Commerce, 243
Central Europe
  banking collapse, 38
  banking system, 4, 11, 24
  universal banking, 19–25 *passim*, 134
Centralbanken for Norge, 29
  see also Norway
Chadzikyriakos, A., 212, 214
chambers of commerce, 59–61, 72, 257,
  260–1, 264, 266
  and industry, 207
Charilaos, E., 212–14
Clark, W. C., 242–3
Commercial Bank of Pest
  and industry, 158–77 *passim*
  'banker's agreement', 164, 167–8
  'gold' balance sheet (1925), 172, 174
  Guiness Mahon & Co., 171
  intern loans, 164, 167–8
  League of Nations, 169
  Niederösterreichische Escompte
    Gesellschaft, 170
  Schweizerischer Bankverein, 171
communism, 34
Compagnie Belge pour l'Industrie, 112
Consorzio per la Sovvenzioni su Valori
  Industriali, 186–7, 193, 197–8
Conti, E., 197
Conuit, *see* Banca Commerciale Italiana
Credit, *see* Credito Italiano
credit market, 34, 53, 80
Crédit Mobilier, 29
Credito Italiano, 179–85, 190–2, 196–9
Credito Nazionale, 193
Crispi, S., 188
CSVI, *see* Consorzio per la Sovvenzioni su
  Valori Industriali
currency depreciation/devaluation
  Britain, 2–3, 220, 263

currency depreciation/devaluation (*cont.*)
  Greece, 1–2, 208
  Japan, 1, 263–4
  Sweden, 2
Czechoslovakia
  hyperinflation, 20

Daiichi Bank, 255, 259–60, 262
Danatbank, *see* Darmstädter und
  Nationalbank
Darmstädter und Nationalbank, 19, 39, 41, 60
Dawes Plan, 38, 40
De Stefani, A., 194
deflation, 6, 7, 11, 20, 23, 86–7, 89, 195, 253,
  256
Denmark
  Bank Inspection Board, 99
  banking crisis, 100
  banking law (1919), 95, 98
  banking system, 95
  commercial banking, 30, 32, 95, 97–9
  Landmandsbanken, 97
  legislation (banks), 33
Deposito- en Administratiebank, *see*
  Rotterdamsche Bankvereeniging
Deutsch, F., 67
Deutsche Bank, 60, 70
Diomedes, A., 216, 221, 227
Dominions' Farm Credit Corporation, 237
Drosopoulos, J., 214
Dual Monarchy, *see* Habsburg Monarchy

Erzberger tax reform, 54

fascists, fascism, 16, 34, 192
Feder, G., 50
Federal Reserve Bank of New York (FRBNY),
  35–6, 41, 45
Fiat, 188, 190
Finlayson, H. C., 220, 222–3
First World War, 1, 4, 15, 18–19, 29–31, 84,
  88, 95, 98, 105, 108, 128, 132, 134, 158–9,
  162, 166, 175, 182, 207, 238, 253
France
  financial stabilization, 40
  see also Banque de France
free market system, 34
free trade, 34
  in gold, 255–7, 263, 268
Friedrich, K., 61

Germany
  Anschluss, 180
  Bank Inquiry (1933), 9
  banking crisis (1931), 8, 17, 40, 49, 51, 75,
    197

Banking Law (1934), 9, 50
banking system, 15–16, 49, 51
corporation, 15, 74
credit market, 53
depression, 52
finance capital, 52
gold standard, 17, 51, 58
hyperinflation, 20
inflation, 20, 40, 50–2, 62, 65, 70, 72, 76
mixed banking, 109, 179
National Socialists, 50
politics, 13–18 *passim*
reparations, 53
Standstill Agreement, 41
state, banks and industry, 49–79 *passim*
Gerschenkron, A., 28, 158, 181
Giolitti, G., 190
gold reserves, 3, 253, 255
gold standard, 1–2, 4–6, 11, 13, 15, 34–5,
  39–40, 42–5, 51, 58, 112, 114, 116, 194,
  214–15, 221, 224–5, 244, 251–7, 262–4,
  267
Goldschmidt, J., 60–1, 66, 70
Goldsmith, R., 2, 34
Göteborgs Bank, 94
Great Britain
  Conservative Party, 44
  currency destabilization, 3
  financial crisis (1931), 35, 45
  gold standard, 13, 17, 35, 42–5, 114, 263
  Labour Party, 43
  Macmillan Committee, 39
  May Committee, 41
Great Depression, 3, 13, 17, 52, 131, 188, 198,
  232–3, 235, 244–5
Great War, *see* First World War
Gregorini, F., 188
Greece
  banking system, 206, 208, 215, 228
  banks and the economy, 206–31 *passim*
  chamber(s) of commerce and industry,
    207, 228
  commercial banks, 207–8, 215–17,
    219–25
  concentration (banks), 228
  deflation, 224
  devaluation, 221, 224–5
  exchange speculation, 208
  financial crisis (1931), 220, 226–7
  gold standard, 13, 214–15, 221, 224–5
  inflation, 208, 224
  League of Nations, 209, 215–18, 220, 223
  legislation (banks), 215–16, 222
  Metaxas dictatorship/regime, 212, 228
  Populist Party, 216, 223
Grenfell, E. (Lord St. Just), 37, 40, 45

Habsburg Monarchy, 122, 134–6, 139, 151, 153, 159, 176, 186
Hahn, L., 72–3
Harjes, 37
Harrison, G. L., 37–9, 43
Harrod—Domar model, 27
Harvey, E., 42, 44
Havenstein, R., 16
Hellenic and General Trust (Hellenic Corporation Ltd), 213–14, 228
Henderson, H. D., 40
Higo Bank, 261
Hilferding, R., 28, 64, 158
Hirsch, J., 55–9, 62
Hoover, H., 38
Hoover Moratorium, 38–9
House of Morgan, 35–40, 42–5
Hungarian General Credit Bank, 159–61
Hungarian National Bank, 166–7
Hungary
    Ausgleich, 161
    banking crisis (1931), 8
    deflation, 170, 174–5
    financial capital circulation, 158
    hyperinflation, 158
    industrial capital concentration, 158
    inflation, 20, 164, 166, 169–70, 172, 174–5
    mixed banks, 1
hyperinflation, 9, 20, 158
Hypothec Bank, 252, 265

Ichiki, O., 254
Ikeda, K., 254
Ikeda, S., 255–6, 260, 262
Ilva, 189
Imai, T., 262
IMI, *see* Istituto Mobiliare Italiano
Incasso Bank, 107
inflation(s), 2, 9, 18, 20, 23, 40, 50–2, 62, 65, 70, 72, 76, 84, 116, 164, 169–70, 172, 208
    see also under countries
Inowe, J., 253–4, 257, 259, 262–3
Inukai, T., 263
Ionian Bank, 210, 219
IRI, *see* Istituto di Riconstruzione Industriale
Ishii, K., 260
Istituto di Riconstruzione Industriale, 8, 17, 179–80, 193, 199, 201, 229
Istituto Mobiliare Italiano, 187, 198
Italy
    banking crisis, 8, 79–80, 198, 200–1
    banking system, 4, 15, 183, 185, 201
    commercial banks, 179, 181–9, 192–5, 199, 201
    corporatism, 15, 201
    deflation, 195

Fascist Party, 201
fascists, fascism, 16, 34, 192
financial crisis (1920–3), 188
gold standard, 194
Great Depression, 188, 198
industrial securities, 180, 182, 185, 194, 197–9, 201
legislation (banks), 200–1
March on Rome, 194, 201
mixed banks, 179–205 *passim*
nationalization (industry), 201
savings banks, 187, 198
war debts, 194–5

Japan
    bank mergers, 258–68 *passim*
    banking crises, 8
    banking system, 258
    chamber(s) of commerce, 257, 260–1, 264, 266
    commercial banks, 251
    corporatism, 15
    deflation, 253. 256
    devaluation, 263–4
    free trade in gold, 255–7, 263, 268
    gold reserves, 253, 255
    gold standard, 251–7, 262–4, 267–8
    legislation (banks), 8, 15, 258, 260
    post-war recession (1920), 253, 255, 258
    zaibatsu, 254, 259, 267
joint-stock companies, 83, 181–2
    foreign, 140
    industrial (Austria), 122–53 *passim*
Jordan, Hans, 55, 57–8, 65
Jordan Plan, 72

Kanellopoulos, N., 212, 214
Keynes, J. M., 34, 38, 215
Kodama, K., 254
Kraemer, H., 55, 61–2, 69, 71
Kreuger, I., 92
Kreuger crash, 33, 91–3
Krupp (Berndorf), 21
Kushida, M., 254–5, 259, 263
Kuznets, S., 27, 34

Lamont, T. W., 37–8, 43
Landmandsbanken, 97
League of Nations, 5, 134, 215, 254
    Commercial Bank of Pest, 169
    Financial Committee, 1, 216–18, 220, 223
    Greece, 209
Leffingwell, R. G., 37
Luther, H., 39–40

MacDonald, R., 41–3
Maddison, A., 2, 34

276   *Index*

Magyar Általános Hitelbank, *see* Hungarian
    General Credit Bank
MAH, *see* Hungarian General Credit Bank
market(s)
    financial, 4
    free, 34
    London, 4
    New York, 4
    world, 1
Marx en Co Bank, 108
Matsumoto, O., 259
Mayer, T., 198
Mellon, A. W., 35
Mendelssohn Bank, 116
Menichella, D., 201
Mitsubishi, 254–6, 259, 262, 264
Mitsui Bank, 255, 257, 259, 262
Miyajima, S., 254
Moret, C., 39
Morgan, J. P., 18
Morgan, J. P. ('Jack'), 37, 41, 43, 45
Morgan & Co., J. P., *see* House of Morgan
Morgan Grenfell & Co., *see* House of
    Morgan
Morgan Harjes (Morgan et Cie, Paris), *see*
    House of Morgan
Mori, K., 263, 265–6
Morrow, D., 37, 39
Müller en Co, 108
Mussolini, B., 193–5, 197
Muto, S., 254
Mynors, H., 45

National Bank of Greece, 5, 14, 207–10, 216,
    219–25, 227
    Hambros Bank, 213
National Bank of Yugoslavia, 225
National Mortgage Bank, 213, 227
Nederlandsche Bank, 116
Nederlandsche Handel-Maatschappij, 107,
    114, 116
Niemeyer, O., 221, 223
Nitti, F. S., 190–1, 201
Noguchi, K., 262
Norman, M., 3–6, 17, 36, 39–42, 218
Norway
    Bank Inspection Board, 99
    banking crisis, 29, 100
    banking law (1924), 95
    banking system, 95
    commercial banks, 32, 95–100
    legislation (banks), 33
    savings banks, 29, 99
Norwegian National Bank, 96
NV Maatschappij voor
    Industriefinancierung, 115

Österreichische Bodencreditanstalt, *see*
    Allgemeine Österreichische Boden-
    Credit-Anstalt
Österreichische Credit-Anstalt, *see*
    Österreichische Credit-Anstalt für
    Handel und Gewerbe
Österreichische Credit-Anstalt für Handel
    und Gewerbe, 1, 8, 10, 19, 23–4, 38,
    122–53 *passim*, 180, 196
    industrial groups, 139
Österreichische Nationalbank, 23–4, 38
'organized capitalism', 74
Osaka Clearing House, 256
Osaka Sanju-yon Bank, 254
Oyama, K., 254

Peacock, E. R., 42, 44
Perrone, M., 189, 191
Perrone, P., 189, 191
Pesti Magyar Kereskedelmi Bank, *see*
    Commercial Bank of Pest
Pirelli, 195
PMKB, *see* Commercial Bank of Pest
post-war stabilization, 3

Reich Economic Bank, 9, 17, 58–9
    see also Germany
Reich Economics Council, 56, 62
    see also Germany
Reichsbank, 5, 16, 39, 50–1, 54–5, 57–61,
    64–6, 68, 71–3, 76
    see also Germany
reparations, 18
Riksbanken, 80, 92
Robaver, *see* Rotterdamsche Bankvereeniging
Rotterdamsche Bank, *see* Rotterdamsche
    Bankvereeniging
Rotterdamsche Bankvereeniging, 107
Royal Bank, 243
RWR (Reichswirtschaftsrat), *see* Reich
    Economics Council

Salomonsohn, A., 66
SBI, *see* Società Bancaria Italiana
Schacht, H., 50
Schäffer, H., 75–6
Scholz, E., 59
Second World War, 9, 27, 106, 115, 117
SFI, *see* Società Finanziaria Italiana
Siezen Bank for Industry and Commerce, 70
Siezen Savings Bank, 70
Skandinaviska Banken, 89, 92–4
Snowdon, P., 41
Social Democrats, 23, 90–1
Società Adriatica di Elettricità (SADE), 195
Società Bancaria Italiana, 182–3, 185

Società Elettrofinanziaria, 197, 199, 200
Società Finanziaria Italiana, 196–8
Société Générale de Belgique, 8, 30, 105, 111–12
Société Nationale de Crédit à l'Industrie, 111
Sofindit, 198
Stimson, H., 38
Stinnes, H., 52, 75
stock exchange/market(s), 107–8
    Athens, 220
    North America, 235
    Prague, 21
    Vienna, 21–2
Stockholms Enskilda Bank, 81, 92–4
Stringher, B., 161, 184–5, 187, 190, 193, 200
Strong, B., 36–7
Sumitomo Bank, 255, 259, 262
Susaki, Y., 255, 259
Suzuki Trading Company, 256
Svenska Handelsbanken, 88–9, 92–4
Sweden
    bank(ing) crisis, 1, 85–7
    Bank Inspection Board, 33, 83–5, 88–9, 91, 93–4
    Banking Committee (1924), 85–90, 93
    Banking law (1911), 84, 88, 90, 94–5; (1933), 33
    banking system, 80–2, 95
    commercial banks, 29–32
    credit market, 80
    deflation, 86–7, 89
    deposit banking, 80
    inflation, 84
    Kreuger crash, 91–3
    mixed banking, 9, 29
    Social Democratic Party, 90–1

Takahashi, K., 258, 265
Tanaka, G., 257
Terauchi, H., 266
The Netherlands
    banking concentration, 107
    banking crisis, 1, 108, 117
    banking system, 117
    commercial banking, 29
    gold, 116
    legislation, 116, 118

mixed banking, 117–18
state, banks and industry, 104–12 *passim*
Thyssen, F., 75
Toeplitz, G., 191, 197
Tokyo Clearing House, 256–7, 265
Tsonderos, E., 217, 222
Twentsche Bank, 107

Ullmann, M., 160
United States of America
    banking collapse, 232
    debtor–creditor, 35
    Federal Reserve System, 232
    gold shipments, 253
    gold standard, 13
    recession, 38

Van Hengel, 136
Van Vlissingen, F., 109
Varvaressos, K., 221
Venizelos, E., 15, 216, 218, 220–4
Volpi, di Mijurata G., 195

Wall Street stock market crash (1929), 15, 38
Wallenberg(s), 92–3, 95
war debts, 18, 38, 194–5
Warburg, M., 5, 64–6, 70
Whigham, C., 38
Wiener Bankverein, 9, 24
    and Commercial Bank of Pest, 161
    merger with Österreichische Credit-Anstalt, 141
Wirth, S., 61
world depression, 1, 9, 19, 30, 179, 262
    see also Great Depression
World Economic Crisis, 18, 100
    see also world depression, Great Depression

Yamamoto, T., 251–2
Yamamuro, S., 256
Yashiro, N., 254, 259, 262–3
Yasuda Bank, 255, 259, 262–6
Yokohama Specie Bank, 254
Young Plan, 38, 40
Yukawa, K., 255
Yuki, T., 255–6, 259, 266

For EU product safety concerns, contact us at Calle de José Abascal, 56–1°, 28003 Madrid, Spain or eugpsr@cambridge.org.

www.ingramcontent.com/pod-product-compliance
Ingram Content Group UK Ltd.
Pitfield, Milton Keynes, MK11 3LW, UK
UKHW042316180425
457623UK00005B/26